PLAYS BY WEBSTER AND FORD

AMS PRESS
NEW YORK

POETS ARE THE TRUMPETS WHICH SING TO BATTLE POETS ARE THE UNACKNOWLEDGED LEGISLATORS OF THE WORLD SHELLEY

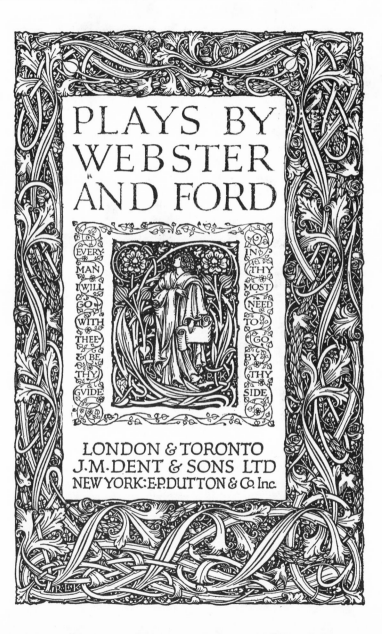

PLAYS BY WEBSTER AND FORD

EVERY-
MAN
I WILL
GO
WITH
THEE
& BE
THY
GVIDE

IN
THY
MOST
NEED
TO
GO
BY
THY
SIDE

LONDON & TORONTO
J·M·DENT & SONS LTD
NEW YORK: E·P·DUTTON & Co. Inc.

Library of Congress Cataloging in Publication Data

Webster, John, 1580?-1625?
  Plays by Webster and Ford.

  Reprint of the 1933 ed. published by J.M. Dent,
London, which was issued as no. 899 of Everyman's
Library: Poetry and the drama.
  CONTENTS: The white devil.—The duchess of
Malfi.—The broken heart.—'Tis pity she's a whore.
  1. English drama—17th century. I. Ford,
John, 1586-ca. 1640. II. Title..
PR1265.5.W4 1977   822'.3   75-41291
ISBN 0-404-14628-7

Reprinted from an original in the collections
of the University of Iowa Library

From the edition of 1933, London
First AMS edition published in 1977
Manufactured in the United States of America

AMS PRESS INC.
NEW YORK, N.Y.

INTRODUCTION

WEBSTER and Ford belong to the third generation of Elizabethan dramatists, and their tragedies are good specimens of the tastes of theatre-goers, and especially of gentlemen of the Stuart Court, in the earlier years of the seventeenth century. It is customary to regard all plays written between 1570 and 1640 as 'Elizabethan'. The label is not very happy; the best plays were written after the death of Queen Elizabeth; and King James the First and his family were more generous and enlightened patrons of the players. But classification has its conveniences, and it is possible to trace, very generally, three stages or generations in this drama.

The first is the generation of the pioneers. So far as is known, English dramatists about 1587 began quite suddenly to write good plays. It is, however, sometimes forgotten that so few plays of the 1570's and 1580's survive that the success of Marlowe and Kyd may have been less sudden and spontaneous than is usually supposed. Compared with their existing predecessors they were bold and successful innovators. They had certain advantages. Good drama was still a novelty; their audiences were unspoiled by surfeit and variety; and Edward Alleyn, who first interpreted the parts of Tamburlaine, the Jew of Malta, Dr. Faustus, and Hieronimo, was a magnificent, if robustious, mouthpiece for high-sounding bombast. Marlowe's themes were simple; his four tragedies are plays of a single hero, and though each hero may be said to embody a theme in his own fate, the plots come to pass chronologically until the hero dies. In *The Spanish Tragedy* Kyd's theme was the revenge of a father for his murdered son, elaborated with all kinds of subsidiary horrors. Kyd had a much greater sense of drama than Marlowe, and, more than any other, he set the fashion for the tragedy of blood and vengeance. As his *Spanish Tragedy* was continually acted and reprinted until the closing of the theatres at the Civil War, it was a permanent example for his successors to copy.

The second generation was that of Shakespeare and his immediate contemporaries—Jonson, Chapman, Dekker, Heywood, Marston. Shakespeare's tragedies were still in essence

vii

simple; his themes were ambition, jealousy, filial ingratitude; and the problems of Macbeth, Othello, and Lear are in some form universal. But, genius apart, Shakespeare was far more skilled in the craft and technique of the stage than those who had gone before him. This skill seems to have been instinctive rather than the result of conscious study of principles and technique. Jonson, on the other hand, and probably Chapman and Marston, were students of theory; nothing ever happened by chance in a Jonsonian play. As a result, in this generation, acting and stage production became subtler, and especially after the renewed vogue of the small indoor playhouses, which began in 1599. Henceforward, at the turn of the century, and notably in the reign of James the First, players and dramatists appealed less to the hearty populace' which had first been attracted by Marlowe's noisy heroes, and rather to the gentlemen spectators who were more sophisticated and discriminating. The art of drama thus grew more complex; problems and situations ceased to be general and universal, but became particular and intricate, psychological rather than moral.

In the third generation the first great names were Beaumont and Fletcher who exactly gauged the taste of this new audience, which had by this time twenty years' critical experience of the drama at its best.

Very little is known either of Webster or of Ford. Webster's name is first found in 1602 in the account book of Philip Henslowe, Alleyn's father-in-law, who financed the players acting at the Rose and Fortune theatres. He was at this time collaborating in the composition of plays both for the Admiral's Men and Worcester's Men, but none of these plays have survived. In 1624 he devised a pageant for Lord Mayor's Day which was published, wherein he calls himself 'Merchant Taylor', and states that he was born free of the company. The dates of his birth and death are unknown; and, apart from a few occasional verses by him or mentioning him, nothing else has been found. All that survives is collected in Mr. F. L. Lucas's edition of *The Works of John Webster*, 4 vols., 1927.

Webster's reputation comes from his two tragedies *The White Devil* and *The Duchess of Malfi*. The first was printed in 1612, and was probably then a new play; the second came out in 1623, but apparently both were written about the same time. *The White Devil* is a dramatization of actual events which had occurred nearly thirty years before. The story of Vittoria Corambona (or Accoramboni) 'the famous Venetian courtesan' was well known, and one of many which accounted for the not unreasonable prejudice of elderly Elizabethan gentlemen that Italy was not a country which young men should visit. It is not known how the story came to Webster, and in his stage version many of the details differ from fact. The reality, however, was not less horrible than the play.

Webster seems to have been a self-conscious artist. His plays were wrought slowly, and his effects came from art, not chance; but in his own way he was superb. He delighted in horror of a peculiar kind, and in both plays the main intent was to create strong passions, horror, and terror, with occasional contrasting flashes of pathos. The impression after seeing one of them acted is not a sense of a tragic theme presented as a whole but rather a series of magnificent scenes, such as the blazing courage of Vittoria before her judges; or the terrible death of Brachiano when the supposed friars reveal themselves to exult over his last agonies. In *The Duchess of Malfi* he achieved even greater horror, especially in the scene where the duchess is deceived by the counterfeit image of her murdered husband and children, tormented by the dance of madmen, and finally strangled by the cardinal's murderers; or again, at the end, when the Duke Ferdinand, driven mad by his own crimes, tries to throttle his own shadow. The story of *The Duchess of Malfi* is taken from Painter's *Palace of Pleasure*. It is, however, in a way a rewriting of the conclusion of *The White Devil*, the story being taken up at the point where Vittoria is left a widow by the death of Brachiano. According to the contemporary account in the *Fugger Letters*, Vittoria, in her widowhood, was urged by Francisco to renounce her fortune and to remain unmarried, and preferably to enter a convent. This is the situation at the beginning of *The Duchess of Malfi*. The chief characters in the play, too, are reincarnations; Duke Francisco, Cardinal Monticelso, and Flamineo reappear as Duke Ferdinand, the cardinal, and Bosola; whilst the duchess herself is a compound of the good qualities of Vittoria and Isabella.

There was little hearty humour in Webster; such laughter as is heard in his tragedies is derisive and bitter. In both plays one of the most important characters acts as a commentator on the action, and the events are thus seen with his vision. In this, Webster was not original, for the railing or

cynical observer had already appeared in Jaques, Touch-
stone, Thersites and Luciano, in Jonson's Macilente and
Asper, and Marston's Feliche and Malevole. Webster, however, gives an important part in the action both to Flamineo
and to Bosola; their observations are mainly responsible for
the tonic bitterness of the plays.

Not the least of Webster's gifts was his way of making his
characters say unforgettable things at high moments:

> My soul, like to a ship in a black storm,
> Is driven, I know not whither. . . .

> A rape! a rape! Yes, you have ravished Justice. . . .

> I am Duchess of Malfi still. . . .

> Cover her face: mine eyes dazzle: she died young. . . .

'The end of the matter is', wrote Rupert Brooke, 'that
Webster was a great writer; and the way in which one uses
great writers is two-fold. There is the exhilarating way of
reading their writing; and there is the essence of the whole
man, or of the man's whole work, which you carry away and
permanently keep with you. This essence generally presents
itself more or less in the form of a view of the universe, re-
cognizable rather by its emotional than by its logical content.
The world called Webster is a peculiar one. It is inhabited
by people driven, like animals, and perhaps like men, only by
their instincts, but more blindly and ruinously. Life there
seems to flow into its forms and shapes with an irregular,
abnormal, and horrible volume. This is ultimately the most
sickly, distressing feature of Webster's characters, their foul
and indestructible vitality. It fills one with the repulsion one
feels at the unending soulless energy that heaves and pulses
through the lowest forms of life. They kill, love, torture one
another blindly and without ceasing. A play of Webster's is
full of the feverish and ghastly turmoil of a nest of maggots.
Maggots are what the inhabitants of this universe most
suggest and resemble. The sight of their fever is only alle-
viated by the permanent calm, unfriendly summits and
darknesses of the background of death and gloom. For that
is equally a part of Webster's universe. Human beings are
writhing grubs in an immense night. And the night is without
stars or moon. But it has sometimes a certain quietude in
its darkness; but not very much.'

Of John Ford a little more is known. On 17th April 1586 he

was baptized at Ilsington in Devonshire, and his father was of good family, related by marriage to Queen Elizabeth's Lord Chief Justice Popham. Apparently Ford was for some time at Exeter College, Oxford, and in November 1602 he was entered at the Middle Temple. He was thus contemporary with an exceptionally brilliant generation in the Inns of Court. His first known work was a poem in memory of Charles Blount, Earl of Devonshire, called *Fame's Memorial*, published in 1606. He began to write plays in 1613, and during the next years collaborated with Dekker, Rowley, and Webster. In 1629 he published *The Lover's Melancholy*, and in 1633 his three tragedies, *'Tis Pity She's a Whore*, *The Broken Heart*, and *Love's Sacrifice*. Some occasional commendatory verses and mentions by contemporaries also survive. He died some time after 1639. One couplet has come down which is worth many records of fact. It runs:

> Deep in a dump John Ford alone was got,
> With folded arms and melancholy hat.

Certain reasonable inferences can be drawn from such facts as remain, which were set out by Professor S. P. Sherman in his long and valuable Introduction to the edition of *'Tis Pity* and *The Broken Heart* in the Belles Lettres Series. Professor Sherman pointed out that the couplet definitely labels Ford as a melancholy lover, of the kind portrayed on the frontispiece of Burton's *Anatomy of Melancholy*. He further deduced from the sentiments uttered in *Fame's Memorial* over the Earl of Devonshire's notorious marriage with the divorced wife of Lord Rich, that Ford had modern and advanced views on love and marriage, which are worked out in his tragedies. '*The Broken Heart* presents a clearly defined moral problem. Penthea, very much in love with Orgilus and betrothed to him, is forced to marry Bassanes. Orgilus, taking a purely rationalistic or idealistic view of the matter, refuses to acknowledge any validity in the union of Penthea and Bassanes. Frantic with indignant passion he cries:

> I would possess my wife; the equity
> Of very reason bids me.

Penthea with a supreme effort preserves self-control, and urges her desperate lover to resign himself to the irrevocable, pleading that the true quality of their mutual affection will best show itself in virtuous submission to necessity. Which of the two is right? In Elizabethan times when parents disposed of their children in a rather more high-handed fashion than now obtains—when Penelope Devereux was carried, protesting, to the altar to marry Lord Rich—was it not a fair question?' To which it may be added that Ford himself in his Prologue declares that his story is founded on fact:

> What may be here thought fiction, when time's youth
> Wanted some riper years, was known a truth.

Ford, indeed, was one of many young men directly influenced by the greatest of English works on sex and psychology— *The Anatomy of Melancholy*, which first appeared in 1621. To 'Democritus Junior' the curious aberrations of human behaviour, especially in the passion of love, were a source of melancholy amusement. Ford, however, was neither amused nor distressed, but interested; he suffered that complete loss of moral indignation which often comes from much study of psychology. He was of the same opinion as his contemporary Thomas Carew, who proclaimed in the *Rapture*:

> All things are lawful there, that may delight
> Nature or unrestrained appetite;
> Like and enjoy, to will and act is one:
> We only sin when Love's rites are not done.

Abnormal passions excited in Ford, not repugnance, but curiosity. In *'Tis Pity She's a Whore* the theme is incest. Ford opens the play with the dispute between the friar and Giovanni who boldly justifies his passion for his sister Annabella; and although the friar's threatenings do for a moment turn Giovanni to prayer, the passion is far beyond human control. He is driven consistently to his fate. Annabella, after her marriage to Soranza, repents somewhat, but Giovanni taunts her with breach of faith, and he stabs her to prevent her defilement. When his own turn comes, he dies exultant at the thought of reunion. Ford's sympathies are clearly with the defiant, not the repentant, sinner.

Ford can be condemned for the choice of an unholy theme, but his skill and insight are subtle, and his frank treatment of the story is vastly preferable to the more prurient methods of Beaumont and Fletcher in *King and No King*. In that play the audience are led on to suppose that the love between Arbaces and Panthea is incestuous, and, after a most powerful scene where each declares the mutual passion, destruction seems inevitable whether passion is to be thwarted or satisfied;

but the tragedy is turned to comedy when it is revealed by the usual stage devices that Arbaces was a changeling and so no brother to Panthea. It was, however, a sign of decadence in Ford and his audience that they needed such a stimulus to arouse their excitment.

In *'Tis Pity* Ford drives straight on to his end; the story begins and ends with the fate of Giovanni. In *The Broken Heart* he begins with Orgilus and his sister Euphranea, but ends with the light concentrated on Calantha, who remains outwardly steadfast as her heart is cracked by the successive news that father, friend, and lover are dead—a scene which moved Lamb to write: 'I do not know where to find, in any play, a catastrophe so grand, so solemn, and so surprising as in this. This is indeed, according to Milton, to describe high passions and high actions. The fortitude of the Spartan boy, who let a beast gnaw out his bowels till he died, without expressing a groan, is a faint bodily image of this dilaceration of the spirit, and the exenteration of the inmost mind, which Calantha, with a holy violence against her nature, keeps closely covered, till the last duties of a wife and a queen are fulfilled. . . . Ford was of the first order of poets. He sought for sublimity, not by parcels, in metaphors or visible images, but directly where she has her full residence, in the heart of man; in the actions and sufferings of the greatest minds. There is a grandeur of the soul, above mountains, seas, and the elements'.

Both Webster and Ford have considerable claims on modern readers. They also belonged to a post-war generation, which found no satisfaction in the older standards or ideals of belief and conduct. They had no particular creed except agnosticism, but they were abominably clever.

G. B. HARRISON.

1933.

BIBLIOGRAPHICAL NOTE

WEBSTER: The chief collected editions are by Alexander Dyce, 1830 and 1857; W. C. Hazlitt, 1857 and 1897; F. L. Lucas, 1927, the most modern and best, indispensable for a serious study.

The White Devil was first published in quarto in 1612: other quartos came out in 1631, 1665, and 1672. It was included in Dodsley's Old Plays (1744, 1780, 1825).

The Duchess of Malfi was first published in quarto in 1623, and reprinted in 1640, 1664, 1678, 1708. An edition by A. H. Thorndike came out in 1917. Both plays were reprinted in The Mermaid Series.

Of critical works the most important are those by E. E. Stoll (1905), and Rupert Brooke (1916), and the introductions in F. L. Lucas's edition.

FORD: The chief collected editions are by W. Gifford, 1827, reissued and with additional matter by Alexander Dyce, 1869, and with additions by A. H. Bullen, 1895; (with Massinger's Plays) by Hartley Coleridge, 1839, 1840, 1848.

'Tis Pity She's a Whore was first printed in 1633. It was reprinted in Dodsley's Old Plays.

The Broken Heart was edited by O. Smeaton for The Temple Dramatists in 1906, and included in W. A. Neilson's Chief Elizabethan Dramatists. Both plays were reprinted in The Mermaid Series with Introduction by Havelock Ellis; and by S. P. Sherman in the Belles-lettres Series (N.D.).

For critical appreciations see the usual histories of Elizabethan literature and drama, and S. P. Sherman's Introduction, mentioned above.

CONTENTS

THE WHITE DEVIL

TO THE READER

In publishing this tragedy, I do but challenge to myself that liberty, which other men have taken before me; not that I affect praise by it, for, nos hæc novimus esse nihil, *only, since it was acted in so dull a time of winter, presented in so open and black a theatre, that it wanted (that which is the only grace and setting-out of a tragedy) a full and understanding auditory; and that since that time I have noted, most of the people that come to that playhouse resemble those ignorant asses (who, visiting stationers' shops, their use is not to inquire for good books, but new books), I present it to the general view with this confidence:*

> Nec rhoncos metues maligniorum,
> Nec scombris tunicas dabis molestas.

If it be objected this is no true dramatic poem, I shall easily confess it, non potes in nugas dicere plura meas, ipse ego quam dixi; *willingly, and not ignorantly, in this kind have I faulted: For should a man present to such an auditory, the most sententious tragedy that ever was written, observing all the critical laws as height of style, and gravity of person, enrich it with the sententious* Chorus, *and, as it were Life and Death, in the passionate and weighty* Nuntius: *yet after all this divine rapture,* O dura messorum ilia, *the breath that comes from the incapable multitude is able to poison it; and, ere it be acted, let the author resolve to fix to every scene this of* Horace:

> —Hæc hodie porcis comedenda relinques.

To those who report I was a long time in finishing this tragedy, I confess I do not write with a goose-quill winged with two feathers; and if they will need make it my fault, I must answer them with that of Euripides *to* Alcestides, *a tragic writer:* Alcestides *objecting that* Euripides *had only, in three days composed three verses, whereas himself had written three hundred: Thou tellest truth (quoth he), but here's the difference, thine shall only be read for three days, whereas mine shall continue three ages.*

Detraction is the sworn friend to ignorance: for mine own part, I have ever truly cherished my good opinion of other men's worthy labours, especially of that full and heightened style of Mr. Chapman, *the laboured and understanding works of* Mr. Johnson, *the no less worthy composures of the both worthily excellent* Mr. Beaumont *and* Mr. Fletcher; *and lastly (without wrong last to be named), the right happy and copious industry of* Mr. Shakespeare, Mr. Dekker, *and* Mr. Heywood, *wishing what I write may be read by their light: protesting that, in the strength of mine own judgment, I know them so worthy, that though I rest silent in my own work, yet to most of theirs I dare (without flattery) fix that of* Martial:

—non norunt hæc monumenta mori.

DRAMATIS PERSONÆ

MONTICELSO, a Cardinal; afterwards Pope PAUL the Fourth.

FRANCISCO DE MEDICIS, Duke of Florence; in the 5th Act disguised for a Moor, under the name of MULINASSAR.

BRACHIANO, otherwise PAULO GIORDANO URSINI, Duke of Brachiano, Husband to ISABELLA, and in love with VITTORIA.

GIOVANNI—his Son by ISABELLA.

LODOVICO, an Italian Count, but decayed.

ANTONELLI,⎫ his Friends, and Dependents of the Duke of
GASPARO, ⎭   Florence.

CAMILLO, Husband to VITTORIA.

HORTENSIO, one of BRACHIANO'S Officers.

MARCELLO, an Attendant of the Duke of Florence, and Brother to VITTORIA.

FLAMINEO, his Brother; Secretary to BRACHIANO.

JAQUES, a Moor, Servant to GIOVANNI.

ISABELLA, Sister to FRANCISCO DE MEDICIS, and Wife to BRACHIANO.

VITTORIA COROMBONA, a Venetian Lady; first married to CAMILLO, afterwards to BRACHIANO.

CORNELIA, Mother to VITTORIA, FLAMINEO, and MARCELLO.

ZANCHE, a Moor, Servant to VITTORIA.

Ambassadors, Courtiers, Lawyers, Officers, Physicians, Conjurer, Armourer, Attendants.

THE SCENE—ITALY

5

ACT I

SCENE I

Enter Count Lodovico, Antonelli, and Gasparo

Lodo. Banish'd!

Ant. It griev'd me much to hear the sentence.

Lodo. Ha, ha, O Democritus, thy gods
That govern the whole world! courtly reward
And punishment.   Fortune 's a right whore:
If she give aught, she deals it in small parcels,
That she may take away all at one swoop.
This 'tis to have great enemies! God 'quite them.
Your wolf no longer seems to be a wolf
Than when she 's hungry.

Gas. You term those enemies,
Are men of princely rank.

Lodo. Oh, I pray for them:
The violent thunder is adored by those
Are pasht in pieces by it.

Ant. Come, my lord,
You are justly doom'd; look but a little back
Into your former life: you have in three years
Ruin'd the noblest earldom.

Gas. Your followers
Have swallowed you, like mummia, and being sick
With such unnatural and horrid physic,
Vomit you up i' th' kennel.

Ant. All the damnable degrees
Of drinking have you stagger'd through.   One citizen,
Is lord of two fair manors, call'd you master,
Only for caviare.

Gas. Those noblemen
Which were invited to your prodigal feasts,
(Wherein the phœnix scarce could 'scape your throats)
Laugh at your misery, as fore-deeming you
An idle meteor, which drawn forth, the earth
Would be soon lost i' the air.

7

Ant. Jest upon you,
    And say you were begotten in an earthquake,
    You have ruin'd such fair lordships.
Lodo. Very good.
    This well goes with two buckets: I must tend
    The pouring out of either.
Gas. Worse than these.
    You have acted certain murders here in Rome,
    Bloody and full of horror.
Lodo. 'Las, they were flea-bitings:
    Why took they not my head then?
Gas. Oh, my lord!
    The law doth sometimes mediate, thinks it good
    Not ever to steep violent sins in blood:
    This gentle penance may both end your crimes,
    And in the example better these bad times.
Lodo. So; but I wonder then some great men 'scape
    This banishment: there 's Paulo Giordano Ursini,
    The Duke of Brachiano, now lives in Rome,
    And by close panderism seeks to prostitute
    The honour of Vittoria Corombona:
    Vittoria, she that might have got my pardon
    For one kiss to the duke.
Ant. Have a full man within you:
    We see that trees bear no such pleasant fruit
    There where they grew first, as where they are new set.
    Perfumes, the more they are chaf'd, the more they render
    Their pleasing scents, and so affliction
    Expresseth virtue fully, whether true,
    Or else adulterate.
Lodo. Leave your painted comforts;
    I 'll make Italian cut-works in their guts
    If ever I return.
Gas. Oh, sir.
Lodo. I am patient.
    I have seen some ready to be executed,
    Give pleasant looks, and money, and grown familiar
    With the knave hangman; so do I; I thank them,
    And would account them nobly merciful,
    Would they dispatch me quickly.
Ant. Fare you well;
    We shall find time, I doubt not, to repeal
    Your banishment.

Lodo. I am ever bound to you.
This is the world's alms; pray make use of it.
Great men sell sheep, thus to be cut in pieces,
When first they have shorn them bare, and sold their fleeces.
[Exeunt.

SCENE II

Enter Brachiano, Camillo, Flamineo, Vittoria

Brach. Your best of rest.
Vit. Unto my lord the duke,
The best of welcome. More lights: attend the duke.
[Exeunt Camillo and Vittoria.

Brach. Flamineo.
Flam. My lord.
Brach. Quite lost, Flamineo.
Flam. Pursue your noble wishes, I am prompt
As lightning to your service. O my lord!
The fair Vittoria, my happy sister,
Shall give you present audience—Gentlemen,   *[Whisper.*
Let the caroch go on—and 'tis his pleasure
You put out all your torches, and depart.
Brach. Are we so happy?
Flam. Can it be otherwise?
Observ'd you not to-night, my honour'd lord,
Which way soe'er you went, she threw her eyes?
I have dealt already with her chambermaid,
Zanche the Moor, and she is wondrous proud
To be the agent for so high a spirit.
Brach. We are happy above thought, because 'bove merit.
Flam. 'Bove merit! we may now talk freely: 'bove merit!
what is 't you doubt? her coyness! that 's but the superficies of
lust most women have; yet why should ladies blush to hear
that nam'd, which they do not fear to handle? Oh, they are
politic; they know our desire is increased by the difficulty of
enjoying; whereas satiety is a blunt, weary, and drowsy
passion. If the buttery-hatch at court stood continually
open, there would be nothing so passionate crowding, nor
hot suit after the beverage.
Brach. Oh, but her jealous husband——
Flam. Hang him; a gilder that hath his brains perished with

quicksilver is not more cold in the liver. The great barriers
moulted not more feathers, than he hath shed hairs, by the
confession of his doctor. An Irish gamester that will play
himself naked, and then wage all downward, at hazard, is not
more venturous. So unable to please a woman, that, like a
Dutch doublet, all his back is shrunk into his breeches.
Shroud you within this closet, good my lord;
Some trick now must be thought on to divide
My brother-in-law from his fair bed-fellow.

Brach. Oh, should she fail to come——

Flam. I must not have your lordship thus unwisely amorous.
I myself have loved a lady, and pursued her with a great deal
of under-age protestation, whom some three or four gallants
that have enjoyed would with all their hearts have been glad
to have been rid of. 'Tis just like a summer bird-cage in a
garden: the birds that are without despair to get in, and the
birds that are within despair and are in a consumption for
fear they shall never get out. Away, away, my lord.

                              [Exit Brachiano as Camillo enters.

See here he comes. This fellow by his apparel
Some men would judge a politician;
But call his wit in question, you shall find it
Merely an ass in 's foot-cloth. How now, brother?
What, travelling to bed to your kind wife?

Cam. I assure you, brother, no. My voyage lies
More northerly, in a far colder clime.
I do not well remember, I protest,
When I last lay with her.

Flam. Strange you should lose your count.

Cam. We never lay together, but ere morning
There grew a flaw between us.

Flam. 'T had been your part
To have made up that flaw.

Cam. True, but she loathes I should be seen in 't.

Flam. Why, sir, what 's the matter?

Cam. The duke your master visits me, I thank him;
And I perceive how, like an earnest bowler,
He very passionately leans that way
He should have his bowl run.

Flam. I hope you do not think——

Cam. That nobleman bowl booty? faith, his cheek
Hath a most excellent bias: it would fain
Jump with my mistress.

Flam. Will you be an ass,
  Despite your Aristotle? or a cuckold,
  Contrary to your Ephemerides,
  Which shows you under what a smiling planet
  You were first swaddled?

Cam. Pew wew, sir; tell not me
  Of planets nor of Ephemerides.
  A man may be made cuckold in the day-time,
  When the stars' eyes are out.

Flam. Sir, good-bye you;
  I do commit you to your pitiful pillow
  Stuffed with horn-shavings.

Cam. Brother!

Flam. God refuse me.
  Might I advise you now, your only course
  Were to lock up your wife.

Cam. 'Twere very good.

Flam. Bar her the sight of revels.

Cam. Excellent.

Flam. Let her not go to church, but, like a hound
  In leon, at your heels.

Cam. 'Twere for her honour.

Flam. And so you should be certain in one fortnight,
  Despite her chastity or innocence,
  To be cuckolded, which yet is in suspense:
  This is my counsel, and I ask no fee for 't.

Cam. Come, you know not where my nightcap wrings me.

Flam. Wear it a' th' old fashion; let your large ears come
  through, it will be more easy—nay, I will be bitter—bar your
  wife of her entertainment: women are more willingly and
  more gloriously chaste, when they are least restrained of their
  liberty. It seems you would be a fine capricious, mathe-
  matically jealous coxcomb; take the height of your own horns
  with a Jacob's staff, afore they are up. These politic en-
  closures for paltry mutton, makes more rebellion in the flesh,
  than all the provocative electuaries doctors have uttered since
  last jubilee.

Cam. This doth not physic me——

Flam. It seems you are jealous: I'll show you the error of it
  by a familiar example: I have seen a pair of spectacles
  fashioned with such perspective art, that lay down but one
  twelve pence a' th' board, 'twill appear as if there were twenty;
  now should you wear a pair of these spectacles, and see your

wife tying her shoe, you would imagine twenty hands were taking up of your wife's clothes, and this would put you into a horrible causeless fury.

Cam. The fault there, sir, is not in the eyesight.

Flam. True, but they that have the yellow jaundice think all objects they look on to be yellow. Jealousy is worse; her fits present to a man, like so many bubbles in a basin of water, twenty several crabbed faces, many times makes his own shadow his cuckold-maker. [*Enter Vittoria Corombona.*] See, she comes; what reason have you to be jealous of this creature? what an ignorant ass or flattering knave might he be counted, that should write sonnets to her eyes, or call her brow the snow of Ida, or ivory of Corinth; or compare her hair to the blackbird's bill, when 'tis liker the blackbird's feather? This is all. Be wise; I will make you friends, and you shall go to bed together. Marry, look you, it shall not be your seeking. Do you stand upon that, by any means: walk you aloof; I would not have you seen in 't.—Sister [my lord attends you in the banqueting-house,] your husband is wondrous discontented.

Vit. I did nothing to displease him; I carved to him at suppertime.

Flam. [You need not have carved him, in faith; they say he is a capon already. I must now seemingly fall out with you.] Shall a gentleman so well descended as Camillo [a lousy slave, that within this twenty years rode with the black guard in the duke's carriage, 'mongst spits and dripping-pans!]—

Cam. Now he begins to tickle her.

Flam. An excellent scholar [one that hath a head fill'd with calves' brains without any sage in them,] come crouching in the hams to you for a night's lodging? [that hath an itch in 's hams, which like the fire at the glass-house hath not gone out this seven years] Is he not a courtly gentleman? [when he wears white satin, one would take him by his black muzzle to be no other creature than a maggot] You are a goodly foil, I confess, well set out [but cover'd with a false stone—yon counterfeit diamond].

Cam. He will make her know what is in me.

Flam. Come, my lord attends you; thou shalt go to bed to my lord.

Cam. Now he comes to 't.

Flam. [With a relish as curious as a vintner going to taste new wine.] [*To Camillo.*] I am opening your case hard.

Cam. A virtuous brother, o' my credit!

Flam. He will give thee a ring with a philosopher's stone in it.

Cam. Indeed, I am studying alchemy.

Flam. Thou shalt lie in a bed stuffed with turtle's feathers; swoon in perfumed linen, like the fellow was smothered in roses. So perfect shall be thy happiness, that as men at sea think land, and trees, and ships, go that way they go; so both heaven and earth shall seem to go your voyage. Shalt meet him; 'tis fix'd, with nails of diamonds to inevitable necessity.

Vit. How shalt rid him hence?

Flam. [I will put brize in 's tail, set him gadding presently.] I have almost wrought her to it; I find her coming: but, might I advise you now, for this night I would not lie with her, I would cross her humour to make her more humble.

Cam. Shall I, shall I?

Flam. It will show in you a supremacy of judgment.

Cam. True, and a mind differing from the tumultuary opinion; for, *quæ negata, grata.*

Flam. Right: you are the adamant shall draw her to you, though you keep distance off.

Cam. A philosophical reason.

Flam. Walk by her a' th' nobleman's fashion, and tell her you will lie with her at the end of the progress.

Cam. Vittoria, I cannot be induc'd, or as a man would say, incited——

Vit. To do what, sir?

Cam. To lie with you to-night. Your silkworm used to fast every third day, and the next following spins the better. To-morrow at night, I am for you.

Vit. You 'll spin a fair thread, trust to 't.

Flam. But do you hear, I shall have you steal to her chamber about midnight.

Cam. Do you think so? why look you, brother, because you shall not think I 'll gull you, take the key, lock me into the chamber, and say you shall be sure of me.

Flam. In troth I will; I 'll be your jailer once. But have you ne'er a false door?

Cam. A pox on 't, as I am a Christian! tell me to-morrow how scurvily she takes my unkind parting.

Flam. I will.

Cam. Didst thou not mark the jest of the silkworm? Good-night; in faith, I will use this trick often.

Flam. Do, do, do.   [*Exit Camillo.*
So, now you are safe.   Ha, ha, ha, thou entanglest thyself in
thine own work like a silkworm.   [*Enter Brachiano.*]   Come,
sister, darkness hides your blush.   Women are like cursed
dogs: civility keeps them tied all daytime, but they are
let loose at midnight; then they do most good, or most
mischief.   My lord, my lord!

*Zanche brings out a carpet, spreads it, and lays on it two fair
cushions.   Enter Cornelia listening, but unperceived.*

Brach. Give credit: I could wish time would stand still,
And never end this interview, this hour;
But all delight doth itself soon'st devour.
Let me into your bosom, happy lady,
Pour out, instead of eloquence, my vows.
Loose me not, madam, for if you forgo me,
I am lost eternally.
Vit. Sir, in the way of pity,
I wish you heart-whole.
Brach. You are a sweet physician.
Vit. Sure, sir, a loathed cruelty in ladies
Is as to doctors many funerals:
It takes away their credit.
Brach. Excellent creature!
We call the cruel fair; what name for you
That are so merciful?
Zan. See now they close.
Flam. Most happy union.
Corn. [*Aside.*] My fears are fall'n upon me: oh, my heart!
My son the pander! now I find our house
Sinking to ruin.   Earthquakes leave behind,
Where they have tyranniz'd, iron, or lead, or stone;
But woe to ruin, violent lust leaves none.
Brach. What value is this jewel?
Vit. 'Tis the ornament of a weak fortune.
Brach. In sooth, I 'll have it; nay, I will but change
My jewel for your jewel.
Flam. Excellent;
His jewel for her jewel: well put in, duke.
Brach. Nay, let me see you wear it.
Vit. Here, sir?
Brach. Nay, lower, you shall wear my jewel lower.

Flam. That 's better: she must wear his jewel lower.
Vit. To pass away the time, I 'll tell your grace
   A dream I had last night.
Brach. Most wishedly.
Vit. A foolish idle dream:
   Methought I walked about the mid of night
   Into a churchyard, where a goodly yew-tree
   Spread her large root in ground: under that yew,
   As I sat sadly leaning on a grave,
   Chequer'd with cross-sticks, there came stealing in
   Your duchess and my husband; one of them
   A pickaxe bore, th' other a rusty spade,
   And in rough terms they 'gan to challenge me
   About this yew.
Brach. That tree?
Vit. This harmless yew;
   They told me my intent was to root up
   That well-grown yew, and plant i' the stead of it
   A wither'd blackthorn; and for that they vow'd
   To bury me alive. My husband straight
   With pickaxe 'gan to dig, and your fell duchess
   With shovel, like a fury, voided out
   The earth and scatter'd bones: Lord, how methought
   I trembled! and yet for all this terror
   I could not pray.
Flam. No; the devil was in your dream.
Vit. When to my rescue there arose, methought,
   A whirlwind, which let fall a massy arm
   From that strong plant;
   And both were struck dead by that sacred yew,
   In that base shallow grave that was their due.
Flam. Excellent devil!
   She hath taught him in a dream
   To make away his duchess and her husband.
Brach. Sweetly shall I interpret this your dream.
   You are lodg'd within his arms who shall protect you
   From all the fevers of a jealous husband,
   From the poor envy of our phlegmatic duchess.
   I 'll seat you above law, and above scandal;
   Give to your thoughts the invention of delight,
   And the fruition; nor shall government
   Divide me from you longer, than a care
   To keep you great: you shall to me at once.

Be dukedom, health, wife, children, friends, and all.

Corn. [*Advancing.*] Woe to light hearts, they still forerun
   our fall!

Flam. What fury raised thee up? away, away.   [*Exit Zanche.*

Corn. What make you here, my lord, this dead of night?
   Never dropp'd mildew on a flower here till now.

Flam. I pray, will you go to bed then,
   Lest you be blasted?

Corn. O that this fair garden
   Had with all poison'd herbs of Thessaly
   At first been planted; made a nursery
   For witchcraft, rather than a burial plot
   For both your honours!

Vit. Dearest mother, hear me.

Corn. Oh, thou dost make my brow bend to the earth.
   Sooner than nature! See the curse of children!
   In life they keep us frequently in tears;
   And in the cold grave leave us in pale fears.

Brach. Come, come, I will not hear you.

Vit. Dear my lord.

Corn. Where is thy duchess now, adulterous duke?
   Thou little dream'st this night she 's come to Rome.

Flam. How! come to Rome!

Vit. The duchess!

Brach. She had been better——

Corn. The lives of princes should like dials move,
   Whose regular example is so strong,
   They make the times by them go right, or wrong.

Flam. So, have you done?

Corn. Unfortunate Camillo!

Vit. I do protest, if any chaste denial,
   If anything but blood could have allay'd
   His long suit to me——

Corn. I will join with thee,
   To the most woeful end e'er mother kneel'd:
   If thou dishonour thus thy husband's bed,
   Be thy life short as are the funeral tears
   In great men's——

Brach. Fie, fie, the woman 's mad.

Corn. Be thy act Judas-like; betray in kissing:
   May'st thou be envied during his short breath,
   And pitied like a wretch after his death!

Vit. O me accurs'd!   [*Exit.*

Flam. Are you out of your wits? my lord,
　　I 'll fetch her back again.
Brach. No, I 'll to bed:
　　Send **Doctor Julio** to me presently.
　　Uncharitable woman! thy rash tongue
　　Hath rais'd a fearful and prodigious storm:
　　Be thou the cause of all ensuing harm.　　　　　　*[Exit.*
Flam. Now, you that stand so much upon your honour,
　　Is this a fitting time a' night, think you,
　　To send a duke home without e'er a man?
　　I would fain know where lies the mass of wealth
　　Which you have hoarded for my maintenance,
　　That I may bear my beard out of the level
　　Of my lord's stirrup.
Corn. What! because we are poor
　　Shall we be vicious?
Flam. Pray, what means have you
　　To keep me from the galleys, or the gallows?
　　My father prov'd himself a gentleman,
　　Sold all 's land, and, like a fortunate fellow,
　　Died ere the money was spent.　You brought me up
　　At Padua, I confess, where I protest,
　　For want of means—the University judge me—
　　I have been fain to heel my tutor's stockings,
　　At least seven years; conspiring with a beard,
　　Made me a graduate; then to this duke's service,
　　I visited the court, whence I return'd
　　More courteous, more lecherous by far,
　　But not a suit the richer.　And shall I,
　　Having a path so open, and so free
　　To my preferment, still retain your milk
　　In my pale forehead? No, this face of mine
　　I 'll arm, and fortify with lusty wine,
　　'Gainst shame and blushing.
Corn. O that I ne'er had borne thee!
Flam. So would I;
　　I would the common'st courtesan in Rome
　　Had been my mother, rather than thyself.
　　Nature is very pitiful to whores,
　　To give them but few children, yet those children
　　Plurality of fathers; they are sure
　　They shall not want.　Go, go,
　　Complain unto my great lord cardinal;

It may be he will justify the act.
Lycurgus wonder'd much, men would provide
Good stallions for their mares, and yet would suffer
Their fair wives to be barren.

Corn. Misery of miseries!   [*Exit.*

Flam. The duchess come to court! I like not that.
We are engag'd to mischief, and must on;
As rivers to find out the ocean
Flow with crook bendings beneath forced banks,
Or as we see, to aspire some mountain's top,
The way ascends not straight, but imitates
The subtle foldings of a winter's snake,
So who knows policy and her true aspect,
Shall find her ways winding and indirect.   [*Exit.*

ACT II

Scene I

Enter Francisco de Medicis, Cardinal Monticelso, Marcello, Isabella, young Giovanni, with little Jaques the Moor

Fran. Have you not seen your husband since you arrived?
Isab. Not yet, sir.
Fran. Surely he is wondrous kind;
  If I had such a dove-house as Camillo's,
  I would set fire on 't were 't but to destroy
  The polecats that haunt to it—My sweet cousin!
Giov. Lord uncle, you did promise me a horse,
  And armour.
Fran. That I did, my pretty cousin.
  Marcello, see it fitted.
Marc. My lord, the duke is here.
Fran. Sister, away; you must not yet be seen.
Isab. I do beseech you,
  Entreat him mildly, let not your rough tongue
  Set us at louder variance; all my wrongs

Are freely pardon'd; and I do not doubt,
As men to try the precious unicorn's horn
Make of the powder a preservative circle,
And in it put a spider, so these arms
Shall charm his poison, force it to obeying,
And keep him chaste from an infected straying.

Fran. I wish it may. Begone. [*Exit Isabella as Brachiano and Flamineo enter.*] Void the chamber.

[*Exeunt Flamineo, Marcello, Giovanni, and Jaques.*]
You are welcome; will you sit?—I pray, my lord,
Be you my orator, my heart 's too full;
I 'll second you anon.

Mont. Ere I begin,
Let me entreat your grace forgo all passion,
Which may be raised by my free discourse.

Brach. As silent as i' th' church: you may proceed.

Mont. It is a wonder to your noble friends,
That you, having as 'twere enter'd the world
With a free sceptre in your able hand,
And having to th' use of nature well applied
High gifts of learning, should in your prime age
Neglect your awful throne for the soft down
Of an insatiate bed. O my lord,
The drunkard after all his lavish cups
Is dry, and then is sober; so at length,
When you awake from this lascivious dream,
Repentance then will follow, like the sting
Plac'd in the adder's tail. Wretched are princes
When fortune blasteth but a petty flower
Of their unwieldy crowns, or ravisheth
But one pearl from their sceptre; but alas!
When they to wilful shipwreck lose good fame,
All princely titles perish with their name.

Brach. You have said, my lord——

Mont. Enough to give you taste
How far I am from flattering your greatness.

Brach. Now you that are his second, what say you?
Do not like young hawks fetch a course about;
Your game flies fair, and for you.

Fran. Do not fear it:
I 'll answer you in your own hawking phrase.
Some eagles that should gaze upon the sun
Seldom soar high, but take their lustful ease,

Since they from dunghill birds their prey can seize.
You know Vittoria?

Brach. Yes.

Fran. You shift your shirt there,
When you retire from tennis?

Brach. Happily.

Fran. Her husband is lord of a poor fortune,
Yet she wears cloth of tissue.

Brach. What of this?
Will you urge that, my good lord cardinal,
As part of her confession at next shrift,
And know from whence it sails?

Fran. She is your strumpet——

Brach. Uncivil sir, there 's hemlock in thy breath,
And that black slander.   Were she a whore of mine,
All thy loud cannons, and thy borrow'd Switzers,
Thy galleys, nor thy sworn confederates,
Durst not supplant her.

Fran. Let 's not talk on thunder.
Thou hast a wife, our sister; would I had given
Both her white hands to death, bound and lock'd fast
In her last winding sheet, when I gave thee
But one.

Brach. Thou hadst given a soul to God then.

Fran. True:
Thy ghostly father, with all his absolution,
Shall ne'er do so by thee.

Brach. Spit thy poison.

Fran. I shall not need; lust carries her sharp whip
At her own girdle.   Look to 't, for our anger
Is making thunderbolts.

Brach. Thunder! in faith,
They are but crackers.

Fran. We 'll end this with the cannon.

Brach. Thou 'lt get naught by it, but iron in thy wounds,
And gunpowder in thy nostrils.

Fran. Better that,
Than change perfumes for plasters.

Brach. Pity on thee!
'Twere good you 'd show your slaves, or men condemn'd,
Your new-plough'd forehead.   Defiance! and I 'll meet thee,
Even in a thicket of thy ablest men.

Mont. My lords, you shall not word it any further
    Without a milder limit.
Fran. Willingly.
Brach. Have you proclaim'd a triumph, that you bait
    A lion thus?
Mont. My lord!
Brach. I am tame, I am tame, sir.
Fran. We send unto the duke for conference
    'Bout levies 'gainst the pirates; my lord duke
    Is not at home: we come ourself in person;
    Still my lord duke is busied. But we fear
    When Tiber to each prowling passenger
    Discovers flocks of wild ducks, then, my lord—
    'Bout moulting time I mean—we shall be certain
    To find you sure enough, and speak with you.
Brach. Ha!
Fran. A mere tale of a tub: my words are idle.
    But to express the sonnet by natural reason,

                         [Enter Giovanni.
    When stags grow melancholic you 'll find the season.
Mont. No more, my lord; here comes a champion
    Shall end the difference between you both;
    Your son, the Prince Giovanni. See, my lords,
    What hopes you store in him; this is a casket
    For both your crowns, and should be held like dear.
    Now is he apt for knowledge; therefore know
    It is a more direct and even way,
    To train to virtue those of princely blood,
    By examples than by precepts: if by examples,
    Whom should he rather strive to imitate
    Than his own father? be his pattern then,
    Leave him a stock of virtue that may last,
    Should fortune rend his sails, and split his mast.
Brach. Your hand, boy: growing to a soldier?
Giov. Give me a pike.
Fran. What, practising your pike so young, fair cousin?
Giov. Suppose me one of Homer's frogs, my lord,
    Tossing my bulrush thus. Pray, sir, tell me,
    Might not a child of good discretion
    Be leader to an army?
Fran. Yes, cousin, a young prince
    Of good discretion might.
Giov. Say you so?

Indeed I have heard, 'tis fit a general
Should not endanger his own person oft;
So that he make a noise when he 's a-horseback,
Like a Danske drummer,—Oh, 'tis excellent!—
He need not fight! methinks his horse as well
Might lead an army for him. If I live,
I 'll charge the French foe in the very front
Of all my troops, the foremost man.

Fran. What! what!

Giov. And will not bid my soldiers up, and follow,
But bid them follow me.

Brach. Forward lapwing!
He flies with the shell on 's head.

Fran. Pretty cousin!

Giov. The first year, uncle, that I go to war,
All prisoners that I take, I will set free,
Without their ransom.

Fran. Ha! without their ransom!
How then will you reward your soldiers,
That took those prisoners for you?

Giov. Thus, my lord:
I 'll marry them to all the wealthy widows
That falls that year.

Fran. Why then, the next year following,
You 'll have no men to go with you to war.

Giov. Why then I 'll press the women to the war,
And then the men will follow.

Mont. Witty prince!

Fran. See, a good habit makes a child a man,
Whereas a bad one makes a man a beast.
Come, you and I are friends.

Brach. Most wishedly:
Like bones which, broke in sunder, and well set,
Knit the more strongly.

Fran. Call Camillo hither.—
You have receiv'd the rumour, how Count Lodowick
Is turn'd a pirate?

Brach. Yes.

Fran. We are now preparing
Some ships to fetch him in. Behold your duchess.
We now will leave you, and expect from you
Nothing but kind entreaty.

Brach. You have charm'd me.

> [*Exeunt Francisco, Monticelso, and Giovanni.*
> *Enter Isabella*

You are in health, we see.

Isab. And above health,
  To see my lord well.

Brach. So: I wonder much
  What amorous whirlwind hurried you to Rome.

Isab. Devotion, my lord.

Brach. Devotion!
  Is your soul charg'd with any grievous sin?

Isab. 'Tis burden'd with too many; and I think
  The oftener that we cast our reckonings up,
  Our sleep will be the sounder.

Brach. Take your chamber.

Isab. Nay, my dear lord, I will not have you angry!
  Doth not my absence from you, now two months,
  Merit one kiss?

Brach. I do not use to kiss:
  If that will dispossess your jealousy,
  I 'll swear it to you.

Isab. Oh, my loved lord,
  I do not come to chide: my jealousy!
  I am to learn what that Italian means.
  You are as welcome to these longing arms,
  As I to you a virgin.

Brach. Oh, your breath!
  Out upon sweetmeats and continued physic,
  The plague is in them!

Isab. You have oft, for these two lips,
  Neglected cassia, or the natural sweets
  Of the spring-violet: they are not yet much wither'd.
  My lord, I should be merry: these your frowns
  Show in a helmet lovely; but on me,
  In such a peaceful interview, methinks
  They are too roughly knit.

Brach. O dissemblance!
  Do you bandy factions 'gainst me? have you learnt
  The trick of impudent baseness to complain
  Unto your kindred?

Isab. Never, my dear lord.

Brach. Must I be hunted out? or was 't your trick

To meet some amorous gallant here in Rome,
That must supply our discontinuance?

Isab. I pray, sir, burst my heart; and in my death
Turn to your ancient pity, though not love.

Brach. Because your brother is the corpulent duke,
That is, the great duke, 'sdeath, I shall not shortly
Racket away five hundred crowns at tennis,
But it shall rest 'pon record! I scorn him
Like a shav'd Polack: all his reverend wit
Lies in his wardrobe; he 's a discreet fellow,
When he 's made up in his robes of state.
Your brother, the great duke, because h' 'as galleys,
And now and then ransacks a Turkish fly-boat,
(Now all the hellish furies take his soul!)
First made this match: accursed be the priest
That sang the wedding-mass, and even my issue!

Isab. Oh, too, too far you have curs'd!

Brach. Your hand I 'll kiss;
This is the latest ceremony of my love.
Henceforth I 'll never lie with thee; by this,
This wedding-ring, I 'll ne'er more lie with thee!
And this divorce shall be as truly kept,
As if the judge had doomed it.   Fare you well:
Our sleeps are sever'd.

Isab. Forbid it the sweet union
Of all things blessed! why, the saints in heaven
Will knit their brows at that.

Brach. Let not thy love
Make thee an unbeliever; this my vow
Shall never, on my soul, be satisfied
With my repentance: let thy brother rage
Beyond a horrid tempest, or sea-fight,
My vow is fixed.

Isab. Oh, my winding-sheet!
Now shall I need thee shortly.   Dear my lord,
Let me hear once more, what I would not hear:
Never?

Brach. Never.

Isab. Oh, my unkind lord! may your sins find mercy,
As I upon a woeful widow'd bed
Shall pray for you, if not to turn your eyes
Upon your wretched wife and hopeful son,
Yet that in time you 'll fix them upon heaven!

Brach. No more; go, go, complain to the great duke.

Isab. No, my dear lord; you shall have present witness
How I 'll work peace between you. I will make
Myself the author of your cursed vow;
I have some cause to do it, you have none.
Conceal it, I beseech you, for the weal
Of both your dukedoms, that you wrought the means
Of such a separation: let the fault
Remain with my supposed jealousy,
And think with what a piteous and rent heart
I shall perform this sad ensuing part.

Enter Francisco, Flamineo, Monticelso, and Camillo

Brach. Well, take your course.—My honourable brother!

Fran. Sister!—This is not well, my lord.—Why, sister!—
She merits not this welcome.

Brach. Welcome, say!
She hath given a sharp welcome.

Fran. Are you foolish?
Come, dry your tears: is this a modest course
To better what is naught, to rail and weep?
Grow to a reconcilement, or, by heaven,
I 'll ne'er more deal between you.

Isab. Sir, you shall not;
No, though Vittoria, upon that condition,
Would become honest.

Fran. Was your husband loud
Since we departed?

Isab. By my life, sir, no,
I swear by that I do not care to lose.
Are all these ruins of my former beauty
Laid out for a whore's triumph?

Fran. Do you hear?
Look upon other women, with what patience
They suffer these slight wrongs, and with what justice
They study to requite them: take that course.

Isab. O that I were a man, or that I had power
To execute my apprehended wishes!
I would whip some with scorpions.

Fran. What! turn'd fury!

Isab. To dig the strumpet's eyes out; let her lie
Some twenty months a-dying; to cut off
Her nose and lips, pull out her rotten teeth;

Preserve her flesh like mummia, for trophies
Of my just anger!   Hell, to my affliction,
Is mere snow-water.   By your favour, sir;—
Brother, draw near, and my lord cardinal;—
Sir, let me borrow of you but one kiss;
Henceforth I 'll never lie with you, by this,
This wedding-ring.

Fran. How, ne'er more lie with him!

Isab. And this divorce shall be as truly kept
As if in thronged court a thousand ears
Had heard it, and a thousand lawyers' hands
Sealed to the separation.

Brach. Ne'er lie with me!

Isab. Let not my former dotage
Make thee an unbeliever; this my vow
Shall never on my soul be satisfied
With my repentance: *manet alta mente repostum.*

Fran. Now, by my birth, you are a foolish, mad,
And jealous woman.

Brach. You see 'tis not my seeking.

Fran. Was this your circle of pure unicorn's horn,
You said should charm your lord! now horns upon thee,
For jealousy deserves them!   Keep your vow
And take your chamber.

Isab. No, sir, I 'll presently to Padua;
I will not stay a minute.

Mont. Oh, good madam!

Brach. 'Twere best to let her have her humour;
Some half-day's journey will bring down her stomach,
And then she 'll turn in post.

Fran. To see her come
To my lord cardinal for a dispensation
Of her rash vow, will beget excellent laughter.

Isab. 'Unkindness, do thy office; poor heart, break:
Those are the killing griefs, which dare not speak.'   [*Exit.*

Marc. Camillo 's come, my lord.

Enter Camillo

Fran. Where 's the commission?

Marc. 'Tis here.

Fran. Give me the signet.

Flam. [*Leading Brachiano aside.*] My lord, do you mark their
whispering?   I will compound a medicine, out of their two

heads, stronger than garlic, deadlier than stibium: the cantharides, which are scarce seen to stick upon the flesh, when they work to the heart, shall not do it with more silence or invisible cunning.

Enter Doctor

Brach. About the murder?

Flam. They are sending him to Naples, but I 'll send him to Candy. Here 's another property too.

Brach. Oh, the doctor!

Flam. A poor quack-salving knave, my lord; one that should have been lashed for 's lechery, but that he confessed a judgment, had an execution laid upon him, and so put the whip to a *non plus*.

Doctor. And was cozened, my lord, by an arranter knave than myself, and made pay all the colourable execution.

Flam. He will shoot pills into a man's guts shall make them have more ventages than a cornet or a lamprey; he will poison a kiss; and was once minded for his masterpiece, because Ireland breeds no poison, to have prepared a deadly vapour in a Spaniard's fart, that should have poisoned all Dublin.

Brach. Oh, Saint Anthony's fire!

Doctor. Your secretary is merry, my lord.

Flam. O thou cursed antipathy to nature! Look, his eye 's bloodshot, like a needle a surgeon stitcheth a wound with. Let me embrace thee, toad, and love thee, O thou abominable, loathsome gargarism, that will fetch up lungs, lights, heart, and liver, by scruples!

Brach. No more.—I must employ thee, honest doctor:
You must to Padua, and by the way,
Use some of your skill for us.

Doctor. Sir, I shall.

Brach. But for Camillo?

Flam. He dies this night, by such a politic strain,
Men shall suppose him by 's own engine slain.
But for your duchess' death——

Doctor. I 'll make her sure.

Brach. Small mischiefs are by greater made secure.

Flam. Remember this, you slave; when knaves come to preferment, they rise as gallows are raised in the Low Countries, one upon another's shoulders.

    [*Exeunt. Monticelso, Camillo, and Francisco come forward.*

Mont. Here is an emblem, nephew, pray peruse it:
  'Twas thrown in at your window.
Cam. At my window!
  Here is a stag, my lord, hath shed his horns,
  And, for the loss of them, the poor beast weeps:
  The word, *Inopem me copia fecit.*
Mont. That is,
  Plenty of horns hath made him poor of horns.
Cam. What should this mean?
Mont. I 'll tell you; 'tis given out
  You are a cuckold.
Cam. Is it given out so?
  I had rather such reports as that, my lord,
  Should keep within doors.
Fran. Have you any children?
Cam. None, my lord.
Fran. You are the happier:
  I 'll tell you a tale.
Cam. Pray, my lord.
Fran. An old tale.
  Upon a time Phœbus, the god of light,
  Or him we call the sun, would need be married:
  The gods gave their consent, and Mercury
  Was sent to voice it to the general world.
  But what a piteous cry there straight arose
  Amongst smiths and felt-makers, brewers and cooks,
  Reapers and butter-women, amongst fishmongers,
  And thousand other trades, which are annoyed
  By his excessive heat! 'twas lamentable.
  They came to Jupiter all in a sweat,
  And do forbid the banns. A great fat cook
  Was made their speaker, who entreats of Jove
  That Phœbus might be gelded; for if now,
  When there was but one sun, so many men
  Were like to perish by his violent heat,
  What should they do if he were married,
  And should beget more, and those children
  Make fireworks like their father? So say I;
  Only I will apply it to your wife;
  Her issue, should not providence prevent it,
  Would make both nature, time, and man repent it.
Mont. Look you, cousin,
  Go, change the air for shame; see if your absence

Will blast your cornucopia.   Marcello
Is chosen with you joint commissioner,
For the relieving our Italian coast
From pirates.
Marc. I am much honour'd in 't.
Cam. But, sir,
   Ere I return, the stag's horns may be sprouted
   Greater than those are shed.
Mont. Do not fear it;
   I 'll be your ranger.
Cam. You must watch i' th' nights;
   Then 's the most danger.
Fran. Farewell, good Marcello:
   All the best fortunes of a soldier's wish
   Bring you a-shipboard.
Cam. Were I not best, now I am turn'd soldier,
   Ere that I leave my wife, sell all she hath,
   And then take leave of her?
Mont. I expect good from you,
   Your parting is so merry.
Cam. Merry, my lord! a' th' captain's humour right,
   I am resolved to be drunk this night.   [*Exeunt.*
Fran. So, 'twas well fitted; now shall we discern
   How his wish'd absence will give violent way
   To Duke Brachiano's lust.
Mont. Why, that was it;
   To what scorn'd purpose else should we make choice
   Of him for a sea-captain? and, besides,
   Count Lodowick, which was rumour'd for a pirate,
   Is now in Padua.
Fran. Is 't true?
Mont. Most certain.
   I have letters from him, which are suppliant
   To work his quick repeal from banishment:
   He means to address himself for pension
   Unto our sister duchess.
Fran. Oh, 'twas well!
   We shall not want his absence past six days:
   I fain would have the Duke Brachiano run
   Into notorious scandal; for there 's naught
   In such cursed dotage, to repair his name,
   Only the deep sense of some deathless shame.
Mont. It may be objected, I am dishonourable

To play thus with my kinsman; but I answer,
For my revenge I 'd stake a brother's life,
That being wrong'd, durst not avenge himself.
Fran. Come, to observe this strumpet.
Mont. Curse of greatness!
　　Sure he 'll not leave her?
Fran. There 's small pity in 't:
　　Like mistletoe on sere elms spent by weather,
　　Let him cleave to her, and both rot together.   [*Exeunt.*

Scene II

Enter Brachiano, with one in the habit of a conjurer

Brach. Now, sir, I claim your promise: 'tis dead midnight,
　　The time prefix'd to show me by your art,
　　How the intended murder of Camillo,
　　And our loath'd duchess, grow to action.
Conj. You have won me by your bounty to a deed
　　I do not often practise.　Some there are,
　　Which by sophistic tricks, aspire that name
　　Which I would gladly lose, of necromancer;
　　As some that use to juggle upon cards,
　　Seeming to conjure, when indeed they cheat;
　　Others that raise up their confederate spirits
　　'Bout windmills, and endanger their own necks
　　For making of a squib; and some there are
　　Will keep a curtal to show juggling tricks,
　　And give out 'tis a spirit; besides these,
　　Such a whole ream of almanac-makers, figure-flingers,
　　Fellows, indeed, that only live by stealth,
　　Since they do merely lie about stol'n goods,
　　They 'd make men think the devil were fast and loose,
　　With speaking fustian Latin.　Pray, sit down;
　　Put on this nightcap, sir, 'tis charm'd; and now
　　I 'll show you, by my strong commanding art,
　　The circumstance that breaks your duchess' heart.

A Dumb Show

*Enter suspiciously Julio and Christophero: they draw a curtain
where Brachiano's picture is; they put on spectacles of glass,*

which cover their eyes and noses, and then burn perfumes before the picture, and wash the lips of the picture; that done, quenching the fire, and putting off their spectacles, they depart laughing.

Enter Isabella in her night-gown, as to bedward, with lights, after her, Count Lodovico, Giovanni, Guidantonio, and others waiting on her: she kneels down as to prayers, then draws the curtain of the picture, does three reverences to it, and kisses it thrice; she faints, and will not suffer them to come near it; dies; sorrow expressed in Giovanni, and in Count Lodovico. She is conveyed out solemnly.

Brach. Excellent! then she 's dead.
Conj. She 's poisoned
  By the fumed picture. 'Twas her custom nightly,
  Before she went to bed, to go and visit
  Your picture, and to feed her eyes and lips
  On the dead shadow: Doctor Julio,
  Observing this, infects it with an oil,
  And other poison'd stuff, which presently
  Did suffocate her spirits.
Brach. Methought I saw
  Count Lodowick there.
Conj. He was; and by my art,
  I find he did most passionately dote
  Upon your duchess. Now turn another way,
  And view Camillo's far more politic fate.
  Strike louder, music, from this charmed ground,
  To yield, as fits the act, a tragic sound!

The Second Dumb Show

Enter Flamineo, Marcello, Camillo, with four more as captains: they drink healths, and dance; a vaulting horse is brought into the room; Marcello and two more whispered out of the room, while Flamineo and Camillo strip themselves into their shirts, as to vault; compliment who shall begin; as Camillo is about to vault, Flamineo pitcheth him upon his neck, and, with the help of the rest, writhes his neck about; seems to see if it be broke, and lays him folded double, as 'twere under the horse; makes shows to call for help; Marcello comes in, laments; sends for the cardinal and duke, who comes forth with armed men; wonders at the act; commands the body to be carried home; apprehends Flamineo, Marcello, and the rest, and go, as 'twere, to apprehend Vittoria.

Brach. 'Twas quaintly done; but yet each circumstance
    I taste not fully.
Conj. Oh, 'twas most apparent!
    You saw them enter, charg'd with their deep healths
    To their boon voyage; and, to second that,
    Flamineo calls to have a vaulting horse
    Maintain their sport; the virtuous Marcello
    Is innocently plotted forth the room;
    Whilst your eye saw the rest, and can inform you
    The engine of all.
Brach. It seems Marcello and Flamineo
    Are both committed.
Conj. Yes, you saw them guarded;
    And now they are come with purpose to apprehend
    Your mistress, fair Vittoria.   We are now
    Beneath her roof: 'twere fit we instantly
    Make out by some back postern.
Brach. Noble friend,
    You bind me ever to you: this shall stand
    As the firm seal annexed to my hand;
    It shall enforce a payment.
Conj. Sir, I thank you.   *[Exit Brachiano.*
    Both flowers and weeds spring, when the sun is warm,
    And great men do great good, or else great harm.   *[Exit.*

ACT III

Scene I

*Enter Francisco de Medicis, and Monticelso, their Chancellor
and Register*

Fran. You have dealt discreetly, to obtain the presence
    Of all the grave lieger ambassadors
    To hear Vittoria's trial.
Mont. 'Twas not ill;
    For, sir, you know we have naught but circumstances
    To charge her with, about her husband's death:
    Their approbation, therefore, to the proofs
    Of her black lust shall make her infamous

To all our neighbouring kingdoms.   I wonder
If Brachiano will be here?

Fran. Oh, fie! 'Twere impudence too palpable.   [*Exeunt.*

Enter Flamineo and Marcello guarded, and a Lawyer

Lawyer. What, are you in by the week? So—I will try now
whether thy wit be close prisoner—methinks none should sit
upon thy sister, but old whore-masters——

Flam. Or cuckolds; for your cuckold is your most terrible
tickler of lechery.   Whore-masters would serve; for none are
judges at tilting, but those that have been old tilters.

Lawyer. My lord duke and she have been very private.

Flam. You are a dull ass; 'tis threatened they have been very
public.

Lawyer. If it can be proved they have but kissed one another——

Flam. What then?

Lawyer. My lord cardinal will ferret them.

Flam. A cardinal, I hope, will not catch conies.

Lawyer. For to sow kisses (mark what I say), to sow kisses is to
reap lechery; and, I am sure, a woman that will endure
kissing is half won.

Flam. True, her upper part, by that rule; if you will win her
nether part too, you know what follows.

Lawyer. Hark! the ambassadors are 'lighted——

Flam. I do put on this feigned garb of mirth,
To gull suspicion.

Marc. Oh, my unfortunate sister!
I would my dagger-point had cleft her heart
When she first saw Brachiano: you, 'tis said,
Were made his engine, and his stalking horse,
To undo my sister.

Flam. I am a kind of path
To her and mine own preferment.

Marc. Your ruin.

Flam. Hum! thou art a soldier,
Followest the great duke, feed'st his victories,
As witches do their serviceable spirits,
Even with thy prodigal blood: what hast got?
But, like the wealth of captains, a poor handful,
Which in thy palm thou bear'st, as men hold water;
Seeking to grip it fast, the frail reward
Steals through thy fingers.

Marc. Sir!

Flam. Thou hast scarce maintenance
  To keep thee in fresh chamois.
Marc. Brother!
Flam. Hear me:
  And thus, when we have even pour'd ourselves
  Into great fights, for their ambition,
  Or idle spleen, how shall we find reward?
  But as we seldom find the mistletoe,
  Sacred to physic, or the builder oak,
  Without a mandrake by it; so in our quest of gain,
  Alas, the poorest of their forc'd dislikes
  At a limb proffers, but at heart it strikes!
  This is lamented doctrine.
Marc. Come, come.
Flam. When age shall turn thee
  White as a blooming hawthorn——
Marc. I 'll interrupt you:
  For love of virtue bear an honest heart,
  And stride o'er every politic respect,
  Which, where they most advance, they most infect.
  Were I your father, as I am your brother,
  I should not be ambitious to leave you
  A better patrimony.
Flam. I 'll think on 't.   [*Enter Savoy Ambassador.*
  The lord ambassadors.

    [*Here there is a passage of the Lieger Ambassadors over the
       stage severally.*

Enter French Ambassador

Lawyer. Oh, my sprightly Frenchman! Do you know him? he 's
  an admirable tilter.
Flam. I saw him at last tilting: he showed like a pewter candle-
  stick fashioned like a man in armour, holding a tilting staff
  in his hand, little bigger than a candle of twelve i' th'
  pound.
Lawyer. Oh, but he 's an excellent horseman!
Flam. A lame one in his lofty tricks; he sleeps a-horseback,
  like a poulterer.

Enter English and Spanish

Lawyer. Lo you, my Spaniard!
Flam. He carries his face in 's ruff, as I have seen a serving-man

carry glasses in a cypress hatband, monstrous steady, for fear
of breaking; he looks like the claw of a blackbird, first salted,
and then broiled in a candle.　　　　　　　　　　*[Exeunt.*

SCENE II

The Arraignment of Vittoria

*Enter Francisco, Monticelso, the six Lieger Ambassadors,
Brachiano, Vittoria, Zanche, Flamineo, Marcello, Lawyer,
and a Guard.*

Mont. Forbear, my lord, here is no place assign'd you.
　This business, by his Holiness, is left
　To our examination.
Brach. May it thrive with you.　　*[Lays a rich gown under him.*
Fran. A chair there for his lordship.
Brach. Forbear your kindness: an unbidden guest
　Should travel as Dutch women go to church,
　Bear their stools with them.
Mont. At your pleasure, sir.
　Stand to the table, gentlewoman.　Now, signior,
　Fall to your plea.
*Lawyer. Domine judex, converte oculos in hanc pestem, mulierum
　corruptissimam.*
Vit. What 's he?
Fran. A lawyer that pleads against you.
Vit. Pray, my lord, let him speak his usual tongue,
　I 'll make no answer else.
Fran. Why, you understand Latin.
Vit. I do, sir, but amongst this auditory
　Which come to hear my cause, the half or more
　May be ignorant in 't.
Mont. Go on, sir.
Vit. By your favour,
　I will not have my accusation clouded
　In a strange tongue: all this assembly
　Shall hear what you can charge me with.
Fran. Signior,
　You need not stand on 't much; pray, change your language.
Mont. Oh, for God's sake—Gentlewoman, your credit
　Shall be more famous by it.

Lawyer. Well then, have at you.
Vit. I am at the mark, sir; I 'll give aim to you,
   And tell you how near you shoot.
Lawyer. Most literated judges, please your lordships
   So to connive your judgments to the view
   Of this debauch'd and diversivolent woman;
   Who such a black concatenation
   Of mischief hath effected, that to extirp
   The memory of 't, must be the consummation
   Of her, and her projections——
Vit. What 's all this?
Lawyer. Hold your peace!
   Exorbitant sins must have exulceration.
Vit. Surely, my lords, this lawyer here hath swallow'd
   Some 'pothecaries' bills, or proclamations;
   And now the hard and undigestible words
   Come up, like stones we use give hawks for physic.
   Why, this is Welsh to Latin.
Lawyer. My lords, the woman
   Knows not her tropes, nor figures, nor is perfect
   In the academic derivation
   Of grammatical elocution.
Fran. Sir, your pains
   Shall be well spar'd, and your deep eloquence
   Be worthily applauded amongst those
   Which understand you.
Lawyer. My good lord.
Fran. Sir,
   Put up your papers in your fustian bag—
             [*Francisco speaks this as in scorn.*
   Cry mercy, sir, 'tis buckram and accept
   My notion of your learn'd verbosity.
Lawyer. I most graduatically thank your lordship:
   I shall have use for them elsewhere.
Mont. I shall be plainer with you, and paint out
   Your follies in more natural red and white
   Than that upon your cheek.
Vit. Oh, you mistake!
   You raise a blood as noble in this cheek
   As ever was your mother's.
Mont. I must spare you, till proof cry whore to that.
   Observe this creature here, my honour'd lords,

A woman of a most prodigious spirit,
  In her effected.
Vit. My honourable lord,
  It doth not suit a reverend cardinal
  To play the lawyer thus.
Mont. Oh, your trade instructs your language!
  You see, my lords, what goodly fruit she seems;
  Yet like those apples travellers report
  To grow where Sodom and Gomorrah stood,
  I will but touch her, and you straight shall see
  She 'll fall to soot and ashes.
Vit. Your envenom'd 'pothecary should do 't.
Mont. I am resolv'd,
  Were there a second paradise to lose,
  This devil would betray it.
Vit. O poor Charity!
  Thou art seldom found in scarlet.
Mont. Who knows not how, when several night by night
  Her gates were chok'd with coaches, and her rooms
  Outbrav'd the stars with several kind of lights;
  When she did counterfeit a prince's court
  In music, banquets, and most riotous surfeits;
  This whore forsooth was holy.
Vit. Ha! whore! what 's that?
Mont. Shall I expound whore to you? sure I shall;
  I 'll give their perfect character.   They are first,
  Sweetmeats which rot the eater; in man's nostrils
  Poison'd perfumes.   They are cozening alchemy;
  Shipwrecks in calmest weather.   What are whores!
  Cold Russian winters, that appear so barren,
  As if that nature had forgot the spring.
  They are the true material fire of hell:
  Worse than those tributes i' th' Low Countries paid,
  Exactions upon meat, drink, garments, sleep,
  Ay, even on man's perdition, his sin.
  They are those brittle evidences of law,
  Which forfeit all a wretched man's estate
  For leaving out one syllable.   What are whores!
  They are those flattering bells have all one tune,
  At weddings, and at funerals.   Your rich whores
  Are only treasuries by extortion fill'd,
  And emptied by curs'd riot.   They are worse,
  Worse than dead bodies which are begg'd at gallows,

And wrought upon by surgeons, to teach man
Wherein he is imperfect.   What 's a whore!
She 's like the guilty counterfeited coin,
Which, whosoe'er first stamps it, brings in trouble
All that receive it.

Vit. This character 'scapes me.

Mont. You, gentlewoman!
Take from all beasts and from all minerals
Their deadly poison——

Vit. Well, what then?

Mont. I 'll tell thee;
I 'll find in thee a 'pothecary's shop,
To sample them all.

Fr. Ambass. She hath liv'd ill.

Eng. Ambass. True, but the cardinal 's too bitter.

Mont. You know what whore is.   Next the devil adultery,
Enters the devil murder.

Fran. Your unhappy husband
Is dead.

Vit. Oh, he 's a happy husband!
Now he owes nature nothing.

Fran. And by a vaulting engine.

Mont. An active plot; he jump'd into his grave.

Fran. What a prodigy was 't,
That from some two yards' height, a slender man
Should break his neck!

Mont. I' th' rushes!

Fran. And what 's more,
Upon the instant lose all use of speech,
All vital motion, like a man had lain
Wound up three days.   Now mark each circumstance.

Mont. And look upon this creature was his wife!
She comes not like a widow; she comes arm'd
With scorn and impudence: is this a mourning-habit?

Vit. Had I foreknown his death, as you suggest,
I would have bespoke my mourning.

Mont. Oh, you are cunning!

Vit. You shame your wit and judgment,
To call it so.   What! is my just defence
By him that is my judge call'd impudence?
Let me appeal then from this Christian court,
To the uncivil Tartar.

Mont. See, my lords,
   She scandals our proceedings.
Vit. Humbly thus,
   Thus low, to the most worthy and respected
   Lieger ambassadors, my modesty
   And womanhood I tender; but withal,
   So entangled in a curs'd accusation,
   That my defence, of force, like Perseus,
   Must personate masculine virtue.   To the point.
   Find me but guilty, sever head from body,
   We 'll part good friends: I scorn to hold my life
   At yours, or any man's entreaty, sir.
Eng. Ambass. She hath a brave spirit.
Mont. Well, well, such counterfeit jewels
   Make true ones oft suspected.
Vit. You are deceiv'd:
   For know, that all your strict-combined heads,
   Which strike against this mine of diamonds,
   Shall prove but glassen hammers: they shall break.
   These are but feigned shadows of my evils.
   Terrify babes, my lord, with painted devils,
   I am past such needless palsy.   For your names
   Of 'whore' and 'murderess', they proceed from you,
   As if a man should spit against the wind,
   The filth returns in 's face.
Mont. Pray you, mistress, satisfy me one question:
   Who lodg'd beneath your roof that fatal night
   Your husband broke his neck?
Brach. That question
   Enforceth me break silence: I was there.
Mont. Your business?
Brach. Why, I came to comfort her,
   And take some course for settling her estate,
   Because I heard her husband was in debt
   To you, my lord.
Mont. He was.
Brach. And 'twas strangely fear'd,
   That you would cozen her.
Mont. Who made you overseer?
Brach. Why, my charity, my charity, which should flow
   From every generous and noble spirit,
   To orphans and to widows.
Mont. Your lust!

Brach. Cowardly dogs bark loudest: sirrah priest,
    I 'll talk with you hereafter.   Do you hear?
    The sword you frame of such an excellent temper,
    I 'll sheathe in your own bowels.
    There are a number of thy coat resemble
    Your common post-boys.
Mont. Ha!
Brach. Your mercenary post-boys;
    Your letters carry truth, but 'tis your guise
    To fill your mouths with gross and impudent lies.
Servant. My lord, your gown.
Brach. Thou liest, 'twas my stool:
    Bestow 't upon thy master, that will challenge
    The rest o' th' household-stuff; for Brachiano
    Was ne'er so beggarly to take a stool
    Out of another's lodging: let him make
    Vallance for his bed on 't, or a demy foot-cloth
    For his most reverend moil.   Monticelso,
    Nemo me impune lacessit.   [*Exit.*
Mont. Your champion 's gone.
Vit. The wolf may prey the better.
Fran. My lord, there 's great suspicion of the murder,
    But no sound proof who did it.   For my part,
    I do not think she hath a soul so black
    To act a deed so bloody; if she have,
    As in cold countries husbandmen plant vines,
    And with warm blood manure them; even so
    One summer she will bear unsavoury fruit,
    And ere next spring wither both branch and root.
    The act of blood let pass; only descend
    To matter of incontinence.
Vit. I discern poison
    Under your gilded pills.
Mont. Now the duke 's gone, I will produce a letter
    Wherein 'twas plotted, he and you should meet
    At an apothecary's summer-house,
    Down by the River Tiber,—view 't, my lords,
    Where after wanton bathing and the heat
    Of a lascivious banquet—I pray read it,
    I shame to speak the rest.
Vit. Grant I was tempted;
    Temptation to lust proves not the act:
    Casta est quam nemo rogavit.

You read his hot love to me, but you want
My frosty answer.

Mont. Frost i' th' dog-days! strange!

Vit. Condemn you me for that the duke did love me?
So may you blame some fair and crystal river,
For that some melancholic distracted man
Hath drown'd himself in 't.

Mont. Truly drown'd, indeed.

Vit. Sum up my faults, I pray, and you shall find,
That beauty and gay clothes, a merry heart,
And a good stomach to feast, are all,
All the poor crimes that you can charge me with.
In faith, my lord, you might go pistol flies,
The sport would be more noble.

Mont. Very good.

Vit. But take your course: it seems you 've beggar'd me first,
And now would fain undo me.   I have houses,
Jewels, and a poor remnant of crusadoes;
Would those would make you charitable!

Mont. If the devil
Did ever take good shape, behold his picture.

Vit. You have one virtue left,
You will not flatter me.

Fran. Who brought this letter?

Vit. I am not compell'd to tell you.

Mont. My lord duke sent to you a thousand ducats
The twelfth of August.

Vit. 'Twas to keep your cousin
From prison; I paid use for 't.

Mont. I rather think,
'Twas interest for his lust.

Vit. Who says so but yourself?
If you be my accuser,
Pray cease to be my judge: come from the bench;
Give in your evidence 'gainst me, and let these
Be moderators.   My lord cardinal,
Were your intelligencing ears as loving
As to my thoughts, had you an honest tongue,
I would not care though you proclaim'd them all.

Mont. Go to, go to.
After your goodly and vainglorious banquet,
I 'll give you a choke-pear.

Vit. O' your own grafting?

Mont. You were born in Venice, honourably descended
 From the Vittelli: 'twas my cousin's fate,
 Ill may I name the hour, to marry you;
 He bought you of your father.

Vit. Ha!

Mont. He spent there in six months
 Twelve thousand ducats, and (to my acquaintance)
 Receiv'd in dowry with you not one julio:
 'Twas a hard pennyworth, the ware being so light.
 I yet but draw the curtain; now to your picture:
 You came from thence a most notorious strumpet,
 And so you have continued.

Vit. My lord!

Mont. Nay, hear me,
 You shall have time to prate.   My Lord Brachiano—
 Alas! I make but repetition
 Of what is ordinary and Rialto talk,
 And ballated, and would be play'd a' th' stage,
 But that vice many times finds such loud friends,
 That preachers are charm'd silent.
 You, gentlemen, Flamineo and Marcello,
 The Court hath nothing now to charge you with,
 Only you must remain upon your sureties
 For your appearance.

Fran. I stand for Marcello.

Flam. And my lord duke for me.

Mont. For you, Vittoria, your public fault,
 Join'd to th' condition of the present time,
 Takes from you all the fruits of noble pity,
 Such a corrupted trial have you made
 Both of your life and beauty, and been styl'd
 No less an ominous fate than blazing stars
 To princes.   Hear your sentence: you are confin'd
 Unto a house of convertites, and your bawd——

Flam. [*Aside.*] Who, I?

Mont. The Moor.

Flam. [*Aside.*] Oh, I am a sound man again.

Vit. A house of convertites! what 's that?

Mont. A house of penitent whores.

Vit. Do the noblemen in Rome
 Erect it for their wives, that I am sent
 To lodge there?

Fran. You must have patience.

Vit. I must first have vengeance!
   I fain would know if you have your salvation
   By patent, that you proceed thus.
Mont. Away with her,
   Take her hence.
Vit. A rape! a rape!
Mont. How?
Vit. Yes, you have ravish'd justice;
   Forc'd her to do your pleasure.
Mont. Fie, she 's mad——
Vit. Die with those pills in your most cursed maw,
   Should bring you health! or while you sit o' th' bench,
   Let your own spittle choke you!
Mont. She 's turn'd fury.
Vit. That the last day of judgment may so find you,
   And leave you the same devil you were before!
   Instruct me, some good horse-leech, to speak treason;
   For since you cannot take my life for deeds,
   Take it for words: O woman's poor revenge,
   Which dwells but in the tongue! I will not weep;
   No, I do scorn to call up one poor tear
   To fawn on your injustice: bear me hence
   Unto this house of—what 's your mitigating title?
Mont. Of convertites.
Vit. It shall not be a house of convertites;
   My mind shall make it honester to me
   Than the Pope's palace, and more peaceable
   Than thy soul, though thou art a cardinal.
   Know this, and let it somewhat raise your spite,
   Through darkness diamonds spread their richest light. [*Exit.*

Enter Brachiano

Brach. Now you and I are friends, sir, we 'll shake hands
   In a friend's grave together; a fit place,
   Being th' emblem of soft peace, t' atone our hatred.
Fran. Sir, what 's the matter?
Brach. I will not chase more blood from that lov'd cheek;
   You have lost too much already; fare you well. [*Exit.*
Fran. How strange these words sound! what 's the interpre-
   tation?
Flam. [*Aside.*] Good; this is a preface to the discovery of the
   duchess' death: he carries it well. Because now I cannot
   counterfeit a whining passion for the death of my lady, I

will feign a mad humour for the disgrace of my sister; and
that will keep off idle questions.   Treason's tongue hath a
villainous palsy in 't; I will talk to any man, hear no man, and
for a time appear a politic madman.   [*Exit.*

Enter Giovanni, and Count Lodovico

Fran. How now, my noble cousin? what, in black!
Giov. Yes, uncle, I was taught to imitate you
     In virtue, and you must imitate me
     In colours of your garments.   My sweet mother
     Is——
Fran. How? where?
Giov. Is there; no, yonder: indeed, sir, I 'll not tell you,
     For I shall make you weep.
Fran. Is dead?
Giov. Do not blame me now,
     I did not tell you so.
Lodo. She 's dead, my lord.
Fran. Dead!
Mont. Bless'd lady, thou art now above thy woes!
     Will 't please your lordships to withdraw a little?
Giov. What do the dead do, uncle? do they eat,
     Hear music, go a-hunting, and be merry,
     As we that live?
Fran. No, coz; they sleep.
Giov. Lord, Lord, that I were dead!
     I have not slept these six nights.   When do they wake?
Fran. When God shall please.
Giov. Good God, let her sleep ever!
     For I have known her wake an hundred nights,
     When all the pillow where she laid her head
     Was brine-wet with her tears.   I am to complain to you, sir;
     I 'll tell you how they have us'd her now she 's dead:
     They wrapp'd her in a cruel fold of lead,
     And would not let me kiss her.
Fran. Thou didst love her?
Giov. I have often heard her say she gave me suck,
     And it should seem by that she dearly lov'd me,
     Since princes seldom do it.
Fran. Oh, all of my poor sister that remains!
     Take him away for God's sake!   [*Exit Giovanni.*
Mont. How now, my lord?

Fran. Believe me, I am nothing but her grave;
And I shall keep her blessed memory
Longer than thousand epitaphs.   [*Exeunt.*

SCENE III

Enter Flamineo as distracted, Marcello, and Lodovico

Flam. We endure the strokes like anvils or hard steel,
Till pain itself make us no pain to feel.
Who shall do me right now? is this the end of service? I 'd
rather go weed garlic; travel through France, and be mine
own ostler; wear sheep-skin linings, or shoes that stink
of blacking; be entered into the list of the forty thousand
pedlars in Poland. [*Enter Savoy Ambassador.*] Would I had
rotted in some surgeon's house at Venice, built upon the
pox as well as on piles, ere I had served Brachiano!

Savoy Ambass. You must have comfort.

Flam. Your comfortable words are like honey: they relish well
in your mouth that 's whole, but in mine that 's wounded, they
go down as if the sting of the bee were in them.   Oh, they have
wrought their purpose cunningly, as if they would not seem to
do it of malice! In this a politician imitates the devil, as the
devil imitates a canon; wheresoever he comes to do mischief,
he comes with his backside towards you.

Enter French Ambassador

Fr. Ambass. The proofs are evident.

Flam. Proof! 'twas corruption.   O gold, what a god art thou!
and O man, what a devil art thou to be tempted by that cursed
mineral! Yon diversivolent lawyer, mark him! knaves turn
informers, as maggots turn to flies, you may catch gudgeons
with either.   A cardinal! I would he would hear me: there 's
nothing so holy but money will corrupt and putrify it, like
victual under the line. [*Enter English Ambassador.*] You are
happy in England, my lord; here they sell justice with those
weights they press men to death with.   O horrible salary!

Eng. Ambass. Fie, fie, Flamineo.

Flam. Bells ne'er ring well, till they are at their full pitch; and

I hope yon cardinal shall never have the grace to pray well,
till he come to the scaffold.   If they were racked now to know
the confederacy: but your noblemen are privileged from the
rack; and well may, for a little thing would pull some of them
a-pieces afore they came to their arraignment.   Religion, oh,
how it is commeddled with policy!   The first blood shed in the
world happened about religion.   Would I were a Jew!

Marc. Oh, there are too many!

Flam. You are deceived; there are not Jews enough, priests
enough, nor gentlemen enough.

Marc. How?

Flam. I'll prove it; for if there were Jews enough, so many
Christians would not turn usurers; if priests enough, one
should not have six benefices; and if gentlemen enough, so
many early mushrooms, whose best growth sprang from a
dunghill, should not aspire to gentility.   Farewell: let others
live by begging: be thou one of them practise the art of Wolner
in England, to swallow all's given thee: and yet let one
purgation make thee as hungry again as fellows that work in
a saw-pit.   I'll go hear the screech-owl.   [*Exit.*

Lodo. This was Brachiano's pander; and 'tis strange
That in such open, and apparent guilt
Of his adulterous sister, he dare utter
So scandalous a passion.   I must wind him.

Re-enter Flamineo

Flam. How dares this banish'd count return to Rome,
His pardon not yet purchas'd! I have heard
The deceased duchess gave him pension,
And that he came along from Padua
I' th' train of the young prince.   There's somewhat in't:
Physicians, that cure poisons, still do work
With counter-poisons.

Marc. Mark this strange encounter.

Flam. The god of melancholy turn thy gall to poison,
And let the stigmatic wrinkles in thy face,
Like to the boisterous waves in a rough tide,
One still overtake another.

Lodo. I do thank thee,
And I do wish ingeniously for thy sake,
The dog-days all year long.

Flam. How croaks the raven?
Is our good duchess dead?

Lodo. Dead.

Flam. O fate!
  Misfortune comes like the coroner's business
  Huddle upon huddle.

Lodo. Shalt thou and I join housekeeping?

Flam. Yes, content:
  Let 's be unsociably sociable.

Lodo. Sit some three days together, and discourse?

Flam. Only with making faces;
  Lie in our clothes.

Lodo. With faggots for our pillows.

Flam. And be lousy.

Lodo. In taffeta linings, that 's genteel melancholy;
  Sleep all day.

Flam. Yes; and, like your melancholic hare,
  Feed after midnight.   [*Enter Antonelli and Gasparo.*
  We are observed: see how yon couple grieve.

Lodo. What a strange creature is a laughing fool!
  As if man were created to no use
  But only to show his teeth.

Flam. I 'll tell thee what,
  It would do well instead of looking-glasses,
  To set one's face each morning by a saucer
  Of a witch's congeal'd blood.

Lodo. Precious rogue!
  We 'll never part.

Flam. Never, till the beggary of courtiers,
  The discontent of churchmen, want of soldiers,
  And all the creatures that hang manacled,
  Worse than strappadoed, on the lowest felly
  Of fortune's wheel, be taught, in our two lives,
  To scorn that world which life of means deprives.

Ant. My lord, I bring good news. The Pope, on 's death-bed,
  At th' earnest suit of the great Duke of Florence,
  Hath sign'd your pardon, and restor'd unto you——

Lodo. I thank you for your news. Look up again,
  Flamineo, see my pardon.

Flam. Why do you laugh?
  There was no such condition in our covenant.

Lodo. Why?

Flam. You shall not seem a happier man than I:
  You know our vow, sir; if you will be merry,
  Do it i' th' like posture, as if some great man

Sat while his enemy were executed:
Though it be very lechery unto thee,
Do 't with a crabbed politician's face.

Lodo. Your sister is a damnable whore.

Flam. Ha!

Lodo. Look you, I spake that laughing.

Flam. Dost ever think to speak again?

Lodo. Do you hear?
Wilt sell me forty ounces of her blood
To water a mandrake?

Flam. Poor lord, you did vow
To live a lousy creature.

Lodo. Yes.

Flam. Like one
That had for ever forfeited the daylight,
By being in debt.

Lodo. Ha, ha!

Flam. I do not greatly wonder you do break,
Your lordship learn'd 't long since.   But I 'll tell you.

Lodo. What?

Flam. And 't shall stick by you.

Lodo. I long for it.

Flam. This laughter scurvily becomes your face:
If you will not be melancholy, be angry.   [*Strikes him.*
See, now I laugh too.

Marc. You are to blame: I 'll force you hence.

Lodo. Unhand me.   [*Exeunt Marcello and Flamineo.*
That e'er I should be forc'd to right myself,
Upon a pander!

Ant. My lord.

Lodo. H' had been as good met with his fist a thunderbolt.

Gas. How this shows!

Lodo. Ud's death! how did my sword miss him?
These rogues that are most weary of their lives
Still 'scape the greatest dangers.
A pox upon him; all his reputation,
Nay, all the goodness of his family,
Is not worth half this earthquake:
I learn'd it of no fencer to shake thus:
Come, I 'll forget him, and go drink some wine.

[*Exeunt.*

ACT IV

SCENE I

Enter Francisco and Monticelso

Mont. Come, come, my lord, untie your folded thoughts,
  And let them dangle loose, as a bride's hair.
  Your sister 's poison'd.
Fran. Far be it from my thoughts
  To seek revenge.
Mont. What, are you turn'd all marble?
Fran. Shall I defy him, and impose a war,
  Most burthensome on my poor subjects' necks,
  Which at my will I have not power to end?
  You know, for all the murders, rapes, and thefts,
  Committed in the horrid lust of war,
  He that unjustly caus'd it first proceed,
  Shall find it in his grave, and in his seed.
Mont. That 's not the course I 'd wish you; pray observe me.
  We see that undermining more prevails
  Than doth the cannon.   Bear your wrongs conceal'd,
  And, patient as the tortoise, let this camel
  Stalk o'er your back unbruis'd: sleep with the lion,
  And let this brood of secure foolish mice
  Play with your nostrils, till the time be ripe
  For th' bloody audit, and the fatal gripe:
  Aim like a cunning fowler, close one eye,
  That you the better may your game espy.
Fran. Free me, my innocence, from treacherous acts!
  I know there 's thunder yonder; and I 'll stand,
  Like a safe valley, which low bends the knee
  To some aspiring mountain: since I know
  Treason, like spiders weaving nets for flies,
  By her foul work is found, and in it dies.
  To pass away these thoughts, my honour'd lord,
  It is reported you possess a book,
  Wherein you have quoted, by intelligence,
  The names of all notorious offenders
  Lurking about the city.
Mont. Sir, I do;

And some there are which call it my black-book.
Well may the title hold; for though it teach not
The art of conjuring, yet in it lurk
The names of many devils.
Fran. Pray let 's see it.
Mont. I 'll fetch it to your lordship.   [*Exit.*
Fran. Monticelso,
   I will not trust thee, but in all my plots
   I 'll rest as jealous as a town besieg'd.
   Thou canst not reach what I intend to act:
   Your flax soon kindles, soon is out again,
   But gold slow heats, and long will hot remain.

Enter Monticelso, with the book

Mont. 'Tis here, my lord.
Fran. First, your intelligencers, pray let 's see.
Mont. Their number rises strangely;
   And some of them
   You 'd take for honest men.
   Next are panders.
   These are your pirates; and these following leaves
   For base rogues, that undo young gentlemen,
   By taking up commodities; for politic bankrupts;
   For fellows that are bawds to their own wives,
   Only to put off horses, and slight jewels,
   Clocks, defac'd plate, and such commodities,
   At birth of their first children.
Fran. Are there such?
Mont. These are for impudent bawds,
   That go in men's apparel; for usurers
   That share with scriveners for their good reportage:
   For lawyers that will antedate their writs:
   And some divines you might find folded there,
   But that I slip them o'er for conscience' sake.
   Here is a general catalogue of knaves:
   A man might study all the prisons o'er,
   Yet never attain this knowledge.
Fran. Murderers?
   Fold down the leaf, I pray;
   Good my lord, let me borrow this strange doctrine.
Mont. Pray, use 't, my lord.
Fran. I do assure your lordship,
   You are a worthy member of the State,

And have done infinite good in your discovery
Of these offenders.
Mont. Somewhat, sir.
Fran. O God!
  Better than tribute of wolves paid in England;
  'Twill hang their skins o' th' hedge.
Mont. I must make bold
  To leave your lordship.
Fran. Dearly, sir, I thank you:
  If any ask for me at court, report
  You have left me in the company of knaves.
[Exit Monticelso.
  I gather now by this, some cunning fellow
  That 's my lord's officer, and that lately skipp'd
  From a clerk's desk up to a justice' chair,
  Hath made this knavish summons, and intends,
  As th' rebels wont were to sell heads,
  So to make prize of these.   And thus it happens:
  Your poor rogues pay for 't, which have not the means
  To present bribe in fist; the rest o' th' band
  Are raz'd out of the knaves' record; or else
  My lord he winks at them with easy will;
  His man grows rich, the knaves are the knaves still.
  But to the use I 'll make of it; it shall serve
  To point me out a list of murderers,
  Agents for any villainy.   Did I want
  Ten leash of courtesans, it would furnish me;
  Nay, laundress three armies.   That in so little paper
  Should lie th' undoing of so many men!
  'Tis not so big as twenty declarations.
  See the corrupted use some make of books:
  Divinity, wrested by some factious blood,
  Draws swords, swells battles, and o'erthrows all good.
  To fashion my revenge more seriously,
  Let me remember my dead sister's face:
  Call for her picture? no, I 'll close mine eyes,
  And in a melancholic thought I 'll frame
[Enter Isabella's Ghost.
  Her figure 'fore me.   Now I ha' 't—how strong
  Imagination works! how she can frame
  Things which are not! methinks she stands afore me,
  And by the quick idea of my mind,
  Were my skill pregnant, I could draw her picture.

Thought, as a subtle juggler, makes us deem
Things supernatural, which have cause
Common as sickness. 'Tis my melancholy.
How cam'st thou by thy death?—how idle am I
To question mine own idleness!—did ever
Man dream awake till now?—remove this object;
Out of my brain with 't: what have I to do
With tombs, or death-beds, funerals, or tears,
That have to meditate upon revenge?   [*Exit Ghost.*
So, now 'tis ended, like an old wife's story.
Statesmen think often they see stranger sights
Than madmen. Come, to this weighty business.
My tragedy must have some idle mirth in 't,
Else it will never pass. I am in love,
In love with Corombona; and my suit
Thus halts to her in verse.—   [*He writes.*
I have done it rarely: Oh, the fate of princes!
I am so us'd to frequent flattery,
That, being alone, I now flatter myself:
But it will serve; 'tis seal'd. [*Enter servant.*] Bear this
To the House of Convertites, and watch your leisure
To give it to the hands of Corombona,
Or to the Matron, when some followers
Of Brachiano may be by. Away!   [*Exit Servant.*
He that deals all by strength, his wit is shallow;
When a man's head goes through, each limb will follow.
The engine for my business, bold Count Lodowick;
'Tis gold must such an instrument procure,
With empty fist no man doth falcons lure.
Brachiano, I am now fit for thy encounter:
Like the wild Irish, I 'll ne'er think thee dead
Till I can play at football with thy head,
Flectere si nequeo superos, Acheronta movebo.   [*Exit.*

SCENE II

Enter the Matron, and Flamineo

Matron. Should it be known the duke hath such recourse
     To your imprison'd sister, I were like
     T' incur much damage by it.
Flam. Not a scruple.

The Pope lies on his death-bed, and their heads
Are troubled now with other business
Than guarding of a lady.

Enter Servant

Servant. Yonder 's Flamineo in conference
  With the Matrona.—Let me speak with you:
  I would entreat you to deliver for me
  This letter to the fair Vittoria.
Matron. I shall, sir.

Enter Brachiano

Servant. With all care and secrecy;
  Hereafter you shall know me, and receive
  Thanks for this courtesy.   [*Exit.*
Flam. How now? what 's that?
Matron. A letter.
Flam. To my sister?   I 'll see 't deliver'd.
Brach. What 's that you read, Flamineo?
Flam. Look.
Brach. Ha! 'To the most unfortunate, his best respected
  Vittoria'.
  Who was the messenger?
Flam. I know not.
Brach. No! who sent it?
Flam. Ud's foot! you speak as if a man
  Should know what fowl is coffin'd in a bak'd meat
  Afore you cut it up.
Brach. I 'll open 't, were 't her heart.   What 's here subscrib'd!
  Florence! this juggling is gross and palpable.
  I have found out the conveyance.   Read it, read it.
Flam. [*Reads the letter.*] *Your tears I 'll turn to triumphs, be but*
      mine;
  Your prop is fallen: I pity, that a vine,
  Which princes heretofore have long'd to gather,
  Wanting supporters, now should fade and wither.
  Wine, i' faith, my lord, with lees would serve his turn.
  Your sad imprisonment I 'll soon uncharm,
  And with a princely uncontrolled arm
  Lead you to Florence, where my love and care
  Shall hang your wishes in my silver hair.
  A halter on his strange equivocation!
  Nor for my years return me the sad willow;
  Who prefer blossoms before fruit that 's mellow?

Rotten, on my knowledge, with lying too long i' th' bedstraw.
And all the lines of age this line convinces;
The gods never wax old, no more do princes.
A pox on 't, tear it; let 's have no more atheists, for God's sake.
Brach. Ud's death! I 'll cut her into atomies,
And let th' irregular north wind sweep her up,
And blow her int' his nostrils: where 's this whore?
Flam. What? what do you call her?
Brach. Oh, I could be mad!
Prevent the curs'd disease she 'll bring me to,
And tear my hair off.   Where 's this changeable stuff?
Flam. O'er head and ears in water, I assure you;
She is not for your wearing.
Brach. In, you pander!
Flam. What, me, my lord? am I your dog?
Brach. A bloodhound: do you brave, do you stand me?
Flam. Stand you! let those that have diseases run;
I need no plasters.
Brach. Would you be kick'd?
Flam. Would you have your neck broke?
I tell you, duke, I am not in Russia;
My shins must be kept whole.
Brach. Do you know me?
Flam. Oh, my lord, methodically!
As in this world there are degrees of evils,
So in this world there are degrees of devils.
You 're a great duke, I your poor secretary.
I do look now for a Spanish fig, or an Italian sallet, daily.
Brach. Pander, ply your convoy, and leave your prating.
Flam. All your kindness to me, is like that miserable courtesy
of Polyphemus to Ulysses; you reserve me to be devoured last:
you would dig turfs out of my grave to feed your larks; that
would be music to you.   Come, I 'll lead you to her.
Brach. Do you face me?
Flam. Oh, sir, I would not go before a politic enemy with my
back towards him, though there were behind me a whirlpool.

Enter Vittoria to Brachiano and Flamineo

Brach. Can you read, mistress? look upon that letter:
There are no characters, nor hieroglyphics.
You need no comment; I am grown your receiver.
God's precious! you shall be a brave great lady,
A stately and advanced whore.

Vit. Say, sir?

Brach. Come, come, let 's see your cabinet, discover
  Your treasury of love-letters.   Death and furies!
  I 'll see them all.

Vit. Sir, upon my soul,
  I have not any.   Whence was this directed?

Brach. Confusion on your politic ignorance!
  You are reclaim'd, are you? I 'll give you the bells,
  And let you fly to the devil.

Flam. Ware hawk, my lord.

Vit. Florence! this is some treacherous plot, my lord;
  To me he ne'er was lovely, I protest,
  So much as in my sleep.

Brach. Right! they are plots.
  Your beauty! Oh, ten thousand curses on 't!
  How long have I beheld the devil in crystal!
  Thou hast led me, like an heathen sacrifice,
  With music, and with fatal yokes of flowers,
  To my eternal ruin.   Woman to man
  Is either a god, or a wolf.

Vit. My lord——

Brach. Away!
  We 'll be as differing as two adamants,
  The one shall shun the other.   What! dost weep?
  Procure but ten of thy dissembling trade,
  Ye 'd furnish all the Irish funerals
  With howling past wild Irish.

Flam. Fie, my lord!

Brach. That hand, that cursed hand, which I have wearied
  With doting kisses!—Oh, my sweetest duchess,
  How lovely art thou now!—My loose thoughts
  Scatter like quicksilver: I was bewitch'd;
  For all the world speaks ill of thee.

Vit. No matter;
  I 'll live so now, I 'll make that world recant,
  And change her speeches.   You did name your duchess.

Brach. Whose death God pardon!

Vit. Whose death God revenge
  On thee, most godless duke!

Flam. Now for ten whirlwinds.

Vit. What have I gain'd by thee, but infamy?
  Thou hast stain'd the spotless honour of my house,
  And frighted thence noble society:

Like those, which sick o' th' palsy, and retain
Ill-scenting foxes 'bout them, are still shunn'd
By those of choicer nostrils.   What do you call this house?
Is this your palace? did not the judge style it
A house of penitent whores? who sent me to it?
Who hath the honour to advance Vittoria
To this incontinent college? is 't not you?
Is 't not your high preferment? go, go, brag
How many ladies you have undone, like me.
Fare you well, sir; let me hear no more of you!
I had a limb corrupted to an ulcer,
But I have cut it off; and now I 'll go
Weeping to heaven on crutches.   For your gifts,
I will return them all, and I do wish
That I could make you full executor
To all my sins.   O that I could toss myself
Into a grave as quickly! for all thou art worth
I 'll not shed one tear more—I 'll burst first.

                       [*She throws herself upon a bed.*

Brach. I have drunk Lethe: Vittoria!
  My dearest happiness! Vittoria!
  What do you ail, my love? why do you weep?
Vit. Yes, I now weep poniards, do you see?
Brach. Are not those matchless eyes mine?
Vit. I had rather
  They were not matches.
Brach. Is not this lip mine?
Vit. Yes; thus to bite it off, rather than give it thee.
Flam. Turn to my lord, good sister.
Vit. Hence, you pander!
Flam. Pander! am I the author of your sin?
Vit. Yes; he 's a base thief that a thief lets in.
Flam. We 're blown up, my lord——
Brach. Wilt thou hear me?
  Once to be jealous of thee, is t' express
  That I will love thee everlastingly,
  And never more be jealous.
Vit. O thou fool,
  Whose greatness hath by much o'ergrown thy wit!
  What dar'st thou do, that I not dare to suffer,
  Excepting to be still thy whore? for that,
  In the sea's bottom sooner thou shalt make
  A bonfire.

Flam. Oh, no oaths, for God's sake!

Brach. Will you hear me?

Vit. Never.

Flam. What a damn'd imposthume is a woman's will!
  Can nothing break it? [*Aside.*] Fie, fie, my lord,
  Women are caught as you take tortoises,
  She must be turn'd on her back.   Sister, by this hand
  I am on your side.—Come, come, you have wrong'd her;
  What a strange credulous man were you, my lord,
  To think the Duke of Florence would love her!
  Will any mercer take another's ware
  When once 'tis tows'd and sullied? And yet, sister,
  How scurvily this forwardness becomes you!
  Young leverets stand not long, and women's anger
  Should, like their flight, procure a little sport;
  A full cry for a quarter of an hour,
  And then be put to th' dead quat.

Brach. Shall these eyes,
  Which have so long time dwelt upon your face,
  Be now put out?

Flam. No cruel landlady i' th' world,
  Which lends forth groats to broom-men, and takes use
  For them, would do 't.
  Hand her, my lord, and kiss her: be not like
  A ferret, to let go your hold with blowing.

Brach. Let us renew right hands.

Vit. Hence!

Brach. Never shall rage, or the forgetful wine,
  Make me commit like fault.

Flam. Now you are i' th' way on 't, follow 't hard.

Brach. Be thou at peace with me, let all the world
  Threaten the cannon.

Flam. Mark his penitence;
  Best natures do commit the grossest faults,
  When they 're given o'er to jealousy, as best wine,
  Dying, makes strongest vinegar.   I 'll tell you:
  The sea 's more rough and raging than calm rivers,
  But not so sweet, nor wholesome.   A quiet woman
  Is a still water under a great bridge;
  A man may shoot her safely.

Vit. O ye dissembling men!

Flam. We suck'd that, sister,
  From women's breasts, in our first infancy.

Vit. To add misery to misery!

Brach. Sweetest!

Vit. Am I not low enough?
Ay, ay, your good heart gathers like a snowball,
Now your affection 's cold.

Flam. Ud's foot, it shall melt
To a heart again, or all the wine in Rome
Shall run o' th' lees for 't.

Vit. Your dog or hawk should be rewarded better
Than I have been.   I 'll speak not one word more.

Flam. Stop her mouth
With a sweet kiss, my lord.   So,
Now the tide 's turn'd, the vessel 's come about.
He 's a sweet armful.   Oh, we curl-hair'd men
Are still most kind to women! This is well.

Brach. That you should chide thus!

Flam. Oh, sir, your little chimneys
Do ever cast most smoke! I sweat for you.
Couple together with as deep a silence,
As did the Grecians in their wooden horse.
My lord, supply your promises with deeds;
You know that painted meat no hunger feeds.

Brach. Stay, ungrateful Rome——

Flam. Rome! it deserves to be call'd Barbary,
For our villainous usage.

Brach. Soft; the same project which the Duke of Florence,
(Whether in love or gullery I know not)
Laid down for her escape, will I pursue.

Flam. And no time fitter than this night, my lord.
The Pope being dead, and all the cardinals enter'd
The conclave, for th' electing a new Pope;
The city in a great confusion;
We may attire her in a page's suit,
Lay her post-horse, take shipping, and amain
For Padua.

Brach. I 'll instantly steal forth the Prince Giovanni,
And make for Padua.   You two with your old mother,
And young Marcello that attends on Florence,
If you can work him to it, follow me:
I will advance you all; for you, Vittoria,
Think of a duchess' title.

Flam. Lo you, sister!
Stay, my lord; I 'll tell you a tale.   The crocodile, which lives

in the River Nilus, hath a worm breeds i' th' teeth of 't, which puts it to extreme anguish: a little bird, no bigger than a wren, is barber-surgeon to this crocodile; flies into the jaws of 't, picks out the worm, and brings present remedy.   The fish, glad of ease, but ungrateful to her that did it, that the bird may not talk largely of her abroad for non-payment, closeth her chaps, intending to swallow her, and so put her to perpetual silence.   But nature, loathing such ingratitude, hath armed this bird with a quill or prick on the head, top o' th' which wounds the crocodile i' th' mouth, forceth her open her bloody prison, and away flies the pretty tooth-picker from her cruel patient.

Brach. Your application is, I have not rewarded
The service you have done me.
Flam. No, my lord.
You, sister, are the crocodile: you are blemish'd in your fame, my lord cures it; and though the comparison hold not in every particle, yet observe, remember, what good the bird with the prick i' th' head hath done you, and scorn ingratitude.
It may appear to some ridiculous
Thus to talk knave and madman, and sometimes
Come in with a dried sentence, stuffed with sage:
But this allows my varying of shapes;
Knaves do grow great by being great men's apes.   [*Exeunt.*

SCENE III

Enter Francisco, Lodovico, Gasparo, and six Ambassadors

Fran. So, my lord, I commend your diligence.
Guard well the conclave; and, as the order is,
Let none have conference with the cardinals.
Lodo. I shall, my lord.   Room for the ambassadors.
Gas. They 're wondrous brave to-day: why do they wear
These several habits?
Lodo. Oh, sir, they 're knights
Of several orders:
That lord i' th' black cloak, with the silver cross,
Is Knight of Rhodes; the next, Knight of St. Michael;
That, of the Golden Fleece; the Frenchman, there,
Knight of the Holy Ghost; my Lord of Savoy,
Knight of th' Annunciation; the Englishman

Is Knight of th' honour'd Garter, dedicated
Unto their saint, St. George. I could describe to you
Their several institutions, with the laws
Annexed to their orders; but that time
Permits not such discovery.

Fran. Where 's Count Lodowick?

Lodo. Here, my lord.

Fran. 'Tis o' th' point of dinner time;
Marshal the cardinals' service.

Lodo. Sir, I shall. [*Enter Servants, with several dishes covered.*
Stand, let me search your dish. Who 's this for?

Servant. For my Lord Cardinal Monticelso.

Lodo. Whose this?

Servant. For my Lord Cardinal of Bourbon.

Fr. Ambass. Why doth he search the dishes? to observe
What meat is dressed?

Eng. Ambass. No, sir, but to prevent
Lest any letters should be convey'd in,
To bribe or to solicit the advancement
Of any cardinal. When first they enter,
'Tis lawful for the ambassadors of princes
To enter with them, and to make their suit
For any man their prince affecteth best;
But after, till a general election,
No man may speak with them.

Lodo. You that attend on the lord cardinals,
Open the window, and receive their viands.

Card. [*Within.*] You must return the service: the lord
cardinals
Are busied 'bout electing of the Pope;
They have given o'er scrutiny, and are fallen
To admiration.

Lodo. Away, away.

Fran. I 'll lay a thousand ducats you hear news
Of a Pope presently. Hark; sure he 's elected:
Behold, my Lord of Arragon appears
On the church battlements. [*A Cardinal on the terrace.*

*Arragon. Denuntio vobis gaudium magnum: Reverendissimus
Cardinalis Lorenzo de Monticelso electus est in sedem apostolicam,
et elegit sibi nomen Paulum Quartum.*

Omnes. Vivat Sanctus Pater Paulus Quartus!

Servant. Vittoria, my lord——

Fran. Well, what of her?

Servant. Is fled the city——

Fran. Ha!

Servant. With Duke Brachiano.

Fran. Fled! where 's the Prince Giovanni?

Servant. Gone with his father.

Fran. Let the Matrona of the Convertites
Be apprehended.   Fled?   O damnable!
How fortunate are my wishes! why, 'twas this
I only labour'd: I did send the letter
T' instruct him what to do.   Thy fame, fond duke,
I first have poison'd; directed thee the way
To marry a whore; what can be worse?   This follows:
The hand must act to drown the passionate tongue,
I scorn to wear a sword and prate of wrong.

Enter Monticelso in State

Mont. *Concedimus vobis Apostolicam benedictionem, et re-*
missionem peccatorum.
My lord reports Vittoria Corombona
Is stol'n from forth the House of Convertites
By Brachiano, and they 're fled the city.
Now, though this be the first day of our seat,
We cannot better please the Divine Power,
Than to sequester from the Holy Church
These cursed persons.   Make it therefore known,
We do denounce excommunication
Against them both: all that are theirs in Rome
We likewise banish.   Set on.
              [*Exeunt all but Francisco and Lodovico.*

Fran. Come, dear Lodovico;
You have ta'en the sacrament to prosecute
Th' intended murder?

Lodo. With all constancy.
But, sir, I wonder you 'll engage yourself
In person, being a great prince.

Fran. Divert me not.
Most of his court are of my faction,
And some are of my council.   Noble friend,
Our danger shall be like in this design:
Give leave part of the glory may be mine.   [*Exit Francisco.*

Enter Monticelso

Mont. Why did the Duke of Florence with such care
    Labour your pardon? say.
Lodo. Italian beggars will resolve you that,
    Who, begging of an alms, bid those they beg of,
    Do good for their own sakes; or 't may be,
    He spreads his bounty with a sowing hand,
    Like kings, who many times give out of measure,
    Not for desert so much, as for their pleasure.
Mont. I know you 're cunning.   Come, what devil was that
    That you were raising?
Lodo. Devil, my lord?
Mont. I ask you,
    How doth the duke employ you, that his bonnet
    Fell with such compliment unto his knee,
    When he departed from you?
Lodo. Why, my lord,
    He told me of a resty Barbary horse
    Which he would fain have brought to the career,
    The sault, and the ring galliard: now, my lord,
    I have a rare French rider.
Mont. Take you heed,
    Lest the jade break your neck.   Do you put me off
    With your wild horse-tricks? Sirrah, you do lie.
    Oh, thou 'rt a foul black cloud, and thou dost threat
    A violent storm!
Lodo. Storms are i' th' air, my lord;
    I am too low to storm.
Mont. Wretched creature!
    I know that thou art fashion'd for all ill,
    Like dogs, that once get blood, they 'll ever kill.
    About some murder, was 't not?
Lodo. I 'll not tell you:
    And yet I care not greatly if I do;
    Marry, with this preparation.   Holy father,
    I come not to you as an intelligencer,
    But as a penitent sinner: what I utter
    Is in confession merely; which, you know,
    Must never be reveal'd.
Mont. You have o'erta'en me.
Lodo. Sir, I did love Brachiano's duchess dearly,
    Or rather I pursued her with hot lust,
    Though she ne'er knew on 't.   She was poison'd;

Upon my soul she was: for which I have sworn
T' avenge her murder.
Mont. To the Duke of Florence?
Lodo. To him I have.
Mont. Miserable creature!
  If thou persist in this, 'tis damnable.
  Dost thou imagine, thou canst slide on blood,
  And not be tainted with a shameful fall?
  Or, like the black and melancholic yew-tree,
  Dost think to root thyself in dead men's graves,
  And yet to prosper? Instruction to thee
  Comes like sweet showers to o'er-harden'd ground;
  They wet, but pierce not deep. And so I leave thee,
  With all the furies hanging 'bout thy neck,
  Till by thy penitence thou remove this evil,
  In conjuring from thy breast that cruel devil.   [*Exit.*
Lodo. I 'll give it o'er; he says 'tis damnable:
  Besides I did expect his suffrage,
  By reason of Camillo's death.

Enter Servant and Francisco

Fran. Do you know that count?
Servant. Yes, my lord.
Fran. Bear him these thousand ducats to his lodging.
  Tell him the Pope hath sent them. Happily
  That will confirm more than all the rest.   [*Exit.*
Servant. Sir.
Lodo. To me, sir?
Servant. His Holiness hath sent you a thousand crowns,
  And wills you, if you travel, to make him
  Your patron for intelligence.
Lodo. His creature ever to be commanded.—
  Why now 'tis come about. He rail'd upon me;
  And yet these crowns were told out, and laid ready,
  Before he knew my voyage. Oh, the art,
  The modest form of greatness! that do sit,
  Like brides at wedding-dinners, with their looks turn'd
  From the least wanton jests, their puling stomach
  Sick of the modesty, when their thoughts are loose,
  Even acting of those hot and lustful sports
  Are to ensue about midnight: such his cunning!
  He sounds my depth thus with a golden plummet.

I am doubly arm'd now.   Now to th' act of blood.
There 's but three furies found in spacious hell,
But in a great man's breast three thousand dwell.   [*Exit.*

ACT V

Scene I

*A passage over the stage of Brachiano, Flamineo, Marcello,
Hortensio, Corombona, Cornelia, Zanche, and others: Flamineo
and Hortensio remain.*

Flam. In all the weary minutes of my life,
　　Day ne'er broke up till now.   This marriage
　　Confirms me happy.
Hort. 'Tis a good assurance.
　　Saw you not yet the Moor that 's come to court?
Flam. Yes, and conferr'd with him i' th' duke's closet.
　　I have not seen a goodlier personage,
　　Nor ever talk'd with man better experienc'd
　　In State affairs, or rudiments of war.
　　He hath, by report, serv'd the Venetian
　　In Candy these twice seven years, and been chief
　　In many a bold design.
Hort. What are those two
　　That bear him company?
Flam. Two noblemen of Hungary, that, living in the emperor's
　　service as commanders, eight years since, contrary to the
　　expectation of all the court, entered into religion, into the
　　strict Order of Capuchins; but, being not well settled in their
　　undertaking, they left their Order, and returned to court; for
　　which, being after troubled in conscience, they vowed their
　　service against the enemies of Christ, went to Malta, were
　　there knighted, and in their return back, at this great
　　solemnity, they are resolved for ever to forsake the world, and
　　settle themselves here in a house of Capuchins in Padua.
Hort. 'Tis strange.
Flam. One thing makes it so: they have vowed for ever to wear,
　　next their bare bodies, those coats of mail they served in.
Hort. Hard penance!
　　Is the Moor a Christian?

Flam. He is.

Hort. Why proffers he his service to our duke?

Flam. Because he understands there 's like to grow
  Some wars between us and the Duke of Florence,
  In which he hopes employment.
  I never saw one in a stern bold look
  Wear more command, nor in a lofty phrase
  Express more knowing, or more deep contempt
  Of our slight airy courtiers.   He talks
  As if he travell'd all the princes' courts
  Of Christendom: in all things strives t' express,
  That all, that should dispute with him, may know,
  Glories, like glow-worms, afar off shine bright,
  But look'd to near, have neither heat nor light.
  The duke.

*Enter Brachiano, Francisco disguised like Mulinassar, Lodovico
  and Gasparo, bearing their swords, their helmets down, Antonelli,
  Farnese.*

Brach. You are nobly welcome.   We have heard at full
  Your honourable service 'gainst the Turk.
  To you, brave Mulinassar, we assign
  A competent pension: and are inly sorry,
  The vows of those two worthy gentlemen
  Make them incapable of our proffer'd bounty.
  Your wish is, you may leave your warlike swords
  For monuments in our chapel: I accept it,
  As a great honour done me, and must crave
  Your leave to furnish out our duchess' revels.
  Only one thing, as the last vanity
  You e'er shall view, deny me not to stay
  To see a barriers prepar'd to-night:
  You shall have private standings.   It hath pleas'd
  The great ambassadors of several princes,
  In their return from Rome to their own countries,
  To grace our marriage, and to honour me
  With such a kind of sport.

Fran. I shall persuade them to stay, my lord.

Brach. Set on there to the presence.
                [Exeunt Brachiano, Flamineo, and Hortensio.

Lodo. Noble my lord, most fortunately welcome;
                    [The conspirators here embrace.
  You have our vows, seal'd with the sacrament,

To second your attempts.
Gas. And all things ready;
   He could not have invented his own ruin
   (Had he despair'd) with more propriety.
Lodo. You would not take my way.
Fran. 'Tis better order'd.
Lodo. T' have poison'd his prayer-book, or a pair of beads,
   The pummel of his saddle, his looking-glass,
   Or th' handle of his racket,—Oh, that, that!
   That while he had been bandying at tennis,
   He might have sworn himself to hell, and strook
   His soul into the hazard! Oh, my lord,
   I would have our plot be ingenious,
   And have it hereafter recorded for example,
   Rather than borrow example.
Fran. There's no way
   More speeding than this thought on.
Lodo. On, then.
Fran. And yet methinks that this revenge is poor,
   Because it steals upon him like a thief:
   To have ta'en him by the casque in a pitch'd field,
   Led him to Florence——
Lodo. It had been rare: and there
   Have crown'd him with a wreath of stinking garlic,
   T' have shown the sharpness of his government,
   And rankness of his lust. Flamineo comes.
            [Exeunt Lodovico, Antonelli, and Gasparo.

    Enter Flamineo, Marcello, and Zanche

Marc. Why doth this devil haunt you, say?
Flam. I know not:
   For by this light, I do not conjure for her.
   'Tis not so great a cunning as men think,
   To raise the devil; for here's one up already;
   The greatest cunning were to lay him down.
Marc. She is your shame.
Flam. I pray thee pardon her.
   In faith, you see, women are like to burs,
   Where their affection throws them, there they'll stick.
Zan. That is my countryman, a goodly person;
   When he's at leisure, I'll discourse with him
   In our own language.
Flam. I beseech you do.   *[Exit Zanche.*

How is 't, brave soldier? Oh, that I had seen
Some of your iron days! I pray relate
Some of your service to us.

Fran. 'Tis a ridiculous thing for a man to be his own chronicle:
I did never wash my mouth with mine own praise, for fear of
getting a stinking breath.

Marc. You 're too stoical. The duke will expect other discourse from you.

Fran. I shall never flatter him: I have studied man too much to
do that. What difference is between the duke and I? no more
than between two bricks, all made of one clay: only 't may be
one is placed on the top of a turret, the other in the bottom
of a well, by mere chance. If I were placed as high as the
duke, I should stick as fast, make as fair a show, and bear out
weather equally.

Flam. If this soldier had a patent to beg in churches, then he
would tell stories.

Marc. I have been a soldier too.

Fran. How have you thrived?

Marc. Faith, poorly.

Fran. That 's the misery of peace: only outsides are then
respected. As ships seem very great upon the river, which
show very little upon the seas, so some men i' th' court seem
Colossuses in a chamber, who, if they came into the field,
would appear pitiful pigmies.

Flam. Give me a fair room yet hung with arras, and some great
cardinal to lug me by th' ears, as his endeared minion.

Fran. And thou mayest do the devil knows what villainy.

Flam. And safely.

Fran. Right: you shall see in the country, in harvest-time,
pigeons, though they destroy never so much corn, the farmer
dare not present the fowling-piece to them: why? because they
belong to the lord of the manor; whilst your poor sparrows,
that belong to the Lord of Heaven, they go to the pot for 't.

Flam. I will now give you some politic instruction. The duke
says he will give you pension; that 's but bare promise; get
it under his hand. For I have known men that have come
from serving against the Turk, for three or four months they
have had pension to buy them new wooden legs, and fresh
plasters; but after, 'twas not to be had. And this miserable
courtesy shows as if a tormentor should give hot cordial drinks
to one three-quarters dead o' th' rack, only to fetch the miserable soul again to endure more dog-days.

*[Exit Francisco.   Enter Hortensio, a young Lord, Zanche, and
    two more.*

How now, gallants? what, are they ready for the barriers?

Young Lord. Yes: the lords are putting on their armour.

Hort. What 's he?

Flam. A new upstart; one that swears like a falconer, and will
lie in the duke's ear day by day, like a maker of almanacs:
and yet I knew him, since he came to th' court, smell worse
of sweat than an under tennis-court keeper.

Hort. Look you, yonder 's your sweet mistress.

Flam. Thou art my sworn brother: I 'll tell thee, I do love that
Moor, that witch, very constrainedly. She knows some of
my villainy. I do love her just as a man holds a wolf by the
ears; but for fear of her turning upon me, and pulling out my
throat, I would let her go to the devil.

Hort. I hear she claims marriage of thee.

Flam. 'Faith, I made to her some such dark promise; and, in
seeking to fly from 't, I run on, like a frighted dog with a
bottle at 's tail, that fain would bite it off, and yet dares not
look behind him. Now, my precious gipsy.

Zan. Ay, your love to me rather cools than heats.

Flam. Marry, I am the sounder lover; we have many wenches
about the town heat too fast.

Hort. What do you think of these perfumed gallants, then?

Flam. Their satin cannot save them: I am confident
They have a certain spice of the disease;
For they that sleep with dogs shall rise with fleas.

Zan. Believe it, a little painting and gay clothes make you
loathe me.

Flam. How, love a lady for painting or gay apparel? I 'll un-
kennel one example more for thee. Æsop had a foolish dog
that let go the flesh to catch the shadow; I would have
courtiers be better diners.

Zan. You remember your oaths?

Flam. Lovers' oaths are like mariners' prayers, uttered in
extremity; but when the tempest is o'er, and that the vessel
leaves tumbling, they fall from protesting to drinking. And
yet, amongst gentlemen, protesting and drinking go together,
and agree as well as shoemakers and Westphalia bacon: they
are both drawers on; for drink draws on protestation, and
protestation draws on more drink. Is not this discourse
better now than the morality of your sunburnt gentleman?

Enter Cornelia

Corn. Is this your perch, you haggard? fly to th' stews.
　　　　　　　　　　　　　　　　[Strikes Zanche.
Flam. You should be clapped by th' heels now: strike i' th' court!
　　　　　　　　　　　　　　　　[Exit Cornelia.
Zan. She 's good for nothing, but to make her maids
　Catch cold a-nights: they dare not use a bedstaff,
　For fear of her light fingers.
Marc. You 're a strumpet,
　An impudent one. 　　　　　　　*[Kicks Zanche.*
Flam. Why do you kick her, say?
　Do you think that she 's like a walnut tree?
　Must she be cudgell'd ere she bear good fruit?
Marc. She brags that you shall marry her.
Flam. What then?
Marc. I had rather she were pitch'd upon a stake,
　In some new-seeded garden, to affright
　Her fellow crows thence.
Flam. You 're a boy, a fool,
　Be guardian to your hound; I am of age.
Marc. If I take her near you, I 'll cut her throat.
Flam. With a fan of feathers?
Marc. And, for you, I 'll whip
　This folly from you.
Flam. Are you choleric?
　I 'll purge 't with rhubarb.
Hort. Oh, your brother!
Flam. Hang him,
　He wrongs me most, that ought t' offend me least:
　I do suspect my mother play'd foul play,
　When she conceiv'd thee.
Marc. Now, by all my hopes,
　Like the two slaughter'd sons of Œdipus,
　The very flames of our affection
　Shall turn two ways. Those words I 'll make thee answer
　With thy heart-blood.
Flam. Do, like the geese in the progress;
　You know where you shall find me.
Marc. Very good. 　　　　　　　*[Exit Flamineo.*
　And thou be'st a noble friend, bear him my sword,
　And bid him fit the length on 't.
Young Lord. Sir, I shall. 　　　*[Exeunt all but Zanche.*
Zan. He comes. Hence petty thought of my disgrace!

Enter Francisco

I ne'er lov'd my complexion till now,
'Cause I may boldly say, without a blush,
I love you.

Fran. Your love is untimely sown; there 's a spring at Michael-
mas, but 'tis but a faint one: I am sunk in years, and I have
vowed never to marry.

Zan. Alas! poor maids get more lovers than husbands: yet
you may mistake my wealth.   For, as when ambassadors are
sent to congratulate princes, there 's commonly sent along
with them a rich present, so that, though the prince like not
the ambassador's person, nor words, yet he likes well of the
presentment; so I may come to you in the same manner, and
be better loved for my dowry than my virtue.

Fran. I 'll think on the motion.

Zan. Do; I 'll now detain you no longer.   At your better
leisure, I 'll tell you things shall startle your blood:
Nor blame me that this passion I reveal;
Lovers die inward that their flames conceal.

Fran. Of all intelligence this may prove the best:
Sure I shall draw strange fowl from this foul nest.   [*Exeunt.*

Scene II

Enter Marcello and Cornelia

Corn. I hear a whispering all about the court,
You are to fight: who is your opposite?
What is the quarrel?

Marc. 'Tis an idle rumour.

Corn. Will you dissemble? sure you do not well
To fright me thus: you never look thus pale,
But when you are most angry.   I do charge you,
Upon my blessing—nay, I 'll call the duke,
And he shall school you.

Marc. Publish not a fear,
Which would convert to laughter: 'tis not so.
Was not this crucifix my father's?

Corn. Yes.

Marc. I have heard you say, giving my brother suck
He took the crucifix between his hands,   [*Enter Flamineo.*
And broke a limb off.

Corn. Yes, but 'tis mended.

Flam. I have brought your weapon back.

　　　　　　　　[*Flamineo runs Marcello through.*

Corn. Ha! Oh, my horror!

Marc. You have brought it home, indeed.

Corn. Help! Oh, he 's murder'd!

Flam. Do you turn your gall up? I 'll to sanctuary,
　　And send a surgeon to you. 　　　　　　　　[*Exit.*

　　　　　Enter Lodovico, Hortensio, and Gasparo

Hort. How! o' th' ground!

Marc. Oh, mother, now remember what I told
　　Of breaking of the crucifix! Farewell.
　　There are some sins, which heaven doth duly punish
　　In a whole family. This it is to rise
　　By all dishonest means! Let all men know,
　　That tree shall long time keep a steady foot,
　　Whose branches spread no wider than the root. 　　[*Dies.*

Corn. Oh, my perpetual sorrow!

Hort. Virtuous Marcello!
　　He 's dead. Pray leave him, lady: come, you shall.

Corn. Alas! he is not dead; he 's in a trance. Why, here 's
　　nobody shall get anything by his death. Let me call him
　　again, for God's sake!

Lodo. I would you were deceived.

Corn. Oh, you abuse me, you abuse me, you abuse me! how
　　many have gone away thus, for lack of 'tendance! rear up 's
　　head, rear up 's head! his bleeding inward will kill him.

Hort. You see he is departed.

Corn. Let me come to him; give me him as he is, if he be turn'd
　　to earth; let me but give him one hearty kiss, and you shall
　　put us both into one coffin. Fetch a looking-glass: see if his
　　breath will not stain it; or pull out some feathers from my
　　pillow, and lay them to his lips. Will you lose him for a
　　little painstaking?

Hort. Your kindest office is to pray for him.

Corn. Alas! I would not pray for him yet. He may live to lay
　　me i' th' ground, and pray for me, if you 'll let me come to him.

　　　*Enter Brachiano, all armed, save the beaver, with Flamineo
　　　　　　　　　and others*

Brach. Was this your handiwork?

Flam. It was my misfortune.

Corn. He lies, he lies! he did not kill him: these have killed him,
  that would not let him be better looked to.
Brach. Have comfort, my griev'd mother.
Corn. Oh, you screech-owl!
Hort. Forbear, good madam.
Corn. Let me go, let me go.

> [*She runs to Flamineo with her knife drawn, and coming to
>   him lets it fall.*

  The God of Heaven forgive thee! Dost not wonder
  I pray for thee? I 'll tell thee what 's the reason,
  I have scarce breath to number twenty minutes;
  I 'd not spend that in cursing. Fare thee well:
  Half of thyself lies there; and mayst thou live
  To fill an hour-glass with his moulder'd ashes,
  To tell how thou shouldst spend the time to come
  In blessed repentance!
Brach. Mother, pray tell me
  How came he by his death? what was the quarrel?
Corn. Indeed, my younger boy presum'd too much
  Upon his manhood, gave him bitter words,
  Drew his sword first; and so, I know not how,
  For I was out of my wits, he fell with 's head
  Just in my bosom.
Page. This is not true, madam.
Corn. I pray thee, peace.
  One arrow 's graz'd already; it were vain
  T' lose this, for that will ne'er be found again.
Brach. Go, bear the body to Cornelia's lodging:
  And we command that none acquaint our duchess
  With this sad accident. For you, Flamineo,
  Hark you, I will not grant your pardon.
Flam. No?
Brach. Only a lease of your life; and that shall last
  But for one day: thou shalt be forc'd each evening
  To renew it, or be hang'd.
Flam. At your pleasure.

> [*Lodovico sprinkles Brachiano's beaver with a poison.*

Enter Francisco

  Your will is law now, I 'll not meddle with it.
Brach. You once did brave me in your sister's lodging:
  I 'll now keep you in awe for 't. Where 's our beaver?
Fran. [*Aside.*] He calls for his destruction. Noble youth,

I pity thy sad fate! Now to the barriers.
This shall his passage to the black lake further;
The last good deed he did, he pardon'd murder.   [*Exeunt.*

SCENE III

*Charges and shouts.   They fight at barriers; first single pairs, then
three to three*

Enter Brachiano and Flamineo, with others

Brach. An armourer! ud's death, an armourer!
Flam. Armourer! where 's the armourer?
Brach. Tear off my beaver.
Flam. Are you hurt, my lord?
Brach. Oh, my brain 's on fire!   [*Enter Armourer.*
    The helmet is poison'd.
Armourer. My lord, upon my soul——
Brach. Away with him to torture.
    There are some great ones that have hand in this,
    And near about me.

Enter Vittoria Corombona

Vit. Oh, my lov'd lord! poison'd!
Flam. Remove the bar.   Here 's unfortunate revels!
    Call the physicians.   [*Enter two Physicians.*
    A plague upon you!
    We have too much of your cunning here already:
    I fear the ambassadors are likewise poison'd.
Brach. Oh, I am gone already! the infection
    Flies to the brain and heart.   O thou strong heart!
    There 's such a covenant 'tween the world and it,
    They 're loath to break.
Giov. Oh, my most loved father!
Brach. Remove the boy away.
    Where 's this good woman?   Had I infinite worlds,
    They were too little for thee: must I leave thee?
    What say you, screech-owls, is the venom mortal?
Physicians. Most deadly.
Brach. Most corrupted politic hangman,
    You kill without book; but your art to save
    Fails you as oft as great men's needy friends.
    I that have given life to offending slaves,

And wretched murderers, have I not power
To lengthen mine own a twelvemonth?
[*To Vittoria.*] Do not kiss me, for I shall poison thee.
This unction 's sent from the great Duke of Florence.
Fran. Sir, be of comfort.
Brach. O thou soft natural death, that art joint-twin
To sweetest slumber! no rough-bearded comet
Stares on thy mild departure; the dull owl
Bears not against thy casement; the hoarse wolf
Scents not thy carrion: pity winds thy corse,
Whilst horror waits on princes'.
Vit. I am lost for ever.
Brach. How miserable a thing it is to die
'Mongst women howling! [*Enter Lodovico and Gasparo, as
Capuchins.*] What are those?
Flam. Franciscans:
They have brought the extreme unction.
Brach. On pain of death, let no man name death to me:
It is a word infinitely terrible.
Withdraw into our cabinet.

[*Exeunt all but Francisco and Flamineo.*

Flam. To see what solitariness is about dying princes! as
heretofore they have unpeopled towns, divorced friends, and
made great houses unhospitable, so now, O justice! where are
their flatterers now? flatterers are but the shadows of princes'
bodies; the least thick cloud makes them invisible.
Fran. There 's great moan made for him.
Flam. 'Faith, for some few hours salt-water will run most
plentifully in every office o' th' court; but, believe it, most of
them do but weep over their stepmothers' graves.
Fran. How mean you?
Flam. Why, they dissemble; as some men do that live within
compass o' th' verge.
Fran. Come, you have thrived well under him.
Flam. 'Faith, like a wolf in a woman's breast; I have been fed
with poultry: but for money, understand me, I had as good a
will to cozen him as e'er an officer of them all; but I had not
cunning enough to do it.
Fran. What didst thou think of him? 'faith, speak freely.
Flam. He was a kind of statesman, that would sooner have
reckoned how many cannon-bullets he had discharged against
a town, to count his expense that way, than how many of his
valiant and deserving subjects he lost before it.

Fran. Oh, speak well of the duke!

Flam. I have done.   [*Enter Lodovico.*
  Wilt hear some of my court-wisdom? To reprehend princes
  is dangerous; and to over-commend some of them is
  palpable lying.

Fran. How is it with the duke?

Lodo. Most deadly ill.
  He 's fall'n into a strange distraction:
  He talks of battles and monopolies,
  Levying of taxes; and from that descends
  To the most brain-sick language. His mind fastens
  On twenty several objects, which confound
  Deep sense with folly. Such a fearful end
  May teach some men that bear too lofty crest,
  Though they live happiest yet they die not best.
  He hath conferr'd the whole state of the dukedom
  Upon your sister, till the prince arrive
  At mature age.

Flam. There 's some good luck in that yet.

Fran. See, here he comes.

     [*Enter Brachiano, presented in a bed, Vittoria and others.*
  There 's death in 's face already.

Vit. Oh, my good lord!

Brach. Away, you have abus'd me:
    [*These speeches are several kinds of distractions, and in the
        action should appear so.*
  You have convey'd coin forth our territories,
  Bought and sold offices, oppress'd the poor,
  And I ne'er dreamt on 't. Make up your accounts,
  I 'll now be mine own steward.

Flam. Sir, have patience.

Brach. Indeed, I am to blame:
  For did you ever hear the dusky raven
  Chide blackness? or was 't ever known the devil
  Rail'd against cloven creatures?

Vit. Oh, my lord!

Brach. Let me have some quails to supper.

Flam. Sir, you shall.

Brach. No, some fried dog-fish; your quails feed on poison.
  That old dog-fox, that politician, Florence!
  I 'll forswear hunting, and turn dog-killer.
  Rare! I 'll be friends with him; for, mark you, sir, one dog

Still sets another a-barking.   Peace, peace!
Yonder 's a fine slave come in now.

Flam. Where?

Brach. Why, there,
In a blue bonnet, and a pair of breeches
With a great cod-piece: ha, ha, ha!
Look you, his cod-piece is stuck full of pins,
With pearls o' th' head of them.   Do not you know him?

Flam. No, my lord.

Brach. Why, 'tis the devil.
I know him by a great rose he wears on 's shoe,
To hide his cloven foot.   I 'll dispute with him;
He 's a rare linguist.

Vit. My lord, here 's nothing.

Brach. Nothing! rare! nothing! when I want money,
Our treasury is empty, there is nothing:
I 'll not be us'd thus.

Vit. Oh, lie still, my lord!

Brach. See, see Flamineo, that kill'd his brother,
Is dancing on the ropes there, and he carries
A money-bag in each hand, to keep him even,
For fear of breaking 's neck: and there 's a lawyer,
In a gown whipped with velvet, stares and gapes
When the money will fall.   How the rogue cuts capers!
It should have been in a halter.   'Tis there; what 's she?

Flam. Vittoria, my lord.

Brach. Ha, ha, ha! her hair is sprinkl'd with orris powder,
That makes her look as if she had sinn'd in the pastry.
What 's he?

Flam. A divine, my lord.

[*Brachiano seems here near his end; Lodovico and Gasparo,
in the habit of Capuchins, present him in his bed with
a crucifix and hallowed candle.*

Brach. He will be drunk; avoid him: th' argument
Is fearful, when churchmen stagger in 't.
Look you, six grey rats that have lost their tails
Crawl up the pillow; send for a rat-catcher:
I 'll do a miracle, I 'll free the court
From all foul vermin.   Where 's Flamineo?

Flam. I do not like that he names me so often,
Especially on 's death-bed; 'tis a sign
I shall not live long.   See, he 's near his end.

Lodo. Pray, give us leave.   *Attende, domine Brachiane.*

Flam. See how firmly he doth fix his eye
   Upon the crucifix.
Vit. Oh, hold it constant!
   It settles his wild spirits; and so his eyes
   Melt into tears.
*Lodo. Domine Brachiane, solebas in bello tutus esse tuo clypeo;
   nunc hunc clypeum hosti tuo opponas infernali.*   [*By the crucifix.*
*Gas. Olim hastâ valuisti in bello; nunc hanc sacram hastam
   vibrabis contra hostem animarum.*   [*By the hallowed taper.*
*Lodo. Attende, Domine Brachiane, si nunc quoque probas ea, quæ
   acta sunt inter nos, flecte caput in dextrum.*
*Gas. Esto securus, Domine Brachiane; cogita, quantum habeas
   meritorum; denique memineris meam animam pro tuâ oppig-
   noratam si quid esset periculi.*
*Lodo. Si nunc quoque probas ea, quæ acta sunt inter nos, flecte
   caput in lævum.*
   He is departing: pray stand all apart,
   And let us only whisper in his ears
   Some private meditations, which our order
   Permits you not to hear.
      [*Here, the rest being departed, Lodovico and Gasparo discover
         themselves.*
Gas. Brachiano.
Lodo. Devil Brachiano, thou art damn'd.
Gas. Perpetually.
Lodo. A slave condemn'd and given up to the gallows,
   Is thy great lord and master.
Gas. True; for thou
   Art given up to the devil.
Lodo. Oh, you slave!
   You that were held the famous politician,
   Whose art was poison.
Gas. And whose conscience, murder.
Lodo. That would have broke your wife's neck down the stairs,
   Ere she was poison'd.
Gas. That had your villainous sallets.
Lodo. And fine embroider'd bottles, and perfumes,
   Equally mortal with a winter plague.
Gas. Now there 's mercury——
Lodo. And copperas——
Gas. And quicksilver——
Lodo. With other devilish 'pothecary stuff,
   A-melting in your politic brains: dost hear?

Gas. This is Count Lodovico.

Lodo. This, Gasparo:
  And thou shalt die like a poor rogue.

Gas. And stink
  Like a dead fly-blown dog.

Lodo. And be forgotten
  Before thy funeral sermon.

Brach. Vittoria! Vittoria!

Lodo. Oh, the cursed devil
  Comes to himself again! we are undone.

Gas. Strangle him in private. [*Enter Vittoria and the Attendants.*
  What! will you call him again
  To live in treble torments? for charity,
  For Christian charity, avoid the chamber.

                        [*Vittoria and the rest retire.*

Lodo. You would prate, sir? This is a true-love-knot
  Sent from the Duke of Florence.   [*Brachiano is strangled.*

Gas. What, is it done?

Lodo. The snuff is out. No woman-keeper i' th' world,
  Though she had practis'd seven year at the pest-house,
  Could have done 't quaintlier. My lords, he 's dead.

Vittoria and the others come forward

Omnes. Rest to his soul!

Vit. Oh me! this place is hell.   [*Exit.*

Fran. How heavily she takes it!

Flam. Oh, yes, yes;
  Had women navigable rivers in their eyes,
  They would dispend them all. Surely, I wonder
  Why we should wish more rivers to the city,
  When they sell water so good cheap. I 'll tell thee,
  These are but moonish shades of griefs or fears;
  There 's nothing sooner dry than women's tears.
  Why, here 's an end of all my harvest; he has given me
    nothing.
  Court promises! let wise men count them curs'd;
  For while you live, he that scores best, pays worst.

Fran. Sure this was Florence' doing.

Flam. Very likely:
  Those are found weighty strokes which come from th' hand,
  But those are killing strokes which come from th' head.
  Oh, the rare tricks of a Machiavellian!
  He doth not come, like a gross plodding slave,

And buffet you to death; no, my quaint knave,
He tickles you to death, makes you die laughing,
As if you had swallow'd down a pound of saffron.
You see the feat, 'tis practis'd in a trice;
To teach court honesty, it jumps on ice.
Fran. Now have the people liberty to talk,
And descant on his vices.
Flam. Misery of princes,
That must of force be censur'd by their slaves!
Not only blam'd for doing things are ill,
But for not doing all that all men will:
One were better be a thresher.
Ud's death! I would fain speak with this duke yet.
Fran. Now he's dead?
Flam. I cannot conjure; but if prayers or oaths
Will get to th' speech of him, though forty devils
Wait on him in his livery of flames,
I'll speak to him, and shake him by the hand,
Though I be blasted.   [*Exit.*
Fran. Excellent Lodovico!
What! did you terrify him at the last gasp?
Lodo. Yes, and so idly, that the duke had like
T' have terrified us.
Fran. How?

Enter the Moor

Lodo. You shall hear that hereafter.
See, yon's the infernal, that would make up sport.
Now to the revelation of that secret
She promis'd when she fell in love with you.
Fran. You're passionately met in this sad world.
Zan. I would have you look up, sir; these court tears
Claim not your tribute to them: let those weep,
That guiltily partake in the sad cause.
I knew last night, by a sad dream I had,
Some mischief would ensue: yet, to say truth,
My dream most concern'd you.
Lodo. Shall's fall a-dreaming?
Fran. Yes, and for fashion sake I'll dream with her.
Zan. Methought, sir, you came stealing to my bed.
Fran. Wilt thou believe me, sweeting? by this light,
I was a-dreamt on thee too; for methought
I saw thee naked.

Zan. Fie, sir! as I told you,
  Methought you lay down by me.
Fran. So dreamt I;
  And lest thou shouldst take cold, I cover'd thee
  With this Irish mantle.
Zan. Verily I did dream
  You were somewhat bold with me: but to come to 't——
Lodo. How! how! I hope you will not go to 't here.
Fran. Nay, you must hear my dream out.
Zan. Well, sir, forth.
Fran. When I threw the mantle o'er thee, thou didst laugh
  Exceedingly, methought.
Zan. Laugh!
Fran. And criedst out, the hair did tickle thee.
Zan. There was a dream indeed!
Lodo. Mark her, I pray thee, she simpers like the suds
  A collier hath been wash'd in.
Zan. Come, sir; good fortune tends you.   I did tell you
  I would reveal a secret: Isabella,
  The Duke of Florence' sister, was empoison'd
  By a fum'd picture; and Camillo's neck
  Was broke by damn'd Flamineo, the mischance
  Laid on a vaulting-horse.
Fran. Most strange!
Zan. Most true.
Lodo. The bed of snakes is broke.
Zan. I sadly do confess, I had a hand
  In the black deed.
Fran. Thou kept'st their counsel.
Zan. Right;
  For which, urg'd with contrition, I intend
  This night to rob Vittoria.
Lodo. Excellent penitence!
  Usurers dream on 't while they sleep out sermons.
Zan. To further our escape, I have entreated
  Leave to retire me, till the funeral,
  Unto a friend i' th' country: that excuse
  Will further our escape.   In coin and jewels
  I shall at least make good unto your use
  An hundred thousand crowns.
Fran. Oh, noble wench!
Lodo. Those crowns we 'll share.
Zan. It is a dowry,

Methinks, should make that sun-burnt proverb false,
And wash the Æthiop white.
Fran. It shall; away.
Zan. Be ready for our flight.
Fran. An hour 'fore day.   [*Exit Zanche.*
Oh, strange discovery! why, till now we knew not
The circumstance of either of their deaths.

Re-enter Zanche

Zan. You 'll wait about midnight in the chapel?
Fran. There.   [*Exit Zanche.*
Lodo. Why, now our action 's justified.
Fran. Tush for justice!
What harms it justice? we now, like the partridge,
Purge the disease with laurel; for the fame
Shall crown the enterprise, and quit the shame.   [*Exeunt.*

Scene IV

*Enter Flamineo and Gasparo, at one door; another way, Giovanni,
attended*

Gas. The young duke: did you e'er see a sweeter prince?
Flam. I have known a poor woman's bastard better favoured—
this is behind him.   Now, to his face—all comparisons were
hateful.   Wise was the courtly peacock, that, being a great
minion, and being compared for beauty by some dottrels that
stood by to the kingly eagle, said the eagle was a far fairer
bird than herself, not in respect of her feathers, but in respect
of her long talons: his will grow out in time.—My gracious
lord.
Giov. I pray leave me, sir.
Flam. Your grace must be merry; 'tis I have cause to mourn;
for wot you, what said the little boy that rode behind his
father on horseback?
Giov. Why, what said he?
Flam. When you are dead, father, said he, I hope then I shall
ride in the saddle.   Oh, 'tis a brave thing for a man to sit by
himself! he may stretch himself in the stirrups, look about,
and see the whole compass of the hemisphere.   You 're now,
my lord, i' th' saddle.

Giov. Study your prayers, sir, and be penitent:
    'Twere fit you 'd think on what hath former been;
    I have heard grief nam'd the eldest child of sin.   [*Exit.*

Flam. Study my prayers! he threatens me divinely! I am
    falling to pieces already. I care not, though, like Anacharsis,
    I were pounded to death in a mortar: and yet that death were
    fitter for usurers, gold and themselves to be beaten together,
    to make a most cordial cullis for the devil.
    He hath his uncle's villainous look already,
    In decimo-sexto. [*Enter Courtier.*] Now, sir, what are you?

Court. It is the pleasure, sir, of the young duke,
    That you forbear the presence, and all rooms
    That owe him reverence.

Flam. So the wolf and the raven are very pretty fools when
    they are young. Is it your office, sir, to keep me out?

Court. So the duke wills.

Flam. Verily, Master Courtier, extremity is not to be used in
    all offices: say, that a gentlewoman were taken out of her bed
    about midnight, and committed to Castle Angelo, to the tower
    yonder, with nothing about her but her smock, would it not
    show a cruel part in the gentleman-porter to lay claim to her
    upper garment, pull it o'er her head and ears, and put her in
    naked?

Court. Very good: you are merry.   [*Exit.*

Flam. Doth he make a court-ejectment of me? a flaming fire-
    brand casts more smoke without a chimney than within 't.
    I 'll smoor some of them.   [*Enter Francisco de Medicis.*
    How now? thou art sad.

Fran. I met even now with the most piteous sight.

Flam. Thou meet'st another here, a pitiful
    Degraded courtier.

Fran. Your reverend mother
    Is grown a very old woman in two hours.
    I found them winding of Marcello's corse;
    And there is such a solemn melody,
    'Tween doleful songs, tears, and sad elegies;
    Such as old grandames, watching by the dead,
    Were wont t' outwear the nights with, that, believe me,
    I had no eyes to guide me forth the room,
    They were so o'ercharg'd with water.

Flam. I will see them.

Fran. 'Twere much uncharity in you; for your sight
    Will add unto their tears.

Flam. I will see them:
    They are behind the traverse; I 'll discover
    Their superstitious howling.
       [*He draws the traverse. Cornelia, the Moor, and three other*
          Ladies discovered winding Marcello's corse. A song.
Corn. This rosemary is wither'd; pray, get fresh.
    I would have these herbs grow up in his grave,
    When I am dead and rotten. Reach the bays,
    I 'll tie a garland here about his head;
    'Twill keep my boy from lightning. This sheet
    I have kept this twenty year, and every day
    Hallow'd it with my prayers; I did not think
    He should have wore it.
Zan. Look you, who are yonder?
Corn. Oh, reach me the flowers!
Zan. Her ladyship 's foolish.
Woman. Alas, her grief
    Hath turn'd her child again!
Corn. You 're very welcome: [*To Flamineo.*
    There 's rosemary for you, and rue for you,
    Heart's-ease for you; I pray make much of it,
    I have left more for myself.
Fran. Lady, who 's this?
Corn. You are, I take it, the grave-maker.
Flam. So.
Zan. 'Tis Flamineo.
Corn. Will you make me such a fool? here 's a white hand:
    Can blood so soon be washed out? let me see;
    When screech-owls croak upon the chimney-tops,
    And the strange cricket i' th' oven sings and hops,
    When yellow spots do on your hands appear,
    Be certain then you of a corse shall hear.
    Out upon 't, how 'tis speckled! h' 'as handled a toad sure.
    Cowslip water is good for the memory:
    Pray, buy me three ounces of 't.
Flam. I would I were from hence.
Corn. Do you hear, sir?
    I 'll give you a saying which my grandmother
    Was wont, when she heard the bell toll, to sing o'er
    Unto her lute.
Flam. Do, an you will, do.
Corn. *Call for the robin redbreast, and the wren,*
        [*Cornelia doth this in several forms of distraction.*

Since o'er shady groves they hover,
And with leaves and flowers do cover
The friendless bodies of unburied men.
Call unto his funeral dole
The ant, the fieldmouse, and the mole,
To rear him hillocks that shall keep him warm,
And (when gay tombs are robb'd) sustain no harm;
But keep the wolf far thence, that's foe to men,
For with his nails he'll dig them up again.
They would not bury him 'cause he died in a quarrel;
But I have an answer for them:
Let holy Church receive him duly,
Since he paid the church-tithes truly.
His wealth is summ'd, and this is all his store,
This poor men get, and great men get no more.
Now the wares are gone, we may shut up shop.
Bless you all, good people.   [*Exeunt Cornelia and Ladies.*
Flam. I have a strange thing in me, to th' which
  I cannot give a name, without it be
  Compassion.   I pray leave me.   [*Exit Francisco.*
  This night I'll know the utmost of my fate;
  I'll be resolv'd what my rich sister means
  T' assign me for my service.   I have liv'd
  Riotously ill, like some that live in court,
  And sometimes when my face was full of smiles,
  Have felt the maze of conscience in my breast.
  Oft gay and honour'd robes those tortures try:
  We think cag'd birds sing, when indeed they cry.

Enter Brachiano's Ghost, in his leather cassock and breeches, boots,
        a cowl, a pot of lily flowers, with a skull in 't

  Ha! I can stand thee: nearer, nearer yet.
  What a mockery hath death made thee! thou look'st sad.
  In what place art thou? in yon starry gallery?
  Or in the cursed dungeon? No? not speak?
  Pray, sir, resolve me, what religion's best
  For a man to die in? or is it in your knowledge
  To answer me how long I have to live?
  That's the most necessary question.
  Not answer? are you still, like some great men
  That only walk like shadows up and down,
  And to no purpose; say——
        [*The Ghost throws earth upon him, and shows him the skull.*

What 's that? O fatal! he throws earth upon me.
A dead man's skull beneath the roots of flowers!
I pray speak, sir: our Italian churchmen
Make us believe dead men hold conference
With their familiars, and many times
Will come to bed with them, and eat with them. [*Exit Ghost.*
He 's gone; and see, the skull and earth are vanish'd.
This is beyond melancholy. I do dare my fate
To do its worst. Now to my sister's lodging,
And sum up all these horrors: the disgrace
The prince threw on me; next the piteous sight
Of my dead brother; and my mother's dotage;
And last this terrible vision: all these
Shall with Vittoria's bounty turn to good,
Or I will drown this weapon in her blood.   [*Exit.*

Scene V

Enter Francisco, Lodovico, and Hortensio

Lodo. My lord, upon my soul you shall no further;
  You have most ridiculously engag'd yourself
  Too far already. For my part, I have paid
  All my debts: so, if I should chance to fall,
  My creditors fall not with me; and I vow,
  To quit all in this bold assembly,
  To the meanest follower. My lord, leave the city,
  Or I 'll forswear the murder.   [*Exit.*
Fran. Farewell, Lodovico:
  If thou dost perish in this glorious act,
  I 'll rear unto thy memory that fame,
  Shall in the ashes keep alive thy name.   [*Exit.*
Hort. There 's some black deed on foot. I 'll presently
  Down to the citadel, and raise some force.
  These strong court-factions, that do brook no checks,
  In the career oft break the riders' necks.   [*Exit.*

Scene VI

Enter Vittoria with a book in her hand, Zanche; Flamineo
following them

Flam. What, are you at your prayers? Give o'er.
Vit. How, ruffian?
Flam. I come to you 'bout worldly business.
  Sit down, sit down. Nay, stay, blowze, you may hear it:
  The doors are fast enough.
Vit. Ha! are you drunk?
Flam. Yes, yes, with wormwood water; you shall taste
  Some of it presently.
Vit. What intends the fury?
Flam. You are my lord's executrix; and I claim
  Reward for my long service.
Vit. For your service!
Flam. Come, therefore, here is pen and ink, set down
  What you will give me.
Vit. There.   [*She writes.*
Flam. Ha! have you done already?
  'Tis a most short conveyance.
Vit. I will read it:
  I give that portion to thee, and no other,
  Which Cain groan'd under, having slain his brother.
Flam. A most courtly patent to beg by.
Vit. You are a villain!
Flam. Is 't come to this? they say affrights cure agues:
  Thou hast a devil in thee; I will try
  If I can scare him from thee. Nay, sit still:
  My lord hath left me yet two case of jewels,
  Shall make me scorn your bounty; you shall see them. [*Exit.*
Vit. Sure he 's distracted.
Zan. Oh, he 's desperate!
  For your own safety give him gentle language.
               [*He enters with two cases of pistols.*
Flam. Look, these are better far at a dead lift,
  Than all your jewel house.
Vit. And yet, methinks,
  These stones have no fair lustre, they are ill set.
Flam. I 'll turn the right side towards you: you shall see
  How they will sparkle.
Vit. Turn this horror from me!

What do you want? what would you have me do?
Is not all mine yours? have I any children?
Flam. Pray thee, good woman, do not trouble me
　With this vain worldly business; say your prayers:
　I made a vow to my deceased lord,
　Neither yourself nor I should outlive him
　The numbering of four hours.
Vit. Did he enjoin it?
Flam. He did, and 'twas a deadly jealousy,
　Lest any should enjoy thee after him,
　That urged him vow me to it.　For my death,
　I did propound it voluntarily, knowing,
　If he could not be safe in his own court,
　Being a great duke, what hope then for us?
Vit. This is your melancholy, and despair.
Flam. Away:
　Fool thou art, to think that politicians
　Do use to kill the effects of injuries
　And let the cause live.　Shall we groan in irons,
　Or be a shameful and a weighty burthen
　To a public scaffold? This is my resolve:
　I would not live at any man's entreaty,
　Nor die at any's bidding.
Vit. Will you hear me?
Flam. My life hath done service to other men,
　My death shall serve mine own turn: make you ready.
Vit. Do you mean to die indeed?
Flam. With as much pleasure,
　As e'er my father gat me.
Vit. Are the doors lock'd?
Zan. Yes, madam.
Vit. Are you grown an atheist? will you turn your body,
　Which is the goodly palace of the soul,
　To the soul's slaughter-house? Oh, the cursed devil,
　Which doth present us with all other sins
　Thrice candied o'er, despair with gall and stibium;
　Yet we carouse it off. [*Aside to Zanche.*] Cry out for help!
　Makes us forsake that which was made for man,
　The world, to sink to that was made for devils,
　Eternal darkness!
Zan. Help, help!
Flam. I'll stop your throat
　With winter plums.

Vit. I pray thee yet remember,
  Millions are now in graves, which at last day
  Like mandrakes shall rise shrieking.
Flam.   Leave your prating,
  For these are but grammatical laments,
  Feminine arguments: and they move me,
  As some in pulpits move their auditory,
  More with their exclamation than sense
  Of reason, or sound doctrine.
Zan. [*Aside.*] Gentle madam,
  Seem to consent, only persuade him teach
  The way to death; let him die first.
Vit. 'Tis good, I apprehend it.—
  To kill one's self is meat that we must take
  Like pills, not chew'd, but quickly swallow it;
  The smart o' th' wound, or weakness of the hand,
  May else bring treble torments.
Flam.   I have held it
  A wretched and most miserable life,
  Which is not able to die.
Vit. Oh, but frailty!
  Yet I am now resolv'd; farewell, affliction!
  Behold, Brachiano, I that while you liv'd
  Did make a flaming altar of my heart
  To sacrifice unto you, now am ready
  To sacrifice heart and all.   Farewell, Zanche!
Zan. How, madam! do you think that I 'll outlive you;
  Especially when my best self, Flamineo,
  Goes the same voyage?
Flam. O most loved Moor!
Zan. Only, by all my love, let me entreat you,
  Since it is most necessary one of us
  Do violence on ourselves, let you or I
  Be her sad taster, teach her how to die.
Flam. Thou dost instruct me nobly; take these pistols,
  Because my hand is stain'd with blood already:
  Two of these you shall level at my breast,
  The other 'gainst your own, and so we 'll die
  Most equally contented: but first swear
  Not to outlive me.
Vit. and Zan. Most religiously.
Flam. Then here 's an end of me; farewell, daylight.
  And, O contemptible physic! that dost take

So long a study, only to preserve
So short a life, I take my leave of thee. [*Showing the pistols.*
These are two cupping-glasses, that shall draw
All my infected blood out. Are you ready?

Both. Ready.

Flam. Whither shall I go now? O Lucian, thy ridiculous
purgatory! to find Alexander the Great cobbling shoes,
Pompey tagging points, and Julius Cæsar making hair-
buttons, Hannibal selling blacking, and Augustus crying
garlic, Charlemagne selling lists by the dozen, and King Pepin
crying apples in a cart drawn with one horse!
Whether I resolve to fire, earth, water, air,
Or all the elements by scruples, I know not,
Nor greatly care.—Shoot! shoot!
Of all deaths, the violent death is best;
For from ourselves it steals ourselves so fast,
The pain, once apprehended, is quite past.
[*They shoot, and run to him, and tread upon him.*

Vit. What, are you dropped?

Flam. I am mix'd with earth already: as you are noble,
Perform your vows, and bravely follow me.

Vit. Whither? to hell?

Zan. To most assur'd damnation?

Vit. Oh, thou most cursed devil!

Zan. Thou art caught——

Vit. In thine own engine. I tread the fire out
That would have been my ruin.

Flam. Will you be perjured? what a religious oath was Styx,
that the gods never durst swear by, and violate! Oh, that we
had such an oath to minister, and to be so well kept in our
courts of justice!

Vit. Think whither thou art going.

Zan. And remember
What villainies thou hast acted.

Vit. This thy death
Shall make me, like a blazing ominous star,
Look up and tremble.

Flam. Oh, I am caught with a spring!

Vit. You see the fox comes many times short home;
'Tis here prov'd true.

Flam. Kill'd with a couple of braches!

Vit. No fitter offering for the infernal furies,
Than one in whom they reign'd while he was living.

Flam. Oh, the way 's dark and horrid! I cannot see:
  Shall I have no company?
Vit. Oh, yes, thy sins
  Do run before thee to fetch fire from hell,
  To light thee thither.
Flam. Oh, I smell soot,
  Most stinking soot! the chimney 's afire:
  My liver 's parboil'd, like Scotch holly-bread;
  There 's a plumber laying pipes in my guts, it scalds.
  Wilt thou outlive me?
Zan. Yes, and drive a stake
  Through thy body; for we 'll give it out,
  Thou didst this violence upon thyself.
Flam. Oh, cunning devils! now I have tried your love,
  And doubled all your reaches: I am not wounded.

  [Flamineo riseth.

  The pistols held no bullets; 'twas a plot
  To prove your kindness to me; and I live
  To punish your ingratitude.   I knew,
  One time or other, you would find a way
  To give a strong potion.   O men,
  That lie upon your death-beds, and are haunted
  With howling wives! ne'er trust them; they 'll re-marry
  Ere the worm pierce your winding-sheet, ere the spider
  Make a thin curtain for your epitaphs.
  How cunning you were to discharge! do you practise at the
  Artillery yard? Trust a woman? never, never; Brachiano be
  my precedent.   We lay our souls to pawn to the devil for a
  little pleasure, and a woman makes the bill of sale.   That
  ever man should marry! For one Hypermnestra that saved her
  lord and husband, forty-nine of her sisters cut their husbands'
  throats all in one night.   There was a shoal of virtuous horse
  leeches! Here are two other instruments.

  Enter Lodovico, Gasparo, still disguised as Capuchins

Vit. Help! help!
Flam. What noise is that? ha! false keys i' th' court!
Lodo. We have brought you a mask.
Flam. A matachin it seems by your drawn swords.
  Churchmen turned revellers!
Gas. Isabella! Isabella!
Lodo. Do you know us now?
Flam. Lodovico! and Gasparo!

Lodo. Yes; and that Moor the duke gave pension to
  Was the great Duke of Florence.
Vit. Oh, we are lost!
Flam. You shall not take justice forth from my hands,
  Oh, let me kill her!—I 'll cut my safety
  Through your coats of steel.   Fate 's a spaniel,
  We cannot beat it from us.   What remains now?
  Let all that do ill, take this precedent:
  Man may his fate foresee, but not prevent;
  And of all axioms this shall win the prize:
  'Tis better to be fortunate than wise.
Gas. Bind him to the pillar.
Vit. Oh, your gentle pity!
  I have seen a blackbird that would sooner fly
  To a man's bosom, than to stay the gripe
  Of the fierce sparrow-hawk.
Gas. Your hope deceives you.
Vit. If Florence be i' th' court, would he would kill me!
Gas. Fool! Princes give rewards with their own hands,
  But death or punishment by the hands of others.
Lodo. Sirrah, you once did strike me; I 'll strike you
  Unto the centre.
Flam. Thou 'lt do it like a hangman, a base hangman,
  Not like a noble fellow, for thou see'st
  I cannot strike again.
Lodo. Dost laugh?
Flam. Wouldst have me die, as I was born, in whining?
Gas. Recommend yourself to heaven.
Flam. No, I will carry mine own commendations thither.
Lodo. Oh, could I kill you forty times a day,
  And use 't four years together, 'twere too little!
  Naught grieves but that you are too few to feed
  The famine of our vengeance.   What dost think on?
Flam. Nothing; of nothing: leave thy idle questions.
  I am i' th' way to study a long silence:
  To prate were idle.   I remember nothing.
  There 's nothing of so infinite vexation
  As man's own thoughts.
Lodo. O thou glorious strumpet!
  Could I divide thy breath from this pure air
  When 't leaves thy body, I would suck it up,
  And breathe 't upon some dunghill.
Vit. You, my death's-man!

Methinks thou dost not look horrid enough,
Thou hast too good a face to be a hangman:
If thou be, do thy office in right form;
Fall down upon thy knees, and ask forgiveness.
Lodo. Oh, thou hast been a most prodigious comet!
But I 'll cut off your train.　Kill the Moor first.
Vit. You shall not kill her first; behold my breast:
I will be waited on in death; my servant
Shall never go before me.
Gas. Are you so brave?
Vit. Yes, I shall welcome death,
As princes do some great ambassadors;
I 'll meet thy weapon half-way.
Lodo. Thou dost tremble:
Methinks, fear should dissolve thee into air.
Vit. Oh, thou art deceiv'd, I am too true a woman!
Conceit can never kill me.　I 'll tell thee what,
I will not in my death shed one base tear;
Or if look pale, for want of blood, not fear.
Gas. Thou art my task, black fury.
Zan. I have blood
As red as either of theirs: wilt drink some?
'Tis good for the falling-sickness.　I am proud:
Death cannot alter my complexion,
For I shall ne'er look pale.
Lodo. Strike, strike,
With a joint motion.　　　　　　　　　*[They strike.*
Vit. 'Twas a manly blow;
The next thou giv'st, murder some sucking infant;
And then thou wilt be famous.
Flam. Oh, what blade is 't?
A Toledo, or an English fox?
I ever thought a culter should distinguish
The cause of my death, rather than a doctor.
Search my wound deeper; tent it with the steel
That made it.
Vit. Oh, my greatest sin lay in my blood!
Now my blood pays for 't.
Flam. Th' art a noble sister!
I love thee now; if woman do breed man,
She ought to teach him manhood.　Fare thee well.
Know, many glorious women that are fam'd
For masculine virtue, have been vicious,

Only a happier silence did betide them:
She hath no faults, who hath the art to hide them.
Vit. My soul, like to a ship in a black storm,
  Is driven, I know not whither.
Flam. Then cast anchor.
  Prosperity doth bewitch men, seeming clear;
  But seas do laugh, show white, when rocks are near.
  We cease to grieve, cease to be fortune's slaves,
  Nay, cease to die by dying.   Art thou gone?
  And thou so near the bottom? false report,
  Which says that women vie with the nine Muses,
  For nine tough durable lives! I do not look
  Who went before, nor who shall follow me;
  No, at myself I will begin the end.
  While we look up to heaven, we confound
  Knowledge with knowledge.   Oh, I am in a mist!
Vit. Oh, happy they that never saw the court,
  Nor ever knew great men but by report!   [*Vittoria dies.*
Flam. I recover like a spent taper, for a flash,
  And instantly go out.
  Let all that belong to great men remember th' old wives'
  tradition, to be like the lions i' th' Tower on Candlemas-day;
  to mourn if the sun shine, for fear of the pitiful remainder of
  winter to come.
  'Tis well yet there 's some goodness in my death;
  My life was a black charnel.   I have caught
  An everlasting cold; I have lost my voice
  Most irrecoverably.   Farewell, glorious villains.
  This busy trade of life appears most vain,
  Since rest breeds rest, where all seek pain by pain.
  Let no harsh flattering bells resound my knell;
  Strike, thunder, and strike loud, to my farewell!   [*Dies.*

Enter Ambassadors and Giovanni

Eng. Ambass. This way, this way! break open the doors! this way!
Lodo. Ha! are we betray'd?
  Why then let 's constantly die all together;
  And having finish'd this most noble deed,
  Defy the worst of fate, nor fear to bleed.
Eng. Ambass. Keep back the prince: shoot! shoot!
Lodo. Oh, I am wounded!
  I fear I shall be ta'en.
Giov. You bloody villains,

By what authority have you committed
This massacre?

Lodo. By thine.

Giov. Mine!

Lodo. Yes; thy uncle, which is a part of thee, enjoined us to 't:
Thou know'st me, I am sure; I am Count Lodowick;
And thy most noble uncle in disguise
Was last night in thy court.

Giov. Ha!

Lodo. Yes, that Moor thy father chose his pensioner.

Giov. He turn'd murderer!
Away with them to prison, and to torture:
All that have hands in this shall taste our justice,
As I hope heaven.

Lodo. I do glory yet,
That I can call this act mine own.   For my part,
The rack, the gallows, and the torturing wheel,
Shall be but sound sleeps to me: here 's my rest;
I limn'd this night-piece, and it was my best.

Giov. Remove the bodies.   See, my honour'd lord,
What use you ought make of their punishment.
Let guilty men remember, their black deeds
Do lean on crutches made of slender reeds.

––––––––––––

Instead of an epilogue, only this of Martial supplies me:

Hæc fuerint nobis præmia, si placui.

For the action of the play, 'twas generally well, and I dare
affirm, with the joint testimony of some of their own quality
(for the true imitation of life, without striving to make nature a
monster), the best that ever became them: whereof as I make a
general acknowledgment, so in particular I must remember the
well-approved industry of my friend Master Perkins, and confess
the worth of his action did crown both the beginning and end.

THE DUCHESS OF MALFI

RIGHT HONOURABLE GEORGE HARDING, BARON BERKELEY, OF BERKELEY CASTLE, AND KNIGHT OF THE ORDER OF THE BATH TO THE ILLUSTRIOUS PRINCE CHARLES

MY NOBLE LORD,

That I may present my excuse why, being a stranger to your lordship, I offer this poem to your patronage, I plead this warrant: men who never saw the sea yet desire to behold that regiment of waters, choose some eminent river to guide them thither, and make that, as it were, their conduct or postilion: by the like ingenious means has your fame arrived at my knowledge, receiving it from some of worth, who both in contemplation and practice owe to your honour their clearest service. I do not altogether look up at your title; the ancientest nobility being but a relic of time past, and the truest honour indeed being for a man to confer honour on himself, which your learning strives to propagate, and shall make you arrive at the dignity of a great example. I am confident this work is not unworthy your honour's perusal; for by such poems as this poets have kissed the hands of great princes, and drawn their gentle eyes to look down upon their sheets of paper when the poets themselves were bound up in their winding-sheets. The like courtesy from your lordship shall make you live in your grave, and laurel spring out of it, when the ignorant scorners of the Muses, that like worms in libraries seem to live only to destroy learning, shall wither neglected and forgotten. This work and myself I humbly present to your approved censure, it being the utmost of my wishes to have your honourable self my weighty and perspicuous comment; which grace so done me shall ever be acknowledged

By your lordship's

in all duty and observance

JOHN WEBSTER.

DRAMATIS PERSONÆ

FERDINAND, Duke of Calabria.

CARDINAL, his brother.

ANTONIO BOLOGNA, steward of the household to the Duchess.

DELIO, his friend.

DANIEL DE BOSOLA, gentleman of the horse to the Duchess.

CASTRUCCIO.

MARQUIS OF PESCARA.

COUNT MALATESTI.

RODERIGO.

SILVIO.

GRISOLAN.

DOCTOR.

The several Madmen.

DUCHESS OF MALFI.

CARIOLA, her woman.

JULIA, Castruccio's wife, and the Cardinal's mistress.

Old Lady.

Ladies, Children, Pilgrims, Executioners, Officers, and
Attendants, etc.

ACT I

Enter Antonio and Delio

Delio. You are welcome to your country, dear Antonio;
   You have been long in France, and you return
   A very formal Frenchman in your habit:
   How do you like the French court?
Ant. I admire it:
   In seeking to reduce both state and people
   To a fix'd order, their judicious king
   Begins at home; quits first his royal palace
   Of flattering sycophants, of dissolute
   And infamous persons,—which he sweetly terms
   His master's masterpiece, the work of heaven;
   Considering duly that a prince's court
   Is like a common fountain, whence should flow
   Pure silver drops in general, but if 't chance
   Some curs'd example poison 't near the head,
   Death and diseases through the whole land spread.
   And what is 't makes this blessed government
   But a most provident council, who dare freely
   Inform him the corruption of the times?
   Though some o' the court hold it presumption
   To instruct princes what they ought to do,
   It is a noble duty to inform them
   What they ought to foresee.—Here comes Bosola,
   The only court-gall; yet I observe his railing
   Is not for simple love of piety:
   Indeed, he rails at those things which he wants;
   Would be as lecherous, covetous, or proud,
   Bloody, or envious, as any man,
   If he had means to be so.—Here 's the cardinal.

Enter Cardinal and Bosola

Bos. I do haunt you still.
Card. So.

Bos. I have done you better service than to be slighted thus.
Miserable age, where only the reward of doing well is the
doing of it!

Card. You enforce your merit too much.

Bos. I fell into the galleys in your service; where, for two years
together, I wore two towels instead of a shirt, with a knot on
the shoulder, after the fashion of a Roman mantle.   Slighted
thus! I will thrive some way: blackbirds fatten best in hard
weather; why not I in these dog-days?

Card. Would you could become honest!

Bos. With all your divinity do but direct me the way to it.   I
have known many travel far for it, and yet return as arrant
knaves as they went forth, because they carried themselves
always along with them. [*Exit Cardinal.*] Are you gone? Some
fellows, they say, are possessed with the devil, but this great
fellow were able to possess the greatest devil, and make him
worse.

Ant. He hath denied thee some suit?

Bos. He and his brother are like plum-trees that grow crooked
over standing-pools; they are rich and o'er-laden with fruit,
but none but crows, pies, and caterpillars feed on them. Could
I be one of their flattering panders, I would hang on their ears
like a horseleech, till I were full, and then drop off.   I pray,
leave me.   Who would rely upon these miserable depen-
dencies, in expectation to be advanced to-morrow? what
creature ever fed worse than hoping Tantalus? nor ever died
any man more fearfully than he that hoped for a pardon.
There are rewards for hawks and dogs when they have done us
service; but for a soldier that hazards his limbs in a battle,
nothing but a kind of geometry is his last supportation.

Delio. Geometry!

Bos. Ay, to hang in a fair pair of slings, take his latter swing in
the world upon an honourable pair of crutches, from hospital
to hospital.   Fare ye well, sir: and yet do not you scorn us;
for places in the court are but like beds in the hospital, where
this man's head lies at that man's foot, and so lower and
lower.   [*Exit.*

Delio. I knew this fellow seven years in the galleys
For a notorious murder; and 'twas thought
The cardinal suborn'd it: he was releas'd
By the French general, Gaston de Foix,
When he recover'd Naples.

Ant. 'Tis great pity

He should be thus neglected: I have heard
He 's very valiant.   This foul melancholy
Will poison all his goodness; for, I 'll tell you,
If too immoderate sleep be truly said
To be an inward rust unto the soul,
It then doth follow want of action
Breeds all black malcontents; and their close rearing,
Like moths in cloth, do hurt for want of wearing.

Delio. The presence 'gins to fill: you promis'd me
To make me the partaker of the natures
Of some of your great courtiers.

Ant. The lord cardinal's,
And other strangers' that are now in court?
I shall.—Here comes the great Calabrian duke.

*Enter Ferdinand, Castruccio, Silvio, Roderigo, Grisolan,
and Attendants*

Ferd. Who took the ring oftenest?

Sil. Antonio Bologna, my lord.

Ferd. Our sister duchess' great-master of her household? give
him the jewel.—When shall we leave this sportive action, and
fall to action indeed?

Cast. Methinks, my lord, you should not desire to go to war in
person.

Ferd. Now for some gravity: why, my lord?

Cast. It is fitting a soldier arise to be a prince, but not necessary
a prince descend to be a captain.

Ferd. No?

Cast. No, my lord; he were far better do it by a deputy.

Ferd. Why should he not as well sleep or eat by a deputy?
this might take idle, offensive, and base office from him,
whereas the other deprives him of honour.

Cast. Believe my experience, that realm is never long in quiet
where the ruler is a soldier.

Ferd. Thou toldest me thy wife could not endure fighting.

Cast. True, my lord.

Ferd. And of a jest she broke of a captain she met full of
wounds: I have forgot it.

Cast. She told him, my lord, he was a pitiful fellow, to lie, like
the children of Ishmael, all in tents.

Ferd. Why, there 's a wit were able to undo all the chirurgeons
o' the city; for although gallants should quarrel, and had

drawn their weapons, and were ready to go to it, yet her
persuasions would make them put up.

Cast. That she would, my lord.—How do you like my Spanish
gennet?

Rod. He is all fire.

Ferd. I am of Pliny's opinion, I think he was begot by the wind;
he runs as if he were ballasted with quicksilver.

Sil. True, my lord, he reels from the tilt often.

Rod., Gris. Ha, ha, ha!

Ferd. Why do you laugh? methinks you that are courtiers should
be my touchwood, take fire when I give fire; that is, laugh
[but] when I laugh, were the subject never so witty.

Cast. True, my lord: I myself have heard a very good jest, and
have scorned to seem to have so silly a wit as to understand it.

Ferd. But I can laugh at your fool, my lord.

Cast. He cannot speak, you know, but he makes faces: my lady
cannot abide him.

Ferd. No?

Cast. Nor endure to be in merry company; for she says too
much laughing, and too much company, fills her too full of
the wrinkle.

Ferd. I would, then, have a mathematical instrument made for
her face, that she might not laugh out of compass.—I shall
shortly visit you at Milan, Lord Silvio.

Sil. Your grace shall arrive most welcome.

Ferd. You are a good horseman, Antonio: you have excellent
riders in France: what do you think of good horsemanship?

Ant. Nobly, my lord: as out of the Grecian horse issued many
famous princes, so out of brave horsemanship arise the first
sparks of growing resolution, that raise the mind to noble
action.

Ferd. You have bespoke it worthily.

Sil. Your brother, the lord cardinal, and sister duchess.

Re-enter Cardinal, with Duchess, Cariola, and Julia

Card. Are the galleys come about?

Gris. They are, my lord.

Ferd. Here 's the Lord Silvio is come to take his leave.

Delio. Now, sir, your promise: what 's that cardinal?
    I mean his temper? they say he 's a brave fellow,
    Will play his five thousand crowns at tennis, dance,
    Court ladies, and one that hath fought single combats.

Ant. Some such flashes superficially hang on him for form; but

observe his inward character: he is a melancholy churchman;
the spring in his face is nothing but the engendering of toads;
where he is jealous of any man, he lays worse plots for them
than ever was imposed on Hercules, for he strews in his way
flatterers, panders, intelligencers, atheists, and a thousand
such political monsters. He should have been Pope; but
instead of coming to it by the primitive decency of the
Church, he did bestow bribes so largely and so impudently as
if he would have carried it away without Heaven's knowledge.
Some good he hath done——

Delio. You have given too much of him. What 's his brother?

Ant. The duke there? a most perverse and turbulent nature:
　　What appears in him mirth is merely outside;
　　If he laugh heartily, it is to laugh
　　All honesty out of fashion.

Delio. Twins?

Ant. In quality.
　　He speaks with others' tongues, and hears men's suits
　　With others' ears; will seem to sleep o' the bench
　　Only to entrap offenders in their answers;
　　Dooms men to death by information;
　　Rewards by hearsay.

Delio. Then the law to him
　　Is like a foul black cobweb to a spider,—
　　He makes it his dwelling and a prison
　　To entangle those shall feed him.

Ant. Most true:
　　He never pays debts unless they be shrewd turns,
　　And those he will confess that he doth owe.
　　Last, for his brother there, the cardinal,
　　They that do flatter him most say oracles
　　Hang at his lips; and verily I believe them,
　　For the devil speaks in them.
　　But for their sister, the right noble duchess,
　　You never fix'd your eye on three fair medals
　　Cast in one figure, of so different temper.
　　For her discourse, it is so full of rapture,
　　You only will begin then to be sorry
　　When she doth end her speech, and wish, in wonder,
　　She held it less vainglory to talk much,
　　Than your penance to hear her: whilst she speaks,
　　She throws upon a man so sweet a look,
　　That it were able to raise one to a galliard

That lay in a dead palsy, and to dote
On that sweet countenance; but in that look
There speaketh so divine a continence
As cuts off all lascivious and vain hope.
Her days are practis'd in such noble virtue,
That sure her nights, nay, more, her very sleeps,
Are more in heaven than other ladies' shrifts.
Let all sweet ladies break their flattering glasses,
And dress themselves in her.

Delio. Fie, Antonio,
You play the wire-drawer with her commendations.

Ant. I 'll case the picture up: only thus much;
All her particular worth grows to this sum,—
She stains the time past, lights the time to come.

Cari. You must attend my lady in the gallery,
Some half an hour hence.

Ant. I shall.   [*Exeunt Antonio and Delio.*

Ferd. Sister, I have a suit to you.

Duch. To me, sir?

Ferd. A gentleman here, Daniel de Bosola,
One that was in the galleys——

Duch. Yes, I know him.

Ferd. A worthy fellow he is: pray, let me entreat for
The provisorship of your horse.

Duch. Your knowledge of him
Commends him and prefers him.

Ferd. Call him hither.   [*Exit Attendant.*
We [are] now upon parting. Good Lord Silvio,
Do us commend to all our noble friends
At the leaguer.

Silvio. Sir, I shall.

Ferd. You are for Milan?

Silvio. I am.

Duch. Bring the caroches.—We 'll bring you down to the haven.
     [*Exeunt Duchess, Silvio, Castruccio, Roderigo, Grisolan,
          Cariola, Julia, and Attendants.*

Card. Be sure you entertain that Bosola
For your intelligence: I would not be seen in 't;
And therefore many times I have slighted him
When he did court our furtherance, as this morning.

Ferd. Antonio, the great-master of her household,
Had been far fitter.

Card. You are deceiv'd in him:

His nature is too honest for such business.—
He comes: I 'll leave you.   [*Exit.*

Re-enter Bosola

Bos. I was lur'd to you.

Ferd. My brother, here, the cardinal could never
Abide you.

Bos. Never since he was in my debt.

Ferd. May be some oblique character in your face
Made him suspect you.

Bos. Doth he study physiognomy?
There 's no more credit to be given to the face
Than to a sick man's urine, which some call
The physician's whore because she cozens him.
He did suspect me wrongfully.

Ferd. For that
You must give great men leave to take their times.
Distrust doth cause us seldom be deceiv'd:
You see the oft shaking of the cedar-tree
Fastens it more at root.

Bos. Yet, take heed;
For to suspect a friend unworthily
Instructs him the next way to suspect you,
And prompts him to deceive you.

Ferd. There 's gold.

Bos. So:
What follows? never rain'd such showers as these
Without thunderbolts i' the tail of them: whose throat must
I cut?

Ferd. Your inclination to shed blood rides post
Before my occasion to use you.   I give you that
To live i' the court here, and observe the duchess;
To note all the particulars of her haviour,
What suitors do solicit her for marriage,
And whom she best affects.   She 's a young widow:
I would not have her marry again.

Bos. No, sir?

Ferd. Do not you ask the reason; but be satisfied
I say I would not.

Bos. It seems you would create me
One of your familiars.

Ferd. Familiar! what 's that?

Bos. Why, a very quaint invisible devil in flesh,—
  An intelligencer.
Ferd. Such a kind of thriving thing
  I would wish thee; and ere long thou mayst arrive
  At a higher place by 't.
Bos. Take your devils,
  Which hell calls angels: these curs'd gifts would make
  You a corrupter, me an impudent traitor;
  And should I take these, they 'd take me [to] hell.
Ferd. Sir, I 'll take nothing from you that I have given:
  There is a place that I procur'd for you
  This morning, the provisorship o' the horse;
  Have you heard on 't?
Bos. No.
Ferd. 'Tis yours: is 't not worth thanks?
Bos. I would have you curse yourself now, that your bounty
  (Which makes men truly noble) e'er should make me
  A villain. Oh, that to avoid ingratitude
  For the good deed you have done me, I must do
  All the ill man can invent! Thus the devil
  Candies all sins o'er; and what heaven terms vile,
  That names he complimental.
Ferd. Be yourself;
  Keep your old garb of melancholy; 'twill express
  You envy those that stand above your reach,
  Yet strive not to come near 'em: this will gain
  Access to private lodgings, where yourself
  May, like a politic dormouse——
Bos. As I have seen some
  Feed in a lord's dish, half asleep, not seeming
  To listen to any talk; and yet these rogues
  Have cut his throat in a dream.   What 's my place?
  The provisorship o' the horse? say, then, my corruption
  Grew out of horse-dung: I am your creature.
Ferd. Away!
Bos. Let good men, for good deeds, covet good fame,
  Since place and riches oft are bribes of shame:
  Sometimes the devil doth preach.   [*Exit.*

Re-enter Duchess, Cardinal, and Cariola

Card. We are to part from you; and your own discretion
  Must now be your director.
Ferd. You are a widow:

You know already what man is; and therefore
Let not youth, high promotion, eloquence——
Card. No,
Nor anything without the addition, honour,
Sway your high blood.
Ferd. Marry! they are most luxurious
Will wed twice.
Card. Oh, fie!
Ferd. Their livers are more spotted
Than Laban's sheep.
Duch. Diamonds are of most value,
They say, that have pass'd through most jewellers' hands.
Ferd. Whores by that rule are precious.
Duch. Will you hear me?
I 'll never marry.
Card. So most widows say;
But commonly that motion lasts no longer
Than the turning of an hour-glass: the funeral sermon
And it end both together.
Ferd. Now hear me:
You live in a rank pasture, here, i' the court;
There is a kind of honey-dew that 's deadly;
'Twill poison your fame; look to 't: be not cunning;
For they whose faces do belie their hearts
Are witches ere they arrive at twenty years,
Ay, and give the devil suck.
Duch. This is terrible good counsel.
Ferd. Hypocrisy is woven of a fine small thread,
Subtler than Vulcan's engine: yet, believe 't,
Your darkest actions, nay, your privat'st thoughts,
Will come to light.
Card. You may flatter yourself,
And take your own choice; privately be married
Under the eves of night——
Ferd. Think 't the best voyage
That e'er you made; like the irregular crab,
Which, though 't goes backward, thinks that it goes right
Because it goes its own way: but observe,
Such weddings may more properly be said
To be executed than celebrated.
Card. The marriage night
Is the entrance into some prison.
Ferd. And those joys,

Those lustful pleasures, are like heavy sleeps
Which do forerun man's mischief.
Card. Fare you well.
Wisdom begins at the end: remember it.   [*Exit.*
Duch. I think this speech between you both was studied,
It came so roundly off.
Ferd. You are my sister;
This was my father's poniard, do you see?
I 'd be loth to see 't look rusty, 'cause 'twas his.
I would have you give o'er these chargeable revels:
A visor and a mask are whispering-rooms
That were never built for goodness;—fare ye well;—
And women like that part which, like the lamprey,
Hath never a bone in 't.
Duch. Fie, sir!
Ferd. Nay,
I mean the tongue; variety of courtship:
What cannot a neat knave with a smooth tale
Make a woman believe? Farewell, lusty widow.   [*Exit*
Duch. Shall this move me? If all my royal kindred
Lay in my way unto this marriage,
I 'd make them my low footsteps: and even now,
Even in this hate, as men in some great battles,
By apprehending danger, have achiev'd
Almost impossible actions (I have heard soldiers say so),
So I through frights and threatenings will assay
This dangerous venture.   Let old wives report
I wink'd and chose a husband.—Cariola,
To thy known secrecy I have given up
More than my life,—my fame.
Cari. Both shall be safe;
For I 'll conceal this secret from the world
As warily as those that trade in poison
Keep poison from their children.
Duch. Thy protestation
Is ingenious and hearty: I believe it.
Is Antonio come?
Cari. He attends you.
Duch. Good dear soul,
Leave me; but place thyself behind the arras,
Where thou mayst overhear us.   Wish me good speed;
For I am going into a wilderness

Where I shall find nor path nor friendly clue
To be my guide.   [*Cariola goes behind the arras.*

Enter Antonio

I sent for you: sit down;
Take pen and ink, and write: are you ready?
Ant. Yes.
Duch. What did I say?
Ant. That I should write somewhat.
Duch. Oh, I remember.
After these triumphs and this large expense,
It 's fit, like thrifty husbands, we inquire
What 's laid up for to-morrow.
Ant. So please your beauteous excellence.
Duch. Beauteous!
Indeed, I thank you: I look young for your sake;
You have ta'en my cares upon you.
Ant. I 'll fetch your grace
The particulars of your revenue and expense.
Duch. Oh, you are
An upright treasurer: but you mistook:
For when I said I meant to make inquiry
What 's laid up for to-morrow, I did mean
What 's laid up yonder for me.
Ant. Where?
Duch. In heaven.
I am making my will (as 'tis fit princes should,
In perfect memory), and, I pray, sir, tell me,
Were not one better make it smiling, thus,
Than in deep groans and terrible ghastly looks,
As if the gifts we parted with procur'd
That violent distraction?
Ant. Oh, much better.
Duch. If I had a husband now, this care were quit:
But I intend to make you overseer.
What good deed shall we first remember? say.
Ant. Begin with that first good deed began i' the world
After man's creation, the sacrament of marriage:
I 'd have you first provide for a good husband;
Give him all.
Duch. All!
Ant. Yes, your excellent self.
Duch. In a winding-sheet?

Ant. In a couple.

Duch. Saint Winifred, that were a strange will!

Ant. 'Twere stranger if there were no will in you
　　To marry again.

Duch. What do you think of marriage?

Ant. I take 't, as those that deny purgatory,
　　It locally contains or heaven or hell;
　　There 's no third place in 't.

Duch. How do you affect it?

Ant. My banishment, feeding my melancholy,
　　Would often reason thus.

Duch. Pray, let 's hear it.

Ant. Say a man never marry, nor have children,
　　What takes that from him? only the bare name
　　Of being a father, or the weak delight
　　To see the little wanton ride a-cock-horse
　　Upon a painted stick, or hear him chatter
　　Like a taught starling.

Duch. Fie, fie, what 's all this?
　　One of your eyes is bloodshot; use my ring to 't,
　　They say 'tis very sovereign: 'twas my wedding-ring,
　　And I did vow never to part with it
　　But to my second husband.

Ant. You have parted with it now.

Duch. Yes, to help your eyesight.

Ant. You have made me stark blind.

Duch. How?

Ant. There is a saucy and ambitious devil
　　Is dancing in this circle.

Duch. Remove him.

Ant. How?

Duch. There needs small conjuration, when your finger
　　May do it: thus; is it fit?
　　　　　　　　　　[*She puts the ring upon his finger: he kneels.*

Ant. What said you?

Duch. Sir,
　　This goodly roof of yours is too low built;
　　I cannot stand upright in 't nor discourse,
　　Without I raise it higher: raise yourself;
　　Or, if you please, my hand to help you: so.　　　[*Raises him.*

Ant. Ambition, madam, is a great man's madness,
　　That is not kept in chains and close-pent rooms,
　　But in fair lightsome lodgings, and is girt

With the wild noise of prattling visitants,
Which makes it lunatic beyond all cure.
Conceive not I am so stupid but I aim
Whereto your favours tend: but he 's a fool
That, being a-cold, would thrust his hands i' the fire
To warm them.
Duch. So, now the ground 's broke,
You may discover what a wealthy mine
I make you lord of.
Ant. Oh, my unworthiness!
Duch. You were ill to sell yourself:
This darkening of your worth is not like that
Which tradesmen use i' the city; their false lights
Are to rid bad wares off: and I must tell you,
If you will know where breathes a cómplete man
(I speak it without flattery), turn your eyes,
And progress through yourself.
Ant. Were there nor heaven nor hell,
I should be honest: I have long serv'd virtue,
And ne'er ta'en wages of her.
Duch. Now she pays it.
The misery of us that are born great!
We are forc'd to woo, because none dare woo us;
And as a tyrant doubles with his words,
And fearfully equivocates, so we
Are forc'd to express our violent passions
In riddles and in dreams, and leave the path
Of simple virtue, which was never made
To seem the thing it is not.   Go, go brag
You have left me heartless; mine is in your bosom:
I hope 'twill multiply love there.   You do tremble:
Make not your heart so dead a piece of flesh,
To fear more than to love me.   Sir, be confident:
What is 't distracts you? This is flesh and blood, sir;
'Tis not the figure cut in alabaster
Kneels at my husband's tomb.   Awake, awake, man!
I do here put off all vain ceremony,
And only do appear to you a young widow
That claims you for her husband, and, like a widow,
I use but half a blush in 't.
Ant. Truth speak for me;
I will remain the constant sanctuary
Of your good name.

Duch. I thank you, gentle love:
　　And 'cause you shall not come to me in debt,
　　Being now my steward, here upon your lips
　　I sign your *Quietus est.*　This you should have begg'd now:
　　I have seen children oft eat sweetmeats thus,
　　As fearful to devour them too soon.
Ant. But for your brothers?
Duch. Do not think of them:
　　All discord without this circumference
　　Is only to be pitied, and not fear'd:
　　Yet, should they know it, time will easily
　　Scatter the tempest.
Ant. These words should be mine,
　　And all the parts you have spoke, if some part of it
　　Would not have savour'd flattery.
Duch. Kneel.　　　　　　*[Cariola comes from behind the arras.*
Ant. Ha!
Duch. Be not amaz'd; this woman 's of my counsel:
　　I have heard lawyers say, a contract in a chamber
　　Per verba presenti is absolute marriage.
　　　　　　　　　　　　　　[She and Antonio kneel.
　　Bless, Heaven, this sacred gordian, which let violence
　　Never untwine!
Ant. And may our sweet affections, like the spheres,
　　Be still in motion!
Duch. Quickening, and make
　　The like soft music!
Ant. That we may imitate the loving palms,
　　Best emblem of a peaceful marriage,
　　That never bore fruit, divided!
Duch. What can the Church force more?
Ant. That fortune may not know an accident,
　　Either of joy or sorrow, to divide
　　Our fixed wishes!
Duch. How can the Church build faster?
　　We now are man and wife, and 'tis the church
　　That must but echo this.—Maid, stand apart:
　　I now am blind.
Ant. What 's your conceit in this?
Duch. I would have you lead your fortune by the hand
　　Unto your marriage-bed:
　　(You speak in me this, for we now are one:)
　　We 'll only lie, and talk together, and plot

To appease my humorous kindred; and if you please,
Like the old tale in Alexander and Lodowick,
Lay a naked sword between us, keep us chaste.
Oh, let me shroud my blushes in your bosom,
Since 'tis the treasury of all my secrets!

[*Exeunt Duchess and Antonio.*

Cari. Whether the spirit of greatness or of woman
Reign most in her, I know not; but it shows
A fearful madness: I owe her much of pity.   [*Exit.*

ACT II

Scene I

Enter Bosola and Castruccio

Bos. You say you would fain be taken for an eminent courtier?
Cast. 'Tis the very main of my ambition.
Bos. Let me see: you have a reasonable good face for 't already,
and your night-cap expresses your ears sufficient largely.   I
would have you learn to twirl the strings of your band with a
good grace, and in a set speech, at the end of every sentence, to
hum three or four times, or blow your nose till it smart again,
to recover your memory.   When you come to be a president in
criminal causes, if you smile upon a prisoner, hang him; but if
you frown upon him and threaten him, let him be sure to
scape the gallows.
Cast. I would be a very merry president.
Bos. Do not sup o' nights; 'twill beget you an admirable wit.
Cast. Rather it would make me have a good stomach to quarrel;
for they say, your roaring boys eat meat seldom, and that
makes them so valiant.   But how shall I know whether the
people take me for an eminent fellow?
Bos. I will teach a trick to know it: give out you lie a-dying, and
if you hear the common people curse you, be sure you are
taken for one of the prime night-caps.   [*Enter an Old Lady.*
You come from painting now.
Old Lady. From what?
Bos. Why, from your scurvy face-physic.   To behold thee not
painted inclines somewhat near a miracle: these in thy face
I 899

here were deep ruts and foul sloughs the last progress.   There
was a lady in France that, having had the smallpox, flayed
the skin off her face to make it more level; and whereas before
she looked like a nutmeg-grater, after she resembled an
abortive hedgehog.

Old Lady. Do you call this painting?

Bos. No, no, but you call [it] careening of an old morphewed
lady, to make her disembogue again: there's rough-cast
phrase to your plastic.

Old Lady. It seems you are well acquainted with my closet.

Bos. One would suspect it for a shop of witchcraft, to find in
it the fat of serpents, spawn of snakes, Jews' spittle, and their
young children's ordure; and all these for the face.   I would
sooner eat a dead pigeon taken from the soles of the feet of
one sick of the plague, than kiss one of you fasting.   Here are
two of you, whose sin of your youth is the very patrimony of
the physician; makes him renew his foot-cloth with the spring,
and change his high-priced courtesan with the fall of the leaf.
I do wonder you do not loathe yourselves.   Observe my
meditation now.

What thing is in this outward form of man
To be belov'd? We account it ominous,
If nature do produce a colt, or lamb,
A fawn, or goat, in any limb resembling
A man, and fly from 't as a prodigy:
Man stands amaz'd to see his deformity
In any other creature but himself.
But in our own flesh though we bear diseases
Which have their true names only ta'en from beasts,—
As the most ulcerous wolf and swinish measle,—
Though we are eaten up of lice and worms,
And though continually we bear about us
A rotten and dead body, we delight
To hide it in rich tissue: all our fear,
Nay, all our terror, is, lest our physician
Should put us in the ground to be made sweet.—
Your wife's gone to Rome: you two couple, and get you to
the wells at Lucca to recover your aches.   I have other work
on foot.   [*Exeunt Castruccio and Old Lady.*
I observe our duchess
Is sick a-days, she pukes, her stomach seethes,
The fins of her eyelids look most teeming blue,
She wanes i' the cheek, and waxes fat i' the flank,

And, contrary to our Italian fashion,
Wears a loose-bodied gown: there 's somewhat in 't.
I have a trick may chance discover it,
A pretty one; I have bought some apricots,
The first our spring yields.

Enter Antonio and Delio

Delio. And so long since married!
　You amaze me.
Ant. Let me seal your lips for ever:
　For did I think that anything but the air
　Could carry these words from you, I should wish
　You had no breath at all.—Now, sir, in your contemplation?
　You are studying to become a great wise fellow.
Bos. Oh, sir, the opinion of wisdom is a foul tetter that runs all
　over a man's body: if simplicity direct us to have no evil, it
　directs us to a happy being; for the subtlest folly proceeds
　from the subtlest wisdom: let me be simply honest.
Ant. I do understand your inside.
Bos. Do you so?
Ant. Because you would not seem to appear to the world
　Puff'd up with your preferment, you continue
　This out-of-fashion melancholy: leave it, leave it.
Bos. Give me leave to be honest in any phrase, in any compli-
　ment whatsoever. Shall I confess myself to you? I look no
　higher than I can reach: they are the gods that must ride on
　winged horses. A lawyer's mule of a slow pace will both suit
　my disposition and business; for, mark me, when a man's
　mind rides faster than his horse can gallop, they quickly
　both tire.
Ant. You would look up to heaven, but I think
　The devil, that rules i' the air, stands in your light.
Bos. Oh, sir, you are lord of the ascendant, chief man with the
　duchess; a duke was your cousin-german removed. Say you
　were lineally descended from King Pepin, or he himself, what
　of this? search the heads of the greatest rivers in the world,
　you shall find them but bubbles of water. Some would think
　the souls of princes were brought forth by some more weighty
　cause than those of meaner persons: they are deceived,
　there 's the same hand to them; the like passions sway them;
　the same reason that makes a vicar to go to law for a tithe-
　pig and undo his neighbours, makes them spoil a whole
　province, and batter down goodly cities with the cannon

Enter Duchess and Ladies

Duch. Your arm, Antonio: do I not grow fat?
   I am exceeding short-winded.—Bosola,
   I would have you, sir, provide for me a litter;
   Such a one as the Duchess of Florence rode in.
Bos. The duchess us'd one when she was great with child.
Duch. I think she did.—Come hither, mend my ruff:
   Here, when? thou art such a tedious lady; and
   Thy breath smells of lemon-pills: would thou hadst done!
   Shall I swoon under thy fingers? I am
   So troubled with the mother!
Bos. [*Aside.*] I fear too much.
Duch. I have heard you say that the French courtiers
   Wear their hats on 'fore the king.
Ant. I have seen it.
Duch. In the presence?
Ant. Yes.
Duch. Why should not we bring up that fashion?
   'Tis ceremony more than duty that consists
   In the removing of a piece of felt:
   Be you the example to the rest o' the court;
   Put on your hat first.
Ant. You must pardon me:
   I have seen, in colder countries than in France,
   Nobles stand bare to the prince; and the distinction
   Methought show'd reverently.
Bos. I have a present for your grace.
Duch. For me, sir?
Bos. Apricots, madam.
Duch. Oh, sir, where are they?
   I have heard of none to-year.
Bos. [*Aside.*] Good; her colour rises.
Duch. Indeed, I thank you: they are wondrous fair ones.
   What an unskilful fellow is our gardener!
   We shall have none this month.
Bos. Will not your grace pare them?
Duch. No: they taste of musk, methinks; indeed they do.
Bos. I know not: yet I wish your grace had par'd 'em.
Duch. Why?
Bos. I forgot to tell you, the knave gardener,
   Only to raise his profit by them the sooner,
   Did ripen them in horse-dung.

Duch. Oh, you jest.—
  You shall judge: pray taste one.
Ant. Indeed, madam,
  I do not love the fruit.
Duch. Sir, you are loth
  To rob us of our dainties: 'tis a delicate fruit;
  They say they are restorative.
Bos. 'Tis a pretty art,
  This grafting.
Duch. 'Tis so; bettering of nature.
Bos. To make a pippin grow upon a crab,
  A damson on a blackthorn.—[*Aside.*] How greedily she eats
    them!
  A whirlwind strike off these bawd farthingales!
  For, but for that and the loose-bodied gown,
  I should have discover'd apparently
  The young springal cutting a caper in her belly.
Duch. I thank you, Bosola: they were right good ones,
  If they do not make me sick.
Ant. How now, madam!
Duch. This green fruit and my stomach are not friends:
  How they swell me!
Bos. [*Aside.*] Nay, you are too much swell'd already.
Duch. Oh, I am in an extreme cold sweat!
Bos. I am very sorry.
Duch. Lights to my chamber!—Oh, good Antonio,
  I fear I am undone!
Delio. Lights there, lights!
      [*Exeunt Duchess and Ladies.—Exit, on the other side, Bosola.*
Ant. Oh, my most trusty Delio, we are lost!
  I fear she's fall'n in labour; and there's left
  No time for her remove.
Delio. Have you prepar'd
  Those ladies to attend her? and procur'd
  That politic safe conveyance for the midwife
  Your duchess plotted?
Ant. I have.
Delio. Make use, then, of this forc'd occasion:
  Give out that Bosola hath poison'd her
  With these apricots; that will give some colour
  For her keeping close.
Ant. Fie, fie, the physicians
  Will then flock to her.

Delio. For that you may pretend
 She 'll use some prepar'd antidote of her own,
 Lest the physicians should re-poison her.
Ant. I am lost in amazement: I know not what to think on 't.
               [Exeunt.

SCENE II

Enter Bosola

Bos. So, so, there 's no question but her techiness and most
 vulturous eating of the apricots are apparent signs of breeding.
             [Enter an Old Lady.
 Now?
Old Lady. I am in haste, sir.
Bos. There was a young waiting-woman had a monstrous desire
 to see the glass-house——
Old Lady. Nay, pray, let me go.
Bos. And it was only to know what strange instrument it was
 should swell up a glass to the fashion of a woman's belly.
Old Lady. I will hear no more of the glass-house. You are still
 abusing women?
Bos. Who, I? no; only, by the way now and then, mention your
 frailties. The orange-tree bears ripe and green fruit and
 blossoms all together; and some of you give entertainment for
 pure love, but more for more precious reward. The lusty
 spring smells well; but drooping autumn tastes well. If we
 have the same golden showers that rained in the time of
 Jupiter the thunderer, you have the same Danaës still, to
 hold up their laps to receive them. Didst thou never study
 the mathematics?
Old Lady. What 's that, sir?
Bos. Why, to know the trick how to make a many lines meet
 in one centre. Go, go, give your foster-daughters good counsel:
 tell them, that the devil takes delight to hang at a woman's
 girdle, like a false rusty watch, that she cannot discern how
 the time passes.   *[Exit Old Lady.*

Enter Antonio, Roderigo, and Grisolan

Ant. Shut up the court-gates.
Rod. Why, sir? what 's the danger?
Ant. Shut up the posterns presently, and call
 All the officers o' the court.
Gris. I shall instantly.   *[Exit.*

Ant. Who keeps the key o' the park-gate?
Rod. Forobosco.
Ant. Let him bring 't presently.

Re-enter Grisolan with Servants

First Serv. Oh, gentlemen o' the court, the foulest treason!
Bos. [*Aside.*] If that these apricots should be poison'd now,
　　Without my knowledge!
First Serv. There was taken even now a Switzer in the duchess'
　　bed-chamber——
Second Serv. A Switzer!
First Serv. With a pistol in his great cod-piece.
Bos. Ha, ha, ha!
First Serv. The cod-piece was the case for 't.
Second Serv. There was a cunning traitor: who would have
　　searched his cod-piece?
First Serv. True, if he had kept out of the ladies' chambers: and
　　all the moulds of his buttons were leaden bullets.
Second Serv. O wicked cannibal! a fire-lock in 's cod-piece!
First Serv. 'Twas a French plot, upon my life.
Second Serv. To see what the devil can do!
Ant. [Are] all the officers here?
Serv. We are.
Ant. Gentlemen,
　　We have lost much plate you know; and but this evening
　　Jewels, to the value of four thousand ducats,
　　Are missing in the duchess' cabinet.
　　Are the gates shut?
Serv. Yes.
Ant. 'Tis the duchess' pleasure
　　Each officer be lock'd into his chamber
　　Till the sun-rising; and to send the keys
　　Of all their chests and of their outward doors
　　Into her bed-chamber.　She is very sick.
Rod. At her pleasure.
Ant. She entreats you take 't not ill; the innocent
　　Shall be the more approv'd by it.
Bos. Gentleman o' the wood-yard, where 's your Switzer now?
First Serv. By this hand, 'twas credibly reported by one o' the
　　black guard.　　　　　[*Exeunt all except Antonio and Delio.*
Delio. How fares it with the duchess?
Ant. She 's expos'd
　　Unto the worst of torture, pain and fear.

Delio. Speak to her all happy comfort.
Ant. How I do play the fool with mine own danger!
  You are this night, dear friend, to post to Rome:
  My life lies in your service.
Delio. Do not doubt me.
Ant. Oh, 'tis far from me: and yet fear presents me
  Somewhat that looks like danger.
Delio. Believe it,
  'Tis but the shadow of your fear, no more:
  How superstitiously we mind our evils!
  The throwing down salt, or crossing of a hare,
  Bleeding at nose, the stumbling of a horse,
  Or singing of a cricket, are of power
  To daunt whole man in us. Sir, fare you well:
  I wish you all the joys of a bless'd father;
  And, for my faith, lay this unto your breast,—
  Old friends, like old swords, still are trusted best.   [*Exit.*

Enter Cariola

Cari. Sir, you are the happy father of a son:
  Your wife commends him to you.
Ant. Blessed comfort!—
  For heaven' sake tend her well: I 'll presently
  Go set a figure for 's nativity.   [*Exeunt.*

Scene III

Enter Bosola, with a dark lantern

Bos. Sure I did hear a woman shriek: list, ha!
  And the sound came, if I receiv'd it right,
  From the duchess' lodgings. There 's some stratagem
  In the confining all our courtiers
  To their several wards: I must have part of it;
  My intelligence will freeze else. List, again!
  It may be 'twas the melancholy bird,
  Best friend of silence and of solitariness,
  The owl, that scream'd so.—Ha! Antonio!

Enter Antonio

Ant. I heard some noise.—Who 's there? what art thou? speak.
Bos. Antonio, put not your face nor body

To such a forc'd expression of fear:
I am Bosola, your friend.

Ant. Bosola!—
[*Aside.*] This mole does undermine me.—Heard you not
A noise even now?

Bos. From whence?

Ant. From the duchess' lodging.

Bos. Not I: did you?

Ant. I did, or else I dream'd.

Bos. Let 's walk towards it.

Ant. No: it may be 'twas
But the rising of the wind.

Bos. Very likely.
Methinks 'tis very cold, and yet you sweat:
You look wildly.

Ant. I have been setting a figure
For the duchess' jewels.

Bos. Ah, and how falls your question?
Do you find it radical?

Ant. What 's that to you?
'Tis rather to be question'd what design,
When all men were commanded to their lodgings,
Makes you a night-walker.

Bos. In sooth, I 'll tell you:
Now all the court 's asleep, I thought the devil
Had least to do here; I came to say my prayers;
And if it do offend you I do so,
You are a fine courtier.

Ant. [*Aside.*] This fellow will undo me.—
You gave the duchess apricots to-day:
Pray heaven they were not poison'd!

Bos. Poison'd! a Spanish fig
For the imputation.

Ant. Traitors are ever confident
Till they are discover'd.   There were jewels stol'n too.
In my conceit, none are to be suspected
More than yourself.

Bos. You are a false steward.

Ant. Saucy slave, I 'll pull thee up by the roots.

Bos. Maybe the ruin will crush you to pieces.

Ant. You are an impudent snake indeed, sir:
Are you scarce warm, and do you show your sting?
You libel well, sir.

Bos. No, sir: copy it out,
  And I will set my hand to 't.
Ant. [*Aside.*] My nose bleeds.
  One that were superstitious would count
  This ominous, when it merely comes by chance:
  Two letters, that are wrote here for my name,
  Are drown'd in blood!
  Mere accident.—For you, sir, I 'll take order
  I' the morn you shall be safe:—[*Aside.*] 'tis that must colour
  Her lying-in:—sir, this door you pass not:
  I do not hold it fit that you come near
  The duchess' lodgings, till you have quit yourself.—
  [*Aside.*] The great are like the base, nay, they are the same,
  When they seek shameful ways to avoid shame.   [*Exit.*
Bos. Antonio hereabout did drop a paper:
  Some of your help, false friend:—Oh, here it is.
  What 's here? a child's nativity calculated!   [*Reads.*
    '*The duchess was delivered of a son, 'tween the hours twelve
  and one in the night, Anno Dom.* 1504*',*—that 's this year—
  '*decimo nono Decembris,*'—that 's this night,—'*taken according
  to the meridian of Malfi,*'—that 's our duchess: happy dis-
  covery!—'*The lord of the first house being combust in the
  ascendant, signifies short life; and Mars being in a human sign,
  joined to the tail of the Dragon, in the eighth house, doth threaten
  a violent death.   Cætera non scrutantur.*'
  Why, now 'tis most apparent: this precise fellow
  Is the duchess' bawd:—I have it to my wish!
  This is a parcel of intelligency
  Our courtiers were cas'd up for: it needs must follow
  That I must be committed on pretence
  Of poisoning her: which I 'll endure, and laugh at.
  If one could find the father now! but that
  Time will discover.   Old Castruccio
  I' the morning posts to Rome: by him I 'll send
  A letter that shall make her brothers' galls
  O'erflow their livers.   This was a thrifty way.
  Though lust do mask in ne'er so strange disguise,
  She 's oft found witty, but is never wise.   [*Exit.*

SCENE IV

Enter Cardinal and Julia

Card. Sit: thou art my best of wishes.   Prithee, tell me
    What trick didst thou invent to come to Rome
    Without thy husband?

Julia. Why, my lord, I told him
    I came to visit an old anchorite
    Here for devotion.

Card. Thou art a witty false one,—
    I mean, to him.

Julia. You have prevail'd with me
    Beyond my strongest thoughts: I would not now
    Find you inconstant.

Card. Do not put thyself
    To such a voluntary torture, which proceeds
    Out of your own guilt.

Julia. How, my lord!

Card. You fear
    My constancy, because you have approv'd
    Those giddy and wild turnings in yourself.

Julia. Did you e'er find them?

Card. Sooth, generally for women,
    A man might strive to make glass malleable,
    Ere he should make them fixed.

Julia. So, my lord.

Card. We had need go borrow that fantastic glass
    Invented by Galileo the Florentine
    To view another spacious world i' the moon,
    And look to find a constant woman there.

Julia. This is very well, my lord.

Card. Why do you weep?
    Are tears your justification? the self-same tears
    Will fall into your husband's bosom, lady,
    With a loud protestation that you love him
    Above the world.   Come, I 'll love you wisely,
    That 's jealously; since I am very certain
    You cannot make me cuckold.

Julia. I 'll go home
    To my husband.

Card. You may thank me, lady,
    I have taken you off your melancholy perch,

Bore you upon my fist, and show'd you game,
And let you fly at it.—I pray thee, kiss me.—
When thou wast with thy husband, thou wast watch'd
Like a tame elephant:—still you are to thank me:—
Thou hadst only kisses from him and high feeding:
But what delight was that? 'twas just like one
That 's come a little fingering on the lute,
Yet cannot tune it:—still you are to thank me.

Julia. You told me of a piteous wound i' the heart
And a sick liver, when you woo'd me first,
And spake like one in physic.

Card. Who 's that?—   [*Enter Servant.*
Rest firm, for my affection to thee,
Lightning moves slow to 't.

Serv. Madam, a gentleman,
That 's come post from Malfi, desires to see you.

Card. Let him enter: I 'll withdraw.   [*Exit.*

Serv. He says
Your husband, old Castruccio, is come to Rome,
Most pitifully tir'd with riding post.   [*Exit.*

Enter Delio

Julia. [*Aside.*] Signior Delio! 'tis one of my old suitors.

Delio. I was bold to come and see you.

Julia. Sir, you are welcome.

Delio. Do you lie here?

Julia. Sure, your own experience
Will satisfy you no: our Roman prelates
Do not keep lodging for ladies.

Delio. Very well:
I have brought you no commendations from your husband,
For I know none by him.

Julia. I hear he 's come to Rome.

Delio. I never knew man and beast, of a horse and a knight,
So weary of each other: if he had had a good back,
He would have undertook to have borne his horse,
His breech was so pitifully sore.

Julia. Your laughter
Is my pity.

Delio. Lady, I know not whether
You want money, but I have brought you some.

Julia. From my husband?

Delio. No, from mine own allowance.

Julia. I must hear the condition, ere I be bound to take it.
Delio. Look on 't, 'tis gold: hath it not a fine colour?
Julia. I have a bird more beautiful.
Delio. Try the sound on 't.
Julia. A lute-string far exceeds it:
    It hath no smell, like cassia or civet;
    Nor is it physical, though some fond doctors
    Persuade us seethe 't in cullises. I 'll tell you,
    This is a creature bred by——

Re-enter Servant

Serv. Your husband 's come,
    Hath deliver'd a letter to the Duke of Calabria
    That, to my thinking, hath put him out of his wits.   [*Exit.*
Julia. Sir, you hear;
    Pray, let me know your business and your suit
    As briefly as can be.
Delio. With good speed: I would wish you,
    At such time as you are non-resident
    With your husband, my mistress.
Julia. Sir, I 'll go ask my husband if I shall,
    And straight return your answer.   [*Exit.*
Delio. Very fine!
    Is this her wit, or honesty, that speaks thus?
    I heard one say the duke was highly mov'd
    With a letter sent from Malfi. I do fear
    Antonio is betray'd: how fearfully
    Shows his ambition now! unfortunate fortune!
    They pass through whirlpools, and deep woes do shun,
    Who the event weigh ere the action 's done.   [*Exit.*

Scene V

Enter Cardinal, and Ferdinand with a letter

Ferd. I have this night digg'd up a mandrake.
Card. Say you?
Ferd. And I am grown mad with 't.
Card. What 's the prodigy?
Ferd. Read there,—a sister damn'd: she 's loose i' the hilts;
    Grown a notorious strumpet.

Card. Speak lower.

Ferd. Lower!

　Rogues do not whisper 't now, but seek to publish 't
　(As servants do the bounty of their lords)
　Aloud; and with a covetous searching eye,
　To mark who note them. Oh, confusion seize her!
　She hath had most cunning bawds to serve her turn,
　And more secure conveyances for lust
　Than towns of garrison for service.

Card. Is 't possible?

　Can this be certain?

Ferd. Rhubarb, oh, for rhubarb
　To purge this choler! here 's the cursed day
　To prompt my memory; and here 't shall stick
　Till of her bleeding heart I make a sponge
　To wipe it out.

Card. Why do you make yourself
　So wild a tempest?

Ferd. Would I could be one,
　That I might toss her palace 'bout her ears,
　Root up her goodly forests, blast her meads,
　And lay her general territory as waste
　As she hath done her honours.

Card. Shall our blood,
　The royal blood of Arragon and Castile,
　Be thus attainted?

Ferd. Apply desperate physic:
　We must not now use balsamum, but fire,
　The smarting cupping-glass, for that 's the mean
　To purge infected blood, such blood as hers.
　There is a kind of pity in mine eye,—
　I 'll give it to my handkercher; and now 'tis here,
　I 'll bequeath this to her bastard.

Card. What to do?

Ferd. Why, to make soft lint for his mother's wounds,
　When I have hew'd her to pieces.

Card. Cursed creature!
　Unequal nature, to place women's hearts
　So far upon the left side!

Ferd. Foolish men,
　That e'er will trust their honour in a bark
　Made of so slight weak bulrush as is woman,
　Apt every minute to sink it!

Card. Thus
Ignorance, when it hath purchas'd honour,
It cannot wield it.

Ferd. Methinks I see her laughing,—
Excellent hyena! Talk to me somewhat quickly,
Or my imagination will carry me
To see her in the shameful act of sin.

Card. With whom?

Ferd. Happily with some strong-thigh'd bargeman,
Or one o' the wood-yard that can quoit the sledge
Or toss the bar, or else some lovely squire
That carries coals up to her privy lodgings.

Card. You fly beyond your reason.

Ferd. Go to, mistress!
'Tis not your whore's milk that shall quench my wild fire,
But your whore's blood.

Card. How idly shows this rage, which carries you,
As men convey'd by witches through the air,
On violent whirlwinds! this intemperate noise
Fitly resembles deaf men's shrill discourse,
Who talk aloud, thinking all other men
To have their imperfection.

Ferd. Have not you
My palsy?

Card. Yes, [but] I can be angry
Without this rupture: there is not in nature
A thing that makes man so deform'd, so beastly,
As doth intemperate anger. Chide yourself.
You have divers men who never yet express'd
Their strong desire of rest but by unrest,
By vexing of themselves. Come, put yourself
In tune.

Ferd. So I will only study to seem
The thing I am not. I could kill her now,
In you, or in myself; for I do think
It is some sin in us heaven doth revenge
By her.

Card. Are you stark mad?

Ferd. I would have their bodies
Burnt in a coal-pit with the ventage stopp'd.
That their curs'd smoke might not ascend to heaven;
Or dip the sheets they lie in in pitch or sulphur,
Wrap them in 't, and then light them like a match;

Or else to-boil their bastard to a cullis,
And give 't his lecherous father to renew
The sin of his back.
Card. I 'll leave you.
Ferd. Nay, I have done.
I am confident, had I been damn'd in hell,
And should have heard of this, it would have put me
Into a cold sweat.   In, in; I 'll go sleep.
Till I know who leaps my sister, I 'll not stir:
That known, I 'll find scorpions to string my whips,
And fix her in a general eclipse.   [*Exeunt.*

ACT III

Scene I

Enter Antonio and Delio

Ant. Our noble friend, my most belovèd Delio!
Oh, you have been a stranger long at court:
Came you along with the Lord Ferdinand?
Delio. I did, sir: and how fares your noble duchess?
Ant. Right fortunately well: she 's an excellent
Feeder of pedigrees; since you last saw her,
She hath had two children more, a son and daughter.
Delio. Methinks 'twas yesterday: let me but wink,
And not behold your face, which to mine eye
Is somewhat leaner, verily I should dream
It were within this half-hour.
Ant. You have not been in law, friend Delio,
Nor in prison, nor a suitor at the court,
Nor begg'd the reversion of some great man's place,
Nor troubled with an old wife, which doth make
Your time so insensibly hasten.
Delio. Pray, sir, tell me,
Hath not this news arriv'd yet to the ear
Of the lord cardinal?
Ant. I fear it hath:
The Lord Ferdinand, that 's newly come to court,

Doth bear himself right dangerously.

Delio. Pray, why?

Ant. He is so quiet that he seems to sleep
    The tempest out, as dormice do in winter:
    Those houses that are haunted are most still
    Till the devil be up.

Delio. What say the common people?

Ant. The common rabble do directly say
    She is a strumpet.

Delio. And your graver heads
    Which would be politic, what censure they?

Ant. They do observe I grow to infinite purchase,
    The left-hand way; and all suppose the duchess
    Would amend it, if she could; for, say they,
    Great princes, though they grudge their officers
    Should have such large and unconfinèd means
    To get wealth under them, will not complain,
    Lest thereby they should make them odious
    Unto the people: for other obligation
    Of love or marriage between her and me
    They never dream of.

Delio. The Lord Ferdinand
    Is going to bed.

Enter Duchess, Ferdinand, and Attendants

Ferd. I 'll instantly to bed,
    For I am weary.—I am to bespeak
    A husband for you.

Duch. For me, sir! pray, who is 't?

Ferd. The great Count Malatesti.

Duch. Fie upon him!
    A count! he 's a mere stick of sugar-candy;
    You may look quite thorough him.   When I choose
    A husband, I will marry for your honour.

Ferd. You shall do well in 't.—How is 't, worthy Antonio?

Duch. But, sir, I am to have private conference with you
    About a scandalous report is spread
    Touching mine honour.

Ferd. Let me be ever deaf to 't;
    One of Pasquil's paper-bullets, court-calumny,
    A pestilent air, which princes' palaces
    Are seldom purg'd of.   Yet say that it were true,
    I pour it in your bosom, my fix'd love

Would strongly excuse, extenuate, nay, deny
Faults, were they apparent in you.   Go, be safe
In your own innocency.
Duch. [*Aside.*] O bless'd comfort!
This deadly air is purg'd.
        [*Exeunt Duchess, Antonio, Delio, and Attendants.*
Ferd. Her guilt treads on
Hot-burning coulters.   [*Enter Bosola.*
Now, Bosola,
How thrives our intelligence?
Bos. Sir, uncertainly:
'Tis rumour'd she hath had three bastards, but
By whom we may go read i' the stars.
Ferd. Why, some
Hold opinion all things are written there.
Bos. Yes, if we could find spectacles to read them.
I do suspect there hath been some sorcery
Us'd on the duchess.
Ferd. Sorcery! to what purpose?
Bos. To make her dote on some desertless fellow
She shames to acknowledge.
Ferd. Can your faith give way
To think there 's power in potions or in charms,
To make us love whether we will or no?
Bos. Most certainly.
Ferd. Away! these are mere gulleries, horrid things,
Invented by some cheating mountebanks
To abuse us.   Do you think that herbs or charms
Can force the will?   Some trials have been made
In this foolish practice, but the ingredients
Were lenitive poisons, such as are of force
To make the patient mad; and straight the witch
Swears by equivocation they are in love.
The witchcraft lies in her rank blood.   This night
I will force confession from her.   You told me
You had got, within these two days, a false key
Into her bed-chamber.
Bos. I have.
Ferd. As I would wish.
Bos. What do you intend to do?
Ferd. Can you guess?
Bos. No.
Ferd. Do not ask, then:

He that can compass me, and know my drifts,
May say he hath put a girdle 'bout the world,
And sounded all her quicksands.
Bos. I do not
Think so.
Ferd. What do you think, then, pray?
Bos. That you are
Your own chronicle too much, and grossly
Flatter yourself.
Ferd. Give me thy hand; I thank thee:
I never gave pension but to flatterers,
Till I entertainèd thee.   Farewell.
That friend a great man's ruin strongly checks,
Who rails into his belief all his defects.   [*Exeunt.*

Scene II

Enter Duchess, Antonio, and Cariola

Duch. Bring me the casket hither, and the glass.—
You get no lodging here to-night, my lord.
Ant. Indeed, I must persuade one.
Duch. Very good:
I hope in time 'twill grow into a custom,
That noblemen shall come with cap and knee
To purchase a night's lodging of their wives.
Ant. I must lie here.
Duch. Must! you are a lord of misrule.
Ant. Indeed, my rule is only in the night.
Duch. To what use will you put me?
Ant. We'll sleep together.
Duch. Alas,
What pleasure can two lovers find in sleep!
Cari. My lord, I lie with her often; and I know
She'll much disquiet you.
Ant. See, you are complain'd of.
Cari. For she's the sprawling'st bedfellow.
Ant. I shall like her the better for that.
Cari. Sir, shall I ask you a question?
Ant. Ay, pray thee, Cariola.
Cari. Wherefore still, when you lie with my lady,
Do you rise so early?

Ant. Labouring men
   Count the clock oftenest, Cariola,
   Are glad when their task 's ended.
Duch. I 'll stop your mouth.   [*Kisses him.*
Ant. Nay, that 's but one; Venus had two soft doves
   To draw her chariot; I must have another.—
                  [*She kisses him again.*
   When wilt thou marry, Cariola?
Cari. Never, my lord.
Ant. Oh, fie upon this single life! forgo it.
   We read how Daphne, for her peevish flight,
   Became a fruitless bay-tree; Syrinx turn'd
   To the pale empty reed; Anaxarete
   Was frozen into marble: whereas those
   Which married, or prov'd kind unto their friends,
   Were by a gracious influence transhap'd
   Into the olive, pomegranate, mulberry,
   Became flowers, precious stones, or eminent stars.
Cari. This is a vain poetry: but I pray you, tell me,
   If there were propos'd me, wisdom, riches, and beauty,
   In three several young men, which should I choose.
Ant. 'Tis a hard question: this was Paris' case,
   And he was blind in 't, and there was great cause;
   For how was 't possible he could judge right,
   Having three amorous goddesses in view,
   And they stark naked? 'twas a motion
   Were able to benight the apprehension
   Of the severest counsellor of Europe.
   Now I look on both your faces so well form'd,
   It puts me in mind of a question I would ask.
Cari. What is 't?
Ant. I do wonder why hard-favour'd ladies,
   For the most part, keep worse-favour'd waiting-women
   To attend them, and cannot endure fair ones.
Duch. Oh, that 's soon answer'd.
   Did you ever in your life know an ill painter
   Desire to have his dwelling next door to the shop
   Of an excellent picture-maker? 'twould disgrace
   His face-making, and undo him.   I pray thee,
   When were we so merry?—My hair tangles.
Ant. Pray thee, Cariola, let 's steal forth the room,
   And let her talk to herself: I have divers times
   Serv'd her the like, when she hath chaf'd extremely.

I love to see her angry.   Softly, Cariola.

[Exeunt Antonio and Cariola.

Duch. Doth not the colour of my hair 'gin to change?
When I wax grey, I shall have all the court
Powder their hair with arras, to be like me.
You have cause to love me; I enter'd you into my heart
Before you would vouchsafe to call for the keys.

[Enter Ferdinand behind.

We shall one day have my brothers take you napping:
Methinks his presence, being now in court,
Should make you keep your own bed; but you 'll say
Love mix'd with fear is sweetest.   I 'll assure you,
You shall get no more children till my brothers
Consent to be your gossips.   Have you lost your tongue?
'Tis welcome:
For know, whether I am doom'd to live or die,
I can do both like a prince.

Ferd. Die, then, quickly!   *[Giving her a poniard.*
Virtue, where art thou hid? what hideous thing
Is it that doth eclipse thee?

Duch. Pray, sir, hear me.

Ferd. Or is it true thou art but a bare name,
And no essential thing?

Duch. Sir,——

Ferd. Do not speak.

Duch. No, sir:
I will plant my soul in mine ears, to hear you.

Ferd. O most imperfect light of human reason,
That mak'st us so unhappy to foresee
What we can least prevent! Pursue thy wishes,
And glory in them: there 's in shame no comfort
But to be past all bounds and sense of shame.

Duch. I pray, sir, hear me: I am married.

Ferd. So!

Duch. Happily, not to your liking: but for that,
Alas, your shears do come untimely now
To clip the bird's wings that 's already flown!
Will you see my husband?

Ferd. Yes, if I could change
Eyes with a basilisk.

Duch. Sure, you came hither
By his confederacy.

Ferd. The howling of a wolf

Is music to thee, screech-owl: prithee, peace.—
Whate'er thou art that hast enjoy'd my sister,
For I am sure thou hear'st me, for thine own sake
Let me not know thee.   I came hither prepar'd
To work thy discovery; yet am now persuaded
It would beget such violent effects
As would damn us both.   I would not for ten millions
I had beheld thee: therefore use all means
I never may have knowledge of thy name;
Enjoy thy lust still, and a wretched life,
On that condition.—And for thee, vile woman,
If thou do wish thy lecher may grow old
In thy embracements, I would have thee build
Such a room for him as our anchorites
To holier use inhabit.   Let not the sun
Shine on him till he 's dead; let dogs and monkeys
Only converse with him, and such dumb things
To whom nature denies use to sound his name;
Do not keep a paraquito, lest she learn it;
If thou do love him, cut out thine own tongue,
Lest it bewray him.

Duch. Why might not I marry?
I have not gone about in this to create
Any new world or custom.

Ferd. Thou art undone;
And thou hast ta'en that massy sheet of lead
That hid thy husband's bones, and folded it
About my heart.

Duch. Mine bleeds for 't.

Ferd. Thine! thy heart!
What snould I name 't unless a hollow bullet
Fill'd with unquenchable wildfire?

Duch. You are in this
Too strict; and were you not my princely brother,
I would say, too wilful: my reputation
Is safe.

Ferd. Dost thou know what reputation is?
I 'll tell thee,—to small purpose, since the instruction
Comes now too late.
Upon a time Reputation, Love, and Death
Would travel o'er the world; and it was concluded
That they should part, and take three several ways.
Death told them, they should find him in great battles,

Or cities plagu'd with plagues: Love gives them counsel
To inquire for him 'mongst unambitious shepherds,
Where dowries were not talk'd of, and sometimes
'Mongst quiet kindred that had nothing left
By their dead parents: 'Stay,' quote Reputation.
'Do not forsake me; for it is my nature,
If once I part from any man I meet,
I am never found again'.   And so for you:
You have shook hands with Reputation,
And made him invisible.   So, fare you well:
I will never see you more.

Duch. Why should only I,
Of all the other princes of the world,
Be cas'd up, like a holy relic? I have youth
And a little beauty.

Ferd. So you have some virgins
That are witches.   I will never see thee more.   [*Exit.*

Re-enter Antonio with a pistol, and Cariola

Duch. You saw this apparition?

Ant. Yes: we are
Betray'd.   How came he hither? I should turn
This to thee, for that.

Cari. Pray, sir, do; and when
That you have cleft my heart, you shall read there
Mine innocence.

Duch. That gallery gave him entrance.

Ant. I would this terrible thing would come again,
That, standing on my guard, I might relate
My warrantable love.—   [*She shows the poniard.*
Ha! what means this?

Duch. He left this with me.

Ant. And it seems did wish
You would use it on yourself.

Duch. His action
Seem'd to intend so much.

Ant. This hath a handle to 't,
As well as a point: turn it towards him,
And so fasten the keen edge in his rank gall. [*Knocking within.*
How now! who knocks? more earthquakes?

Duch. I stand
As if a mine beneath my feet were ready
To be blown up.

Cari. 'Tis Bosola.

Duch. Away!

  O misery! methinks unjust actions
  Should wear these masks and curtains, and not we.
  You must instantly part hence: I have fashion'd it already.

                                                 [Exit Antonio.

Enter Bosola

Bos. The duke your brother is ta'en up in a whirlwind;
  Hath took horse, and 's rid post to Rome.

Duch. So late?

Bos. He told me, as he mounted into the saddle,
  You were undone.

Duch. Indeed, I am very near it.

Bos. What 's the matter?

Duch. Antonio, the master of our household,
  Hath dealt so falsely with me in 's accounts:
  My brother stood engag'd with me for money
  Ta'en up of certain Neapolitan Jews,
  And Antonio lets the bonds be forfeit.

Bos. Strange!—[*Aside.*] This is cunning.

Duch. And hereupon
  My brother's bills at Naples are protested
  Against.—Call up our officers.

Bos. I shall.   *[Exit.*

Re-enter Antonio

Duch. The place that you must fly to is Ancona:
  Hire a house there; I 'll send after you
  My treasure and my jewels.   Our weak safety
  Runs upon enginous wheels: short syllables
  Must stand for periods.   I must now accuse you
  Of such a feignèd crime as Tasso calls
  Magnanima menzogna, a noble lie,
  'Cause it must shield our honours.—Hark! they are coming.

Re-enter Bosola and Officers

Ant. Will your grace hear me?

Duch. I have got well by you: you have yielded me
  A million of loss: I am like to inherit
  The people's curses for your stewardship.
  You had the trick in audit-time to be sick,
  Till I had sign'd your quietus; and that cur'd you
  Without help of a doctor.—Gentlemen,

I would have this man be an example to you all;
So shall you hold my favour; I pray, let him;
For h' 'as done that, alas, you would not think of,
And, because I intend to be rid of him,
I mean not to publish.—Use your fortune elsewhere.

Ant. I am strongly arm'd to brook my overthrow,
As commonly men bear with a hard year:
I will not blame the cause on 't; but do think
The necessity of my malevolent star
Procures this, not her humour. Oh, the inconstant
And rotten ground of service! you may see,
'Tis even like him, that in a winter night,
Takes a long slumber o'er a dying fire,
A-loath to part from 't; yet parts thence as cold
As when he first sat down.

Duch. We do confiscate,
Towards the satisfying of your accounts,
All that you have.

Ant. I am all yours; and 'tis very fit
All mine should be so.

Duch. So, sir, you have your pass.

Ant. You may see, gentlemen, what 'tis to serve
A prince with body and soul.   [*Exit.*

Bos. Here 's an example for extortion: what moisture is drawn
out of the sea, when foul weather comes, pours down, and
runs into the sea again.

Duch. I would know what are your opinions
Of this Antonio.

Sec. Off. He could not abide to see a pig's head gaping: I
thought your grace would find him a Jew.

Third Off. I would you had been his officer, for your own sake.

Fourth Off. You would have had more money.

First Off. He stopped his ears with black wool, and to those
came to him for money said he was thick of hearing.

Sec. Off. Some said he was an hermaphrodite, for he could not
abide a woman.

Fourth Off. How scurvy proud he would look when the treasury
was full! Well, let him go.

First Off. Yes, and the chippings of the buttery fly after him,
to scour his gold chain.

Duch. Leave us.   [*Exeunt Officers.*
What do you think of these?

Bos. That these are rogues that in 's prosperity,

But to have waited on his fortune, could have wish'd
His dirty stirrup riveted through their noses,
And follow'd after 's mule, like a bear in a ring;
Would have prostituted their daughters to his lust;
Made their first-born intelligencers; thought none happy
But such as were born under his blest planet,
And wore his livery: and do these lice drop off now?
Well, never look to have the like again:
He hath left a sort of flattering rogues behind him;
Their doom must follow.   Princes pay flatterers
In their own money: flatterers dissemble their vices,
And they dissemble their lies; that 's justice.
Alas, poor gentleman!

Duch. Poor! he hath amply fill'd his coffers.

Bos. Sure, he was too honest.   Pluto, the god of riches,
When he 's sent by Jupiter to any man,
He goes limping, to signify that wealth
That comes on God's name comes slowly; but when he 's sent
On the devil's errand, he rides post and comes in by scuttles.
Let me show you what a most unvalu'd jewel
You have in a wanton humour thrown away,
To bless the man shall find him.   He was an excellent
Courtier and most faithful; a soldier that thought it
As beastly to know his own value too little
As devilish to acknowledge it too much.
Both his virtue and form deserv'd a far better fortune:
His discourse rather delighted to judge itself than show itself:
His breast was fill'd with all perfection,
And yet it seem'd a private whispering-room,
It made so little noise of 't.

Duch. But he was basely descended.

Bos. Will you make yourself a mercenary herald,
Rather to examine men's pedigrees than virtues?
You shall want him:
For know an honest statesman to a prince
Is like a cedar planted by a spring;
The spring bathes the tree's root, the grateful tree
Rewards it with his shadow: you have not done so.
I would sooner swim to the Bermoothes on
Two politicians' rotten bladders, tied
Together with an intelligencer's heart-string,
Than depend on so changeable a prince's favour.
Fare thee well, Antonio! since the malice of the world

Would needs down with thee, it cannot be said yet
That any ill happen'd unto thee, considering thy fall
Was accompanied with virtue.
Duch. Oh, you render me excellent music!
Bos. Say you?
Duch. This good one that you speak of is my husband.
Bos. Do I not dream? can this ambitious age
Have so much goodness in 't as to prefer
A man merely for worth, without these shadows
Of wealth and painted honours? possible?
Duch. I have had three children by him.
Bos. Fortunate lady!
For you have made your private nuptial bed
The humble and fair seminary of peace.
No question but many an unbenefic'd scholar
Shall pray for you for this deed, and rejoice
That some preferment in the world can yet
Arise from merit. The virgins of your land
That have no dowries shall hope your example
Will raise them to rich husbands. Should you want
Soldiers, 'twould make the very Turks and Moors
Turn Christians, and serve you for this act.
Last, the neglected poets of your time,
In honour of this trophy of a man,
Rais'd by that curious engine, your white hand,
Shall thank you, in your grave, for 't; and make that
More reverend than all the cabinets
Of living princes. For Antonio,
His fame shall likewise flow from many a pen,
When heralds shall want coats to sell to men.
Duch. As I taste comfort in this friendly speech,
So would I find concealment.
Bos. Oh, the secret of my prince,
Which I will wear on the inside of my heart!
Duch. You shall take charge of all my coin and jewels,
And follow him; for he retires himself
To Ancona.
Bos. So.
Duch. Whither, within few days,
I mean to follow thee.
Bos. Let me think:
I would wish your grace to feign a pilgrimage
To our Lady of Loretto, scarce seven leagues

From fair Ancona; so may you depart
Your country with more honour, and your flight
Will seem a princely progress, retaining
Your usual train about you.
Duch. Sir, your direction
Shall lead me by the hand.
Cari. In my opinion,
She were better progress to the baths at Lucca,
Or go visit the Spa
In Germany; for, if you will believe me,
I do not like this jesting with religion,
This feignèd pilgrimage.
Duch. Thou art a superstitious fool:
Prepare us instantly for our departure.
Past sorrows, let us moderately lament them,
For those to come, seek wisely to prevent them.
                    [*Exeunt Duchess and Cariola.*
Bos. A politician is the devil's quilted anvil;
He fashions all sins on him, and the blows
Are never heard: he may work in a lady's chamber,
As here for proof.   What rests but I reveal
All to my lord? Oh, this base quality
Of intelligencer! why, every quality i' the world
Prefers but gain or commendation:
Now, for this act I am certain to be rais'd,
And men that paint weeds to the life are prais'd.   [*Exit.*

Scene III

Enter Cardinal, Ferdinand, Malatesti, Pescara, Delio, and Silvio

Card. Must we turn soldier, then?
Mal. The emperor,
Hearing your worth that way, ere you attain'd
This reverend garment, joins you in commission
With the right fortunate soldier the Marquis of Pescara,
And the famous Lannoy.
Card. He that had the honour
Of taking the French king prisoner?
Mal. The same.
Here 's a plot drawn for a new fortification
At Naples.

Ferd. This great Count Malatesti, I perceive,
Hath got employment?
Delio. No employment, my lord;
A marginal note in the muster-book, that he is
A voluntary lord.
Ferd. He 's no soldier.
Delio. He has worn gunpowder in 's hollow tooth for the
toothache.
Sil. He comes to the leaguer with a full intent
To eat fresh beef and garlic, means to stay
Till the scent be gone, and straight return to court.
Delio. He hath read all the late service
As the City-Chronicle relates it;
And keeps two pewterers going, only to express
Battles in model.
Sil. Then he 'll fight by the book.
Delio. By the almanac, I think,
To choose good days and shun the critical;
That 's his mistress' scarf.
Sil. Yes, he protests
He would do much for that taffeta.
Delio. I think he would run away from a battle,
To save it from taking prisoner.
Sil. He is horribly afraid
Gunpowder will spoil the perfume on 't.
Delio. I saw a Dutchman break his pate once
For calling him pot-gun; he made his head
Have a bore in 't like a musket.
Sil. I would he had made a touch-hole to 't.
He is indeed a guarded sumpter-cloth,
Only for the remove of the court.

Enter Bosola

Pes. Bosola arriv'd! what should be the business?
Some falling-out amongst the cardinals.
These factions amongst great men, they are like
Foxes, when their heads are divided,
They carry fire in their tails, and all the country
About them goes to wreck for 't.
Sil. What 's that Bosola?
Delio. I knew him in Padua,—a fantastical scholar, like such
who study to know how many knots was in Hercules' club, of
what colour Achilles' beard was, or whether Hector were not

troubled with the toothache. He hath studied himself half
blear-eyed to know the true symmetry of Cæsar's nose by a
shoeing-horn; and this he did to gain the name of a speculative
man.

Pes. Mark Prince Ferdinand:
    A very salamander lives in 's eye,
    To mock the eager violence of fire.

Sil. That cardinal hath made more bad faces with his oppression
    than ever Michael Angelo made good ones: he lifts up 's nose,
    like a foul porpoise before a storm.

Pes. The Lord Ferdinand laughs.

Delio. Like a deadly cannon
    That lightens ere it smokes.

Pes. These are your true pangs of death,
    The pangs of life, that struggle with great statesmen.

Delio. In such a deformed silence witches whisper their charms.

Card. Doth she make religion her riding-hood
    To keep her from the sun and tempest?

Ferd. That,
    That damns her. Methinks her fault and beauty,
    Blended together, show like leprosy,
    The whiter, the fouler. I make it a question
    Whether her beggarly brats were ever christen'd.

Card. I will instantly solicit the state of Ancona
    To have them banish'd.

Ferd. You are for Loretto:
    I shall not be at your ceremony; fare you well.—
    Write to the Duke of Malfi, my young nephew
    She had by her first husband, and acquaint him
    With 's mother's honesty.

Bos. I will.

Ferd. Antonio!
    A slave that only smell'd of ink and counters,
    And never in 's life look'd like a gentleman,
    But in the audit-time.—Go, go presently,
    Draw me out an hundred and fifty of our horse,
    And meet me at the fort-bridge.   [*Exeunt*.

SCENE IV

Enter Two Pilgrims to the Shrine of our Lady of Loretto

First Pil. I have not seen a goodlier shrine than this;
   Yet I have visited many.
Sec. Pil.   The Cardinal of Arragon
   Is this day to resign his cardinal's hat:
   His sister duchess likewise is arriv'd
   To pay her vow of pilgrimage.   I expect
   A noble ceremony.
First Pil.   No question.—They come.

*Here the ceremony of the Cardinal's instalment, in the habit of
a soldier, performed in delivering up his cross, hat, robes, and
ring, at the shrine, and investing him with sword, helmet, shield,
and spurs; then Antonio, the Duchess, and their children,
having presented themselves at the shrine, are, by a form of
banishment in dumb-show expressed towards them by the
Cardinal and the state of Ancona, banished: during all which
ceremony, this ditty is sung, to very solemn music, by divers
churchmen: and then exeunt all except the Two Pilgrims.*

Arms and honours deck thy story,
To thy fame's eternal glory!
Adverse fortune ever fly thee;
No disastrous fate come nigh thee!
I alone will sing thy praises,
Whom to honour virtue raises;
And thy study, that divine is,
Bent to martial discipline is.
Lay aside all those robes lie by thee;
Crown thy arts with arms, they 'll beautify thee.
O worthy of worthiest name, adorn'd in this manner,
Lead bravely thy forces on under war's warlike banner!
O mayst thou prove fortunate in all martial courses!
Guide thou still by skill in arts and forces!
Victory attend thee nigh, whilst fame sings loud thy powers;
Triumphant conquest crown thy head, and blessings pour down
     showers!

First Pil. Here 's a strange turn of state! who would have
     thought
   So great a lady would have match'd herself

Unto so mean a person? yet the cardinal
Bears himself much too cruel.
Sec. Pil. They are banish'd.
First Pil. But I would ask what power hath this state
Of Ancona to determine of a free prince?
Sec. Pil. They are a free state, sir, and her brother show'd
How that the Pope, fore-hearing of her looseness,
Hath seiz'd into the protection of the church
The dukedom which she held as dowager.
First Pil. But by what justice?
Sec. Pil. Sure, I think by none,
Only her brother's instigation.
First Pil. What was it with such violence he took
Off from her finger?
Sec. Pil. 'Twas her wedding-ring;
Which he vow'd shortly he would sacrifice
To his revenge.
First Pil. Alas, Antonio!
If that a man be thrust into a well,
No matter who sets hand to 't, his own weight
Will bring him sooner to the bottom.   Come, let 's hence.
Fortune makes this conclusion general,
All things do help the unhappy man to fall.   [*Exeunt.*

SCENE V

Enter Duchess, Antonio, Children, Cariola, and Servants

Duch. Banish'd Ancona!
Ant. Yes, you see what power
Lightens in great men's breath.
Duch. Is all our train
Shrunk to this poor remainder?
Ant. These poor men,
Which have got little in your service, vow
To take your fortune: but your wiser buntings,
Now they are fledg'd, are gone.
Duch. They have done wisely.
This puts me in mind of death: physicians thus,
With their hands full of money, use to give o'er
Their patients.
Ant. Right the fashion of the world:

From decay'd fortunes every flatterer shrinks;
Men cease to build where the foundation sinks.
Duch. I had a very strange dream to-night.
Ant. What was 't?
Duch. Methought I wore my coronet of state,
  And on a sudden all the diamonds
  Were chang'd to pearls.
Ant. My interpretation
  Is, you 'll weep shortly; for to me the pearls
  Do signify your tears.
Duch. The birds that live i' the field
  On the wild benefit of nature live
  Happier than we; for they may choose their mates,
  And carol their sweet pleasures to the spring.

Enter Bosola with a letter

Bos. You are happily o'erta'en.
Duch. From my brother?
Bos. Yes, from the Lord Ferdinand your brother
  All love and safety.
Duch. Thou dost blanch mischief,
  Wouldst make it white. See, see, like to calm weather
  At sea before a tempest, false hearts speak fair
  To those they intend most mischief.   [*Reads.*

Send Antonio to me; I want his head in a business.

A politic equivocation!
He doth not want your counsel, but your head:
That is, he cannot sleep till you be dead.
And here 's another pitfall that 's strew'd o'er
With roses; mark it, 'tis a cunning one: [*Reads.*

*I stand engaged for your husband for several debts at Naples:
let not that trouble him; I had rather have his heart than his
money:—*

And I believe so too.
Bos. What do you believe?
Duch. That he so much distrusts my husband's love,
  He will by no means believe his heart is with him
  Until he see it: the devil is not cunning enough
  To circumvent us in riddles.
Bos. Will you reject that noble and free league
  Of amity and love which I present you?
Duch. Their league is like that of some politic kings,
  L 899

Only to make themselves of strength and power
To be our after-ruin: tell them so.

Bos. And what from you?

Ant. Thus tell him; I will not come.

Bos. And what of this?

Ant. My brothers have dispers'd
Bloodhounds abroad; which till I hear are muzzled,
No truce, though hatch'd with ne'er such politic skill,
Is safe, that hangs upon our enemies' will.
I 'll not come at them.

Bos. This proclaims your breeding:
Every small thing draws a base mind to fear,
As the adamant draws iron.　Fare you well, sir:
You shall shortly hear from 's.　　　　　[*Exit.*

Duch. I suspect some ambush:
Therefore by all my love I do conjure you
To take your eldest son, and fly towards Milan.
Let us not venture all this poor remainder
In one unlucky bottom.

Ant. You counsel safely.
Best of my life, farewell, since we must part:
Heaven hath a hand in 't; but no otherwise
Than as some curious artist takes in sunder
A clock or watch, when it is out of frame,
To bring 't in better order.

Duch. I know not which is best,
To see you dead, or part with you.—Farewell, boy:
Thou art happy that thou hast not understanding
To know thy misery; for all our wit
And reading brings us to a truer sense
Of sorrow.—In the eternal church, sir,
I do hope we shall not part thus.

Ant. Oh, be of comfort!
Make patience a noble fortitude,
And think not how unkindly we are us'd:
Man, like to cassia, is prov'd best, being bruis'd.

Duch. Must I, like to a slave-born Russian,
Account it praise to suffer tyranny?
And yet, O Heaven, thy heavy hand is in 't!
I have seen my little boy oft scourge his top,
And compar'd myself to 't: naught made me e'er
Go right but heaven's scourge-stick.

Ant. Do not weep:

Heaven fashion'd us of nothing; and we strive
To bring ourselves to nothing.—Farewell, Cariola,
And thy sweet armful.—If I do never see thee more,
Be a good mother to your little ones,
And save them from the tiger: fare you well.
Duch. Let me look upon you once more, for that speech
Came from a dying father: your kiss is colder
Than that I have seen an holy anchorite
Give to a dead man's skull.
Ant. My heart is turn'd to a heavy lump of lead,
With which I sound my danger: fare you well.
            [*Exeunt Antonio and his son.*
Duch. My laurel is all wither'd.
Cari. Look, madam, what a troop of armèd men
Make toward us.
Duch. Oh, they are very welcome:
When Fortune's wheel is overcharg'd with princes,
The weight makes it move swift: I would have my ruin
Be sudden.   [*Re-enter Bosola vizarded, with a guard.*
I am your adventure, am I not?
Bos. You are: you must see your husband no more.
Duch. What devil art thou that counterfeit'st heaven's thunder?
Bos. Is that terrible? I would have you tell me whether
Is that note worse that frights the silly birds
Out of the corn, or that which doth allure them
To the nets? you have hearken'd to the last too much.
Duch. O misery! like to a rusty o'ercharg'd cannon,
Shall I never fly in pieces?—Come, to what prison?
Bos. To none.
Duch. Whither, then?
Bos. To your palace.
Duch. I have heard
That Charon's boat serves to convey all o'er
The dismal lake, but brings none back again.
Bos. Your brothers mean you safety and pity.
Duch. Pity!
With such a pity men preserve alive
Pheasants and quails, when they are not fat enough
To be eaten.
Bos. These are your children?
Duch. Yes.
Bos. Can they prattle?
Duch. No:

But I intend, since they were born accurs'd,
Curses shall be their first language.

Bos. Fie, madam!
Forget this base, low fellow,——

Duch. Were I a man,
I 'd beat that counterfeit face into thy other.

Bos. One of no birth.

Duch. Say that he was born mean,
Man is most happy when 's own actions
Be arguments and examples of his virtue.

Bos. A barren, beggarly virtue.

Duch. I prithee, who is greatest? can you tell?
Sad tales befit my woe: I 'll tell you one.
A salmon, as she swam unto the sea,
Met with a dog-fish, who encounters her
With this rough language: 'Why art thou so bold
To mix thyself with our high state of floods,
Being no eminent courtier, but one
That for the calmest and fresh time o' the year
Dost live in shallow rivers, rank'st thyself
With silly smelts and shrimps? and darest thou
Pass by our dogship without reverence?'
'Oh,' quoth the salmon, 'sister, be at peace:
Thank Jupiter we both have pass'd the net!
Our value never can be truly known,
Till in the fisher's basket we be shown:
I' the market then my price may be the higher,
Even when I am nearest to the cook and fire.'
So to great men the moral may be stretch'd;
Men oft are valu'd high, when they 're most wretch'd.—
But come, whither you please.   I am arm'd 'gainst misery;
Bent to all sways of the oppressor's will:
There 's no deep valley but near some great hill.   [*Exeunt.*

ACT IV

Scene I

Enter Ferdinand and Bosola

Ferd. How doth our sister duchess bear herself
   In her imprisonment?
Bos. Nobly: I 'll describe her.
   She 's sad as one long us'd to 't, and she seems
   Rather to welcome the end of misery
   Than shun it; a behaviour so noble
   As gives a majesty to adversity:
   You may discern the shape of loveliness
   More perfect in her tears than in her smiles:
   She will muse four hours together; and her silence,
   Methinks, expresseth more than if she spake.
Ferd. Her melancholy seems to be fortified
   With a strange disdain.
Bos.   'Tis so; and this restraint,
   Like English mastiffs that grow fierce with tying,
   Makes her too passionately apprehend
   Those pleasures she 's kept from.
Ferd. Curse upon her!
   I will no longer study in the book
   Of another's heart.   Inform her what I told you.   [*Exit.*

Enter Duchess

Bos. All comfort to your grace!
Duch. I will have none.
   Pray thee, why dost thou wrap thy poison'd pills
   In gold and sugar?
Bos. Your elder brother, the Lord Ferdinand,
   Is come to visit you, and sends you word,
   'Cause once he rashly made a solemn vow
   Never to see you more, he comes i' the night;
   And prays you gently neither torch nor taper
   Shine in your chamber: he will kiss your hand,
   And reconcile himself; but for his vow
   He dares not see you.
Duch. At his pleasure.—
   Take hence the lights.—He 's come.

Enter Ferdinand

Ferd. Where are you?

Duch. Here, sir.

Ferd. This darkness suits you well.

Duch. I would ask you pardon.

Ferd. You have it;
   For I account it the honourabl'st revenge,
   Where I may kill, to pardon.—Where are your cubs?

Duch. Whom?

Ferd. Call them your children;
   For though our national law distinguish bastards
   From true legitimate issue, compassionate nature
   Makes them all equal.

Duch. Do you visit me for this?
   You violate a sacrament o' the Church
   Shall make you howl in hell for 't.

Ferd. It had been well,
   Could you have liv'd thus always; for, indeed,
   You were too much i' the light:—but no more;
   I come to seal my peace with you.   Here 's a hand
                    [*Gives her a dead man's hand.*
   To which you have vow'd much love; the ring upon 't
   You gave.

Duch. I affectionately kiss it.

Ferd. Pray, do, and bury the print of it in your heart.
   I will leave this ring with you for a love token;
   And the hand as sure as the ring; and do not doubt
   But you shall have the heart too: when you need a friend,
   Send it to him that own'd it; you shall see
   Whether he can aid you.

Duch. You are very cold:
   I fear you are not well after your travel.—
   Ha! lights!—Oh, horrible!

Ferd. Let her have lights enough.   [*Exit.*

Duch. What witchcraft doth he practise, that he hath left
   A dead man's hand here?

        [*Here is discovered, behind a traverse, the artificial figures
            of Antonio and his children, appearing as if they
            were dead.*

Bos. Look you, here 's the piece from which 'twas ta'en.
   He doth present you this sad spectacle,
   That, now you know directly they are dead,

Hereafter you may wisely cease to grieve
For that which cannot be recoverèd.

Duch. There is not between heaven and earth one wish
I stay for after this: it wastes me more
Than were 't my picture, fashion'd out of wax,
Stuck with a magical needle, and then buried
In some foul dunghill; and yond 's an excellent property
For a tyrant, which I would account mercy.

Bos. What 's that?

Duch. If they would bind me to that lifeless trunk,
And let me freeze to death.

Bos. Come, you must live.

Duch. That 's the greatest torture souls feel in hell,
In hell, that they must live, and cannot die.
Portia, I 'll new kindle thy coals again,
And revive the rare and almost dead example
Of a loving wife.

Bos. Oh, fie! despair? remember
You are a Christian.

Duch. The Church enjoins fasting:
I 'll starve myself to death.

Bos. Leave this vain sorrow.
Things being at the worst begin to mend: the bee
When he hath shot his sting into your hand,
May then play with your eyelid.

Duch. Good comfortable fellow,
Persuade a wretch that 's broke upon the wheel
To have all his bones new set; entreat him live
To be executed again.   Who must dispatch me?
I account this world a tedious theatre,
For I do play a part in 't 'gainst my will.

Bos. Come, be of comfort; I will save your life.

Duch. Indeed, I have not leisure to tend
So small a business.

Bos. Now, by my life, I pity you.

Duch. Thou art a fool, then,
To waste thy pity on a thing so wretched
As cannot pity itself.   I am full of daggers.
Puff, let me blow these vipers from me.   [*Enter Servant.*
What are you?

Serv. One that wishes you long life.

Duch. I would thou wert hang'd for the horrible curse
Thou hast given me: I shall shortly grow one

Of the miracles of pity.   I 'll go pray;
No, I 'll go curse.
Bos. Oh, fie!
Duch. I could curse the stars.
Bos. Oh, fearful!
Duch. And those three smiling seasons of the year
Into a Russian winter: nay, the world
To its first chaos.
Bos. Look you, the stars shine still.
Duch. Oh, but you must
Remember, my curse hath a great way to go.—
Plagues, that make lanes through largest families,
Consume them!—
Bos. Fie, lady!
Duch. Let them, like tyrants,
Never be remember'd but for the ill they have done;
Let all the zealous prayers of mortified
Churchmen forget them!—
Bos. Oh, uncharitable!
Duch. Let heaven a little while cease crowning martyrs,
To punish them!—
Go, howl them this, and say, I long to bleed:
It is some mercy when men kill with speed.   [*Exit.*

Re-enter Ferdinand

Ferd. Excellent, as I would wish; she 's plagu'd in art:
These presentations are but fram'd in wax
By the curious master in that quality,
Vincentio Lauriola, and she takes them
For true substantial bodies.
Bos. Why do you do this?
Ferd. To bring her to despair.
Bos. Faith, end here,
And go no farther in your cruelty:
Send her a penitential garment to put on
Next to her delicate skin, and furnish her
With beads and prayer-books.
Ferd. Damn her! that body of hers,
While that my blood ran pure in 't, was more worth
Than that which thou wouldst comfort, call'd a soul.
I will send her masks of common courtesans,
Have her meat serv'd up by bawds and ruffians,
And, 'cause she 'll needs be mad, I am resolv'd

To remove forth the common hospital
All the mad folk, and place them near her lodging;
There let them practise together, sing and dance,
And act their gambols to the full o' the moon:
If she can sleep the better for it, let her.
Your work is almost ended.

Bos. Must I see her again?

Ferd. Yes.

Bos. Never.

Ferd. You must.

Bos. Never in mine own shape;
That's forfeited by my intelligence
And this last cruel lie: when you send me next,
The business shall be comfort.

Ferd. Very likely;
Thy pity is nothing of kin to thee.   Antonio
Lurks about Milan: thou shalt shortly thither,
To feed a fire as great as my revenge,
Which never will slack till it have spent his fuel:
Intemperate agues make physicians cruel.   [*Exeunt.*

SCENE II

Enter Duchess and Cariola

Duch. What hideous noise was that?

Cari. 'Tis the wild consort
Of madmen, lady, which your tyrant brother
Hath plac'd about your lodging: this tyranny,
I think, was never practis'd till this hour.

Duch. Indeed, I thank him: nothing but noise and folly
Can keep me in my right wits; whereas reason
And silence make me stark mad.   Sit down;
Discourse to me some dismal tragedy.

Cari. Oh, 'twill increase your melancholy.

Duch. Thou art deceiv'd:
To hear of greater grief would lessen mine.
This is a prison?

Cari. Yes, but you shall live
To shake this durance off.

Duch. Thou art a fool:

The robin-redbreast and the nightingale
  Never live long in cages.
Cari. Pray, dry your eyes.
  What think you of, madam?
Duch. Of nothing;
  When I muse thus, I sleep.
Cari. Like a madman, with your eyes open?
Duch. Dost thou think we shall know one another
  In the other world?
Cari. Yes, out of question.
Duch. Oh, that it were possible we might
  But hold some two days' conference with the dead!
  From them I should learn somewhat, I am sure,
  I never shall know here. I'll tell thee a miracle;
  I am not mad yet, to my cause of sorrow:
  The heaven o'er my head seems made of molten brass,
  The earth of flaming sulphur, yet I am not mad.
  I am acquainted with sad misery
  As the tann'd galley-slave is with his oar;
  Necessity makes me suffer constantly,
  And custom makes it easy. Who do I look like now?
Cari. Like to your picture in the gallery,
  A deal of life in show, but none in practice;
  Or rather like some reverend monument
  Whose ruins are even pitied.
Duch. Very proper;
  And Fortune seems only to have her eyesight
  To behold my tragedy.—How now!
  What noise is that?

Enter Servant

Serv. I am come to tell you
  Your brother hath intended you some sport.
  A great physician, when the Pope was sick
  Of a deep melancholy, presented him
  With several sorts of madmen, which wild object
  Being full of change and sport, forc'd him to laugh,
  And so the imposthume broke: the selfsame cure
  The duke intends on you.
Duch. Let them come in.
Serv. There's a mad lawyer; and a secular priest;
  A doctor that hath forfeited his wits
  By jealousy; an astrologian

That in his works said such a day o' the month
Should be the day of doom, and, failing of 't,
Ran mad; an English tailor craz'd in the brain
With the study of new fashions; a gentleman-usher
Quite beside himself with care to keep in mind
The number of his lady's salutations
Or 'How do you' she employ'd him in each morning;
A farmer, too, an excellent knave in grain,
Mad 'cause he was hinder'd transportation:
And let one broker that 's mad loose to these,
You 'd think the devil were among them.
Duch. Sit, Cariola.—Let them loose when you please,
For I am chain'd to endure all your tyranny.

Enter Madmen

Here by a Madman this song is sung to a dismal kind of music.

> *Oh, let us howl some heavy note,*
>   *Some deadly doggèd howl,*
> *Sounding as from the threatening throat*
>   *Of beasts and fatal fowl!*
> *As ravens, screech-owls, bulls, and bears,*
>   *We 'll bell, and bawl our parts,*
> *Till irksome noise have cloy'd your ears*
>   *And córrosiv'd your hearts.*
> *At last, whenas our choir wants breath,*
>   *Our bodies being blest,*
> *We 'll sing, like swans, to welcome death,*
>   *And die in love and rest.*

First Madman. Doomsday not come yet! I 'll draw it nearer
by a perspective, or make a glass that shall set all the world
on fire upon an instant. I cannot sleep; my pillow is stuffed
with a litter of porcupines.
Second Madman. Hell is a mere glass-house, where the devils are
continually blowing up women's souls on hollow irons, and the
fire never goes out.
Third Madman. I will lie with every woman in my parish the
tenth night; I will tythe them over like hay-cocks.
Fourth Madman. Shall my pothecary outgo me because I am
a cuckold? I have found out his roguery; he makes allum of
his wife's urine, and sells it to Puritans that have sore throats
with over-straining.

First Madman. I have skill in heraldry.

Second Madman. Hast?

First Madman. You do give for your crest a woodcock's head with the brains picked out on 't; you are a very ancient gentleman.

Third Madman. Greek is turned Turk: we are only to be saved by the Helvetian translation.

First Madman. Come on, sir, I will lay the law to you.

Second Madman. Oh, rather lay a corrosive: the law will eat to the bone.

Third Madman. He that drinks but to satisfy nature is damned.

Fourth Madman. If I had my glass here, I would show a sight should make all the women here call me mad doctor.

First Madman. What 's he? a rope-maker?

Second Madman. No, no, no, a snuffling knave that, while he shows the tombs, will have his hand in a wench's placket.

Third Madman. Woe to the caroche that brought home my wife from the mask at three o'clock in the morning! it had a large feather-bed in it.

Fourth Madman. I have pared the devil's nails forty times, roasted them in raven's eggs, and cured agues with them.

Third Madman. Get me three hundred milch-bats, to make possets to procure sleep.

Fourth Madman. All the college may throw their caps at me: I have made a soap-boiler costive; it was my masterpiece.

> [*Here the dance, consisting of Eight Madmen, with music answerable thereunto; after which, Bosola, like an old man, enters.*

Duch. Is he mad too?

Serv. Pray, question him.   I 'll leave you.

> [*Exeunt Servant and Madmen.*

Bos. I am come to make thy tomb.

Duch. Ha! my tomb!
   Thou speak'st as if I lay upon my death-bed,
   Gasping for breath: dost thou perceive me sick?

Bos. Yes, and the more dangerously, since thy sickness is insensible.

Duch. Thou art not mad, sure: dost know me?

Bos. Yes.

Duch. Who am I?

Bos. Thou art a box of worm-seed, at best but a salvatory of green mummy. What 's this flesh? a little crudded milk, fantastical puff-paste. Our bodies are weaker than those paper-prisons boys use to keep flies in; more contemptible, since ours is to preserve earth-worms. Didst thou ever see a lark in a cage? Such is the soul in the body: this world is like her little turf of grass, and the heaven o'er our heads like her looking-glass, only gives us a miserable knowledge of the small compass of our prison.

Duch. Am not I thy duchess?

Bos. Thou art some great woman, sure, for riot begins to sit on thy forehead (clad in grey hairs) twenty years sooner than on a merry milkmaid's. Thou sleepest worse than if a mouse should be forced to take up her lodging in a cat's ear: a little infant that breeds its teeth, should it lie with thee, would cry out, as if thou wert the more unquiet bedfellow.

Duch. I am Duchess of Malfi still.

Bos. That makes thy sleeps so broken:
    Glories, like glow-worms, afar off shine bright,
    But, look'd to near, have neither heat nor light.

Duch. Thou art very plain.

Bos. My trade is to flatter the dead, not the living; I am a tomb-maker.

Duch. And thou comest to make my tomb?

Bos. Yes.

Duch. Let me be a little merry: of what stuff wilt thou make it?

Bos. Nay, resolve me first, of what fashion?

Duch. Why, do we grow fantastical in our death-bed? do we affect fashion in the grave?

Bos. Most ambitiously. Princes' images on their tombs do not lie, as they were wont, seeming to pray up to heaven; but with their hands under their cheeks, as if they died of the tooth-ache: they are not carved with their eyes fixed upon the stars; but as their minds were wholly bent upon the world, the self-same way they seem to turn their faces.

Duch. Let me know fully therefore the effect
    Of this thy dismal preparation,
    This talk fit for a charnel.

Bos. Now I shall:—
            [*Enter Executioners, with a coffin, cords, and a bell.*
    Here is a present from your princely brothers;
    And may it arrive welcome, for it brings
    Last benefit, last sorrow.

Duch. Let me see it:
    I have so much obedience in my blood,
    I wish it in their veins to do them good.

Bos. This is your last presence-chamber.
Cari. Oh, my sweet lady!
Duch. Peace; it affrights not me.
Bos. I am the common bellman,
 That usually is sent to condemn'd persons
 The night before they suffer.
Duch. Even now thou said'st
 Thou wast a tomb-maker.
Bos. 'Twas to bring you
 By degrees to mortification. Listen:

> Hark, now everything is still,
> The screech-owl and the whistler shrill
> Call upon our dame aloud,
> And bid her quickly don her shroud!
> Much you had of land and rent;
> Your length in clay 's now competent:
> A long war disturb'd your mind;
> Here your perfect peace is sign'd.
> Of what is 't fools make such vain keeping?
> Sin their conception, their birth weeping,
> Their life a general mist of error,
> Their death a hideous storm of terror.
> Strew your hair with powders sweet,
> Don clean linen, bathe your feet,
> And (the foul fiend more to check)
> A crucifix let bless your neck:
> 'Tis now full tide 'tween night and day;
> End your groan, and come away.

Cari. Hence, villains, tyrants, murderers! alas!
 What will you do with my lady?—Call for help.
Duch. To whom? to our next neighbours? they are mad folks.
Bos. Remove that noise.
Duch. Farewell, Cariola.
 In my last will I have not much to give:
 A many hungry guests have fed upon me;
 Thine will be a poor reversion.
Cari. I will die with her.
Duch. I pray thee, look thou giv'st my little boy
 Some syrup for his cold, and let the girl
 Say her prayers ere she sleep.
      [Cariola is forced out by the Executioners.

Now what you please:
What death?

Bos. Strangling; here are your executioners.

Duch. I forgive them:
The apoplexy, catarrh, or cough o' the lungs,
Would do as much as they do.

Bos. Doth not death fright you?

Duch. Who would be afraid on 't,
Knowing to meet such excellent company
In the other world?

Bos. Yet, methinks,
The manner of your death should much afflict you:
This cord should terrify you.

Duch. Not a whit:
What would it pleasure me to have my throat cut
With diamonds? or to be smotherèd
With cassia? or to be shot to death with pearls?
I know death hath ten thousand several doors
For men to take their exits; and 'tis found
They go on such strange geometrical hinges,
You may open them both ways: any way, for heaven sake,
So I were out of your whispering.   Tell my brothers
That I perceive death, now I am well awake,
Best gift is they can give or I can take.
I would fain put off my last woman's fault,
I 'd not be tedious to you.

First Execut. We are ready.

Duch. Dispose my breath how please you; but my body
Bestow upon my women, will you?

First Execut. Yes.

Duch. Pull, and pull strongly, for your able strength
Must pull down heaven upon me:
Yet stay; heaven gates are not so highly arch'd
As princes' palaces; they that enter there
Must go upon their knees.   [*Kneels.*]—Come, violent death,
Serve for mandragora to make me sleep!—
Go tell my brothers, when I am laid out,
They then may feed in quiet.
                    [*The Executioners strangle the Duchess.*

Bos. Where 's the waiting-woman?
Fetch her: some other strangle the children.
            [*Cariola and Children are brought in by the Executioners;
                who presently strangle the Children.*

Look you, there sleeps your mistress.

Cari. Oh, you are damn'd
Perpetually for this! My turn is next;
Is 't not so order'd?

Bos. Yes, and I am glad
You are so well prepar'd for 't.

Cari. You are deceiv'd, sir,
I am not prepar'd for 't, I will not die;
I will first come to my answer, and know
How I have offended.

Bos. Come, dispatch her.—
You kept her counsel; now you shall keep ours.

Cari. I will not die, I must not; I am contracted
To a young gentleman.

First Execut. Here 's your wedding-ring.

Cari. Let me but speak with the duke; I 'll discover
Treason to his person.

Bos. Delays:—throttle her.

First Execut. She bites and scratches.

Cari. If you kill me now,
I am damn'd; I have not been at confession
This two years.

Bos. [*To Executioners.*] When?

Cari. I am quick with child.

Bos. Why, then,
Your credit 's sav'd.   [*The Executioners strangle Cariola.*
Bear her into the next room;
Let these lie still.

                    [*Exeunt the Executioners with the body of Cariola.*

Enter Ferdinand

Ferd. Is she dead?

Bos. She is what
You 'd have her.   But here begin your pity:
                    [*Shows the Children strangled.*
Alas, how have these offended?

Ferd. The death
Of young wolves is never to be pitied.

Bos. Fix your eye here.

Ferd. Constantly.

Bos. Do you not weep?
Other sins only speak; murder shrieks out:

The element of water moistens the earth,
But blood flies upwards and bedews the heavens.

Ferd. Cover her face; mine eyes dazzle: she died young.

Bos. I think not so; her infelicity
  Seem'd to have years too many.

Ferd. She and I were twins;
  And should I die this instant, I had liv'd
  Her time to a minute.

Bos. It seems she was born first:
  You have bloodily approv'd the ancient truth,
  That kindred commonly do worse agree
  Than remote strangers.

Ferd. Let me see her face
  Again. Why didst not thou pity her? what
  An excellent honest man mightst thou have been,
  If thou hadst borne her to some sanctuary!
  Or, bold in a good cause, oppos'd thyself,
  With thy advancèd sword above thy head,
  Between her innocence and my revenge!
  I bade thee, when I was distracted of my wits,
  Go kill my dearest friend, and thou hast done 't.
  For let me but examine well the cause:
  What was the meanness of her match to me?
  Only I must confess I had a hope,
  Had she continu'd widow, to have gain'd
  An infinite mass of treasure by her death:
  And what was the main cause? her marriage,
  That drew a stream of gall quite through my heart.
  For thee, as we observe in tragedies
  That a good actor many times is curs'd
  For playing a villain's part, I hate thee for 't,
  And, for my sake, say, thou hast done much ill well.

Bos. Let me quicken your memory, for I perceive
  You are falling into ingratitude: I challenge
  The reward due to my service.

Ferd. I 'll tell thee
  What I 'll give thee.

Bos. Do.

Ferd. I 'll give thee a pardon
  For this murder.

Bos. Ha!

Ferd. Yes, and 'tis
  The largest bounty I can study to do thee.

By what authority didst thou execute
This bloody sentence?
Bos. By yours.
Ferd. Mine! was I her judge?
Did any ceremonial form of law
Doom her to not-being? did a cómplete jury
Deliver her conviction up i' the court?
Where shalt thou find this judgment register'd,
Unless in hell? See, like a bloody fool,
Thou 'st forfeited thy life, and thou shalt die for 't.
Bos. The office of justice is perverted quite
When one thief hangs another.   Who shall dare
To reveal this?
Ferd. Oh, I 'll tell thee;
The wolf shall find her grave, and scrape it up,
Not to devour the corpse, but to discover
The horrid murder.
Bos. You, not I, shall quake for 't.
Ferd. Leave me.
Bos. I will first receive my pension.
Ferd. You are a villain.
Bos. When your ingratitude
Is judge, I am so.
Ferd. Oh, horror,
That not the fear of him which binds the devils
Can prescribe man obedience!—
Never look upon me more.
Bos. Why, fare thee well.
Your brother and yourself are worthy men:
You have a pair of hearts are hollow graves,
Rotten, and rotting others; and your vengeance,
Like two chain'd bullets, still goes arm in arm:
You may be brothers; for treason, like the plague,
Doth take much in a blood.   I stand like one
That long hath ta'en a sweet and golden dream:
I am angry with myself, now that I wake.
Ferd. Get thee into some unknown part o' the world,
That I may never see thee.
Bas. Let me know
Wherefore I should be thus neglected.   Sir,
I serv'd your tyranny, and rather strove
To satisfy yourself than all the world:

And though I loath'd the evil, yet I lov'd
You that did counsel it; and rather sought
To appear a true servant than an honest man.
Ferd. I 'll go hunt the badger by owl-light:
'Tis a deed of darkness. [*Exit.*
Bos. He 's much distracted. Off, my painted honour!
While with vain hopes our faculties we tire,
We seem to sweat in ice and freeze in fire.
What would I do, were this to do again?
I would not change my peace of conscience
For all the wealth of Europe.—She stirs; here 's life:
Return, fair soul, from darkness, and lead mine
Out of this sensible hell:—she 's warm, she breathes:—
Upon thy pale lips I will melt my heart,
To store them with fresh colour.—Who 's there!
Some cordial drink!—Alas! I dare not call:
So pity would destroy pity.—Her eye opes,
And heaven in it seems to ope, that late was shut,
To take me up to mercy.
Duch. Antonio!
Bos. Yes, madam, he is living;
The dead bodies you saw were but feign'd statues:
He 's reconcil'd to your brothers; the Pope hath wrought
The atonement.
Duch. Mercy! [*Dies.*
Bos. Oh, she 's gone again! there the cords of life broke.
O sacred innocence, that sweetly sleeps
On turtles' feathers, whilst a guilty conscience
Is a black register wherein is writ
All our good deeds and bad, a perspective
That shows us hell! That we cannot be suffer'd
To do good when we have a mind to it!
This is manly sorrow;
These tears, I am very certain, never grew
In my mother's milk: my estate is sunk
Below the degree of fear: where were
These penitent fountains while she was living?
Oh, they were frozen up! Here is a sight
As direful to my soul as is the sword
Unto a wretch hath slain his father. Come,
I 'll bear thee hence,
And execute thy last will; that 's deliver
Thy body to the reverend dispose

Of some good women: that the cruel tyrant
Shall not deny me.   Then I 'll post to Milan,
Where somewhat I will speedily enact
Worth my dejection.   [*Exit.*

ACT V

Scene I

Enter Antonio and Delio

Ant. What think you of my hope of reconcilement
   To the Arragonian brethren?
Delio. I misdoubt it;
   For though they have sent their letters of safe-conduct
   For your repair to Milan, they appear
   But nets to entrap you.   The Marquis of Pescara,
   Under whom you hold certain land in cheat,
   Much 'gainst his noble nature hath been mov'd
   To seize those lands; and some of his dependants
   Are at this instant making it their suit
   To be invested in your revenues.
   I cannot think they mean well to your life
   That do deprive you of your means of life,
   Your living.
Ant. You are still an heretic
   To any safety I can shape myself.
Delio. Here comes the marquis: I will make myself
   Petitioner for some part of your land,
   To know whither it is flying.
Ant. I pray, do.

Enter Pescara

Delio. Sir, I have a suit to you.
Pes. To me?
Delio. An easy one:
   There is the Citadel of Saint Bennet,
   With some demesnes, of late in the possession
   Of Antonio Bologna,—please you bestow them on me.
Pes. You are my friend; but this is such a suit,
   Nor fit for me to give, nor you to take.

Delio. No, sir?

Pes. I will give you ample reason for 't
Soon in private:—here 's the cardinal's mistress.

Enter Julia

Julia. My lord, I am grown your poor petitioner,
And should be an ill beggar, had I not
A great man's letter here, the cardinal's,
To court you in my favour. [*Gives a letter.*

Pes. He entreats for you
The Citadel of Saint Bennet, that belong'd
To the banish'd Bologna.

Julia. Yes.

Pes. I could not have thought of a friend I could rather
Pleasure with it: 'tis yours.

Julia. Sir, I thank you;
And he shall know how doubly I am engag'd
Both in your gift, and speediness of giving
Which makes your grant the greater. [*Exit.*

Ant. How they fortify
Themselves with my ruin!

Delio. Sir, I am
Little bound to you.

Pes. Why?

Delio. Because you denied this suit to me, and gave 't
To such a creature.

Pes. Do you know what it was?
It was Antonio's land; not forfeited
By course of law, but ravish'd from his throat
By the cardinal's entreaty: it were not fit
I should bestow so main a piece of wrong
Upon my friend; 'tis a gratification
Only due to a strumpet, for it is injustice.
Shall I sprinkle the pure blood of innocents
To make those followers I call my friends
Look ruddier upon me? I am glad
This land, ta'en from the owner by such wrong,
Returns again unto so foul an use
As salary for his lust. Learn, good Delio,
To ask noble things of me, and you shall find
I 'll be a noble giver.

Delio. You instruct me well.

Ant. Why, here 's a man now would fright impudence
　　From sauciest beggars.
Pes. Prince Ferdinand 's come to Milan,
　　Sick, as they give out, of an apoplexy;
　　But some say 'tis a frenzy; I am going
　　To visit him.   [*Exit.*
Ant. 'Tis a noble old fellow.
Delio. What course do you mean to take, Antonio?
Ant. This night I mean to venture all my fortune,
　　Which is no more than a poor lingering life,
　　To the cardinal's worst of malice: I have got
　　Private access to his chamber; and intend
　　To visit him about the mid of night,
　　As once his brother did our noble duchess.
　　It may be that the sudden apprehension
　　Of danger,—for I 'll go in mine own shape,—
　　When he shall see it fraught with love and duty,
　　May draw the poison out of him, and work
　　A friendly reconcilement: if it fail,
　　Yet it shall rid me of this infamous calling:
　　For better fall once than be ever falling.
Delio. I 'll second you in all danger; and, howe'er,
　　My life keeps rank with yours.
Ant. You are still my lov'd and best friend.   [*Exeunt.*

Scene II

Enter Pescara and Doctor

Pes. Now, doctor, may I visit your patient?
Doc. If 't please your lordship: but he 's instantly
　　To take the air here in the gallery
　　By my direction.
Pes. Pray thee, what 's his disease?
Doc. A very pestilent disease, my lord,
　　They call lycanthropia.
Pes. What 's that?
　　I need a dictionary to 't.
Doc. I 'll tell you.
　　In those that are possess'd with 't there o'erflows
　　Such melancholy humour they imagine
　　Themselves to be transformèd into wolves;

Steal forth to churchyards in the dead of night,
And dig dead bodies up: as two nights since
One met the duke 'bout midnight in a lane
Behind Saint Mark's Church, with the leg of a man
Upon his shoulder; and he howl'd fearfully;
Said he was a wolf, only the difference
Was, a wolf's skin was hairy on the outside,
His on the inside; bade them take their swords,
Rip up his flesh, and try: straight I was sent for,
And, having minister'd to him, found his grace
Very well recover'd.

Pes. I am glad on 't.

Doc. Yet not without some fear
Of a relapse. If he grow to his fit again,
I 'll go a nearer way to work with him
Than ever Paracelsus dream'd of; if
They 'll give me leave, I 'll buffet his madness out of him.
Stand aside; he comes.

Enter Ferdinand, Cardinal, Malatesti, and Bosola

Ferd. Leave me.

Mal. Why doth your lordship love this solitariness?

Ferd. Eagles commonly fly alone: they are crows, daws, and
starlings that flock together. Look, what 's that follows me?

Mal. Nothing, my lord.

Ferd. Yes.

Mal. 'Tis your shadow.

Ferd. Stay it; let it not haunt me.

Mal. Impossible, if you move, and the sun shine.

Ferd. I will throttle it. [*Throws himself down on his shadow.*

Mal. Oh, my lord, you are angry with nothing.

Ferd. You are a fool: how is 't possible I should catch my
shadow, unless I fall upon 't? When I go to hell, I mean to
carry a bribe; for, look you, good gifts evermore make way
for the worst persons.

Pes. Rise, good my lord.

Ferd. I am studying the art of patience.

Pes. 'Tis a noble virtue.

Ferd. To drive six snails before me from this town to Moscow;
neither use goad nor whip to them, but let them take their
own time;—the patient'st man i' the world match me for an
experiment;—and I 'll crawl after like a sheep-biter.

Card. Force him up. [*They raise him.*

Ferd. Use me well, you were best.   What I have done, I have done: I 'll confess nothing.

Doc. Now let me come to him.—Are you mad, my lord? are you out of your princely wits?

Ferd. What 's he?

Pes. Your doctor.

Ferd. Let me have his beard sawed off, and his eyebrows filed more civil.

Doc. I must do mad tricks with him, for that 's the only way on 't.—I have brought your grace a salamander's skin to keep you from sun-burning.

Ferd. I have cruel sore eyes.

Doc. The white of a cockatrix's egg is present remedy.

Ferd. Let it be a new-laid one, you were best.—
Hide me from him: physicians are like kings,—
They brook no contradiction.

Doc. Now he begins to fear me: now let me alone with him.

Card. How now! put off your gown!

Doc. Let me have some forty urinals filled with rose water: he and I 'll go pelt one another with them.—Now he begins to fear me.—Can you fetch a frisk, sir?—Let him go, let him go, upon my peril: I find by his eye he stands in awe of me; I 'll make him as tame as a dormouse.

Ferd. Can you fetch your frisks, sir!—I will stamp him into a cullis, flay off his skin, to cover one of the anatomies this rogue hath set i' the cold yonder in Barber-Chirurgeon's Hall.—Hence, hence! you are all of you like beasts for sacrifice: there 's nothing left of you but tongue and belly, flattery and lechery.   [*Exit.*

Pes. Doctor, he did not fear you throughly

Doc. True; I was somewhat too forward.

Bos. Mercy upon me, what a fatal judgment
Hath fall'n upon this Ferdinand!

Pes. Knows your grace
What accident hath brought unto the prince
This strange distraction?

Card. [*Aside.*] I must feign somewhat.—Thus they say it grew.
You have heard it rumour'd, for these many years
None of our family dies but there is seen
The shape of an old woman, which is given
By tradition to us to have been murder'd
By her nephews for her riches.   Such a figure
One night, as the prince sat up late at 's book,

Appear'd to him; when crying out for help,
The gentlemen of 's chamber found his grace
All on a cold sweat, alter'd much in face
And language: since which apparition,
He hath grown worse and worse, and I much fear
He cannot live.

Bos. Sir, I would speak with you.

Pes. We 'll leave your grace,
Wishing to the sick prince, our noble lord,
All health of mind and body.

Card. You are most welcome.

> [*Exeunt Pescara, Malatesti, and Doctor.*

Are you come? so.—[*Aside.*] This fellow must not know
By any means I had intelligence
In our duchess' death; for, though I counsell'd it,
The full of all the engagement seem'd to grow
From Ferdinand.—Now, sir, how fares our sister?
I do not think but sorrow makes her look
Like to an oft-dy'd garment: she shall now
Taste comfort from me.   Why do you look so wildly?
Oh, the fortune of your master here the prince
Dejects you; but be you of happy comfort:
If you 'll do one thing for me I 'll entreat,
Though he had a cold tombstone o'er his bones,
I 'd make you what you would be.

Bos. Anything;
Give it me in a breath, and let me fly to 't:
They that think long small expedition win,
For musing much o' the end cannot begin.

> *Enter Julia*

Julia. Sir, will you come in to supper?

Card. I am busy; leave me.

Julia. [*Aside.*] What an excellent shape hath that fellow!   [*Exit.*

Card. 'Tis thus.   Antonio lurks here in Milan:
Inquire him out, and kill him.   While he lives,
Our sister cannot marry; and I have thought
Of an excellent match for her.   Do this, and style me
Thy advancement.

Bos. But by what means shall I find him out?

Card. There is a gentleman call'd Delio
Here in the camp, that hath been long approv'd
His loyal friend.   Set eye upon that fellow;
Follow him to mass; may be Antonio,

Although he do account religion
But a school-name, for fashion of the world
May accompany him; or else go inquire out
Delio's confessor, and see if you can bribe
Him to reveal it.   There are a thousand ways
A man might find to trace him; as to know
What fellows haunt the Jews for taking up
Great sums of money, for sure he 's in want;
Or else to go to the picture-makers, and learn
Who bought her picture lately: some of these
Happily may take.

Bos. Well, I 'll not freeze i' the business:
I would see that wretched thing, Antonio,
Above all sights i' the world.

Card. Do, and be happy.   [*Exit.*

Bos. This fellow doth breed basilisks in 's eyes,
He 's nothing else but murder; yet he seems
Not to have notice of the duchess' death.
'Tis his cunning: I must follow his example;
There cannot be a surer way to trace
Than that of an old fox.

Re-enter Julia

Julia. So, sir, you are well met.

Bos. How now!

Julia. Nay, the doors are fast enough:
Now, sir, I will make you confess your treachery.

Bos. Treachery!

Julia. Yes, confess to me
Which of my women 'twas you hir'd to put
Love-powder into my drink?

Bos. Love-powder!

Julia. Yes, when I was at Malfi.
Why should I fall in love with such a face else?
I have already suffer'd for thee so much pain,
The only remedy to do me good
Is to kill my longing.

Bos. Sure, your pistol holds
Nothing but perfumes or kissing-comfits.
Excellent lady!
You have a pretty way on 't to discover
Your longing.   Come, come, I 'll disarm you,
And arm you thus: yet this is wondrous strange.

Julia. Compare thy form and my eyes together,
   You 'll find my love no such great miracle.
   Now you 'll say
   I am wanton: this nice modesty in ladies
   Is but a troublesome familiar
   That haunts them.
Bos. Know you me, I am a blunt soldier.
Julia. The better:
   Sure, there wants fire where there are no lively sparks
   Of roughness.
Bos. And I want compliment.
Julia. Why, ignorance
   In courtship cannot make you do amiss,
   If you have a heart to do well.
Bos. You are very fair.
Julia. Nay, if you lay beauty to my charge,
   I must plead unguilty.
Bos. Your bright eyes
   Carry a quiver of darts in them sharper
   Than sunbeams.
Julia. You will mar me with commendation,
   Put yourself to the charge of courting me,
   Whereas now I woo you.
Bos. [*Aside*.] I have it, I will work upon this creature.—
   Let us grow most amorously familiar:
   If the great cardinal now should see me thus,
   Would he not count me a villain?
Julia. No; he might count me a wanton,
   Not lay a scruple of offence on you;
   For if I see and steal a diamond,
   The fault is not i' the stone, but in me the thief
   That purloins it.   I am sudden with you:
   We that are great women of pleasure use to cut off
   These uncertain wishes and unquiet longings,
   And in an instant join the sweet delight
   And the pretty excuse together.   Had you been i' the street,
   Under my chamber-window, even there
   I should have courted you.
Bos. Oh, you are an excellent lady!
Julia. Bid me do somewhat for you presently
   To express I love you.
Bos. I will; and if you love me,
   Fail not to effect it.

The cardinal is grown wondrous melancholy;
Demand the cause, let him not put you off
With feign'd excuse; discover the main ground on 't.

Julia. Why would you know this?

Bos. I have depended on him,
And I hear that he is fall'n in some disgrace
With the emperor: if he be, like the mice
That forsake falling houses, I would shift
To other dependence.

Julia. You shall not need
Follow the wars: I 'll be your maintenance.

Bos. And I your loyal servant: but I cannot
Leave my calling.

Julia. Not leave an ungrateful
General for the love of a sweet lady!
You are like some cannot sleep in feather-beds,
But must have blocks for their pillows.

Bos. Will you do this?

Julia. Cunningly.

Bos. To-morrow I 'll expect the intelligence.

Julia. To-morrow! get you into my cabinet;
You shall have it with you.   Do not delay me,
No more than I do you: I am like one
That is condemn'd; I have my pardon promis'd,
But I would see it seal'd.   Go, get you in:
You shall see me wind my tongue about his heart
Like a skein of silk.   [*Exit Bosola.*

Re-enter Cardinal

Card. Where are you?

Enter Servants

Serv. Here.

Card. Let none, upon your lives, have conference
With the Prince Ferdinand, unless I know it.—
[*Aside.*] In this distraction he may reveal
The murder.   [*Exeunt Servants.*
Yond 's my lingering consumption:
I am weary of her, and by any means
Would be quit of.

Julia. How now, my lord! what ails you?

Card. Nothing.

Julia. Oh, you are much alter'd:
Come, I must be your secretary, and remove
This lead from off your bosom: what 's the matter?

Card. I may not tell you.

Julia. Are you so far in love with sorrow
    You cannot part with part of it? or think you
    I cannot love your grace when you are sad
    As well as merry? or do you suspect
    I, that have been a secret to your heart
    These many winters, cannot be the same
    Unto your tongue?

Card. Satisfy thy longing,—
    The only way to make thee keep my counsel
    Is, not to tell thee.

Julia. Tell your echo this,
    Or flatterers, that like echoes still report
    What they hear though most imperfect, and not me;
    For if that you be true unto yourself,
    I 'll know.

Card. Will you rack me?

Julia. No, judgment shall
    Draw it from you: it is an equal fault,
    To tell one's secrets unto all or none.

Card. The first argues folly.

Julia. But the last tyranny.

Card. Very well: why, imagine I have committed
    Some secret deed which I desire the world
    May never hear of.

Julia. Therefore may not I know it?
    You have conceal'd for me as great a sin
    As adultery. Sir, never was occasion
    For perfect trial of my constancy
    Till now: sir, I beseech you——

Card. You 'll repent it.

Julia. Never.

Card. It hurries thee to ruin: I 'll not tell thee.
    Be well advis'd, and think what danger 'tis
    To receive a prince's secrets: they that do,
    Had need have their breasts hoop'd with adamant
    To contain them. I pray thee, yet be satisfied;
    Examine thine own frailty; 'tis more easy
    To tie knots than unloose them: 'tis a secret
    That, like a lingering poison, may chance lie
    Spread in thy veins, and kill thee seven year hence.

Julia. Now you dally with me.

Card. No more; thou shalt know it.

By my appointment the great Duchess of Malfi
And two of her young children, four nights since,
Were strangl'd.

Julia. O heaven! sir, what have you done!

Card. How now? how settles this? think you your bosom
Will be a grave dark and obscure enough
For such a secret?

Julia. You have undone yourself, sir.

Card. Why?

Julia. It lies not in me to conceal it.

Card. No?
Come, I will swear you to 't upon this book.

Julia. Most religiously.

Card. Kiss it.   [*She kisses the book.*
Now you shall never utter it; thy curiosity
Hath undone thee: thou 'rt poison'd with that book;
Because I knew thou couldst not keep my counsel,
I have bound thee to 't by death.

Re-enter Bosola

Bos. For pity sake, hold!

Card. Ha, Bosola!

Julia. I forgive you
This equal piece of justice you have done;
For I betray'd your counsel to that fellow:
He overheard it; that was the cause I said
It lay not in me to conceal it.

Bos. Oh, foolish woman,
Couldst not thou have poison'd him?

Julia. 'Tis weakness,
Too much to think what should have been done.   I go,
I know not whither.   [*Dies.*

Card. Wherefore com'st thou hither?

Bos. That I might find a great man like yourself,
Not out of his wits as the Lord Ferdinand,
To remember my service.

Card. I 'll have thee hew'd in pieces.

Bos. Make not yourself such a promise of that life
Which is not yours to dispose of.

Card. Who plac'd thee here?

Bos. Her lust, as she intended.

Card. Very well:
  Now you know me for your fellow-murderer.
Bos. And wherefore should you lay fair marble colours
  Upon your rotten purposes to me?
  Unless you imitate some that do plot great treasons,
  And when they have done, go hide themselves i' the graves
  Of those were actors in 't?
Card. No more; there is
  A fortune attends thee.
Bos. Shall I go sue to Fortune any longer?
  'Tis the fool's pilgrimage.
Card. I have honours in store for thee.
Bos. There are many ways that conduct to seeming honour,
  And some of them very dirty ones.
Card. Throw to the devil
  Thy melancholy.   The fire burns well;
  What need we keep a stirring of 't, and make
  A greater smother? Thou wilt kill Antonio?
Bos. Yes.
Card. Take up that body.
Bos. I think I shall
  Shortly grow the common bier for churchyards.
Card. I will allow thee some dozen of attendants
  To aid thee in the murder.
Bos. Oh, by no means.   Physicians that apply horse-leeches to
  any rank swelling use to cut off their tails, that the blood may
  run through them the faster: let me have no train when I go to
  shed blood, lest it make me have a greater when I ride to the
  gallows.
Card. Come to me after midnight, to help to remove
  That body to her own lodging: I 'll give out
  She died o' the plague; 'twill breed the less inquiry
  After her death.
Bos. Where 's Castruccio her husband?
Card. He 's rode to Naples, to take possession
  Of Antonio's citadel.
Bos. Believe me, you have done a very happy turn.
Card. Fail not to come: there is the master-key
  Of our lodgings; and by that you may conceive
  What trust I plant in you.
Bos. You shall find me ready.   [*Exit Cardinal.*
  Oh, poor Antonio, though nothing be so needful
  To thy estate as pity, yet I find

Nothing so dangerous! I must look to my footing:
In such slippery ice-pavements men had need
To be frost-nail'd well, they may break their necks else;
The precedent's here afore me. How this man
Bears up in blood! seems fearless! Why, 'tis well:
Security some men call the suburbs of hell,
Only a dead wall between. Well, good Antonio,
I'll seek thee out; and all my care shall be
To put thee into safety from the reach
Of these most cruel biters that have got
Some of thy blood already. It may be,
I'll join with thee in a most just revenge:
The weakest arm is strong enough that strikes
With the sword of justice. Still methinks the duchess
Haunts me: there, there!—'Tis nothing but my melancholy.
O Penitence, let me truly taste thy cup,
That throws men down only to raise them up!   [*Exit.*

Scene III

Enter Antonio and Delio

Delio. Yond's the cardinal's window. This fortification
    Grew from the ruins of an ancient abbey;
    And to yond side o' the river lies a wall,
    Piece of a cloister, which in my opinion
    Gives the best echo that you ever heard,
    So hollow and so dismal, and withal
    So plain in the distinction of our words,
    That many have suppos'd it is a spirit
    That answers.
Ant. I do love these ancient ruins.
    We never tread upon them but we set
    Our foot upon some reverend history:
    And, questionless, here in this open court,
    Which now lies naked to the injuries
    Of stormy weather, some men lie interr'd
    Lov'd the church so well, and gave so largely to 't,
    They thought it should have canopied their bones
    Till doomsday; but all things have their end:
    Churches and cities, which have diseases like to men,
    Must have like death that we have.

Echo. Like death that we have.

Delio. Now the echo hath caught you.

Ant. It groan'd, methought, and gave
A very deadly accent.

Echo. Deadly accent.

Delio. I told you 'twas a pretty one: you may make it
A huntsman, or a falconer, a musician,
Or a thing of sorrow.

Echo. A thing of sorrow.

Ant. Ay, sure, that suits it best.

Echo. That suits it best.

Ant. 'Tis very like my wife's voice.

Echo. Ay, wife's voice.

Delio. Come, let us walk farther from 't.
I would not have you go to the cardinal's to-night:
Do not.

Echo. Do not.

Delio. Wisdom doth not more moderate wasting sorrow
Than time: take time for 't; be mindful of thy safety.

Echo. Be mindful of thy safety.

Ant. Necessity compels me:
Make scrutiny throughout the passages
Of your own life, you 'll find it impossible
To fly your fate.

Echo. Oh, fly your fate!

Delio. Hark! the dead stones seem to have pity on you,
And give you good counsel.

Ant. Echo, I will not talk with thee,
For thou art a dead thing.

Echo. Thou art a dead thing.

Ant. My duchess is asleep now,
And her little ones, I hope, sweetly: O heaven,
Shall I never see her more?

Echo. Never see her more.

Ant. I mark'd not one repetition of the echo
But that; and on the sudden a clear light
Presented me a face folded in sorrow.

Delio. Your fancy merely.

Ant. Come, I 'll be out of this ague,
For to live thus is not indeed to live;
It is a mockery and abuse of life:
I will not henceforth save myself by halves;
Lose all, or nothing.

N 899

Delio. Your own virtue save you!
　I 'll fetch your eldest son, and second you:
　It may be that the sight of his own blood
　Spread in so sweet a figure may beget
　The more compassion.　However, fare you well.
　Though in our miseries Fortune have a part,
　Yet in our noble sufferings she hath none:
　Contempt of pain, that we may call our own.　　　　*[Exeunt.*

SCENE IV

Enter Cardinal, Pescara, Malatesti, Roderigo, and Grisolan

Card. You shall not watch to-night by the sick prince;
　His grace is very well recover'd.
Mal. Good my lord, suffer us.
Card. Oh, by no means;
　The noise, and change of object in his eye,
　Doth more distract him: I pray, all to bed;
　And though you hear him in his violent fit,
　Do not rise, I entreat you.
Pes. So, sir; we shall not.
Card. Nay, I must have you promise
　Upon your honours, for I was enjoin'd to 't
　By himself; and he seem'd to urge it sensibly.
Pes. Let our honours bind this trifle.
Card. Nor any of your followers.
Mal. Neither.
Card. It may be, to make trial of your promise,
　When he 's asleep, myself will rise and feign
　Some of his mad tricks, and cry out for help,
　And feign myself in danger.
Mal. If your throat were cutting,
　I 'd not come at you, now I have protested against it.
Card. Why, I thank you.
Gris. 'Twas a foul storm to-night.
Rod. The Lord Ferdinand's chamber shook like an osier.
Mal. 'Twas nothing but pure kindness in the devil,
　To rock his own child.　　　*[Exeunt all except the Cardinal.*
Card. The reason why I would not suffer these
　About my brother, is, because at midnight

I may with better privacy convey
Julia's body to her own lodging.   Oh, my conscience!
I would pray now; but the devil takes away my heart
For having any confidence in prayer.
About this hour I appointed Bosola
To fetch the body: when he hath serv'd my turn,
He dies.   [*Exit.*

Enter Bosola

Bos. Ha! 'twas the cardinal's voice; I heard him name
Bosola and my death.   Listen: I hear one's footing.

Enter Ferdinand

Ferd. Strangling is a very quiet death.
Bos. [*Aside.*] Nay, then, I see I must stand upon my guard.
Ferd. What say [you] to that? whisper softly; do you agree
to 't? So; it must be done i' the dark: the cardinal would not
for a thousand pounds the doctor should see it.   [*Exit.*
Bos. My death is plotted; here 's the consequence of murder.
We value not desert nor Christian breath,
When we know black deeds must be cur'd with death.

Enter Antonio and Servant

Serv. Here stay, sir, and be confident, I pray:
I 'll fetch you a dark lantern.   [*Exit.*
Ant. Could I take him at his prayers,
There were hope of pardon.
Bos. Fall right, my sword!—   [*Stabs him.*
I 'll not give thee so much leisure as to pray.
Ant. Oh, I am gone! Thou hast ended a long suit
In a minute.
Bos. What art thou?
Ant. A most wretched thing,
That only have thy benefit in death,
To appear myself.

Re-enter Servant with a lantern

Serv. Where are you, sir?
Ant. Very near my home.—Bosola!
Serv. Oh, misfortune!
Bos. Smother thy pity, thou art dead else.—Antonio!
The man I would have sav'd 'bove mine own life!
We are merely the stars' tennis-balls, struck and banded

Which way please them.—Oh, good Antonio,
I 'll whisper one thing in thy dying ear
Shall make thy heart break quickly! thy fair duchess
And two sweet children——

Ant. Their very names
Kindle a little life in me.

Bos. Are murder'd.

Ant. Some men have wish'd to die
At the hearing of sad tidings; I am glad
That I shall do 't in sadness: I would not now
Wish my wounds balm'd nor heal'd, for I have no use
To put my life to.   In all our quest of greatness,
Like wanton boys, whose pastime is their care,
We follow after bubbles blown in the air.
Pleasure of life, what is 't? only the good hours
Of an ague; merely a preparative to rest,
To endure vexation.   I do not ask
The process of my death; only commend me
To Delio.

Bos. Break, heart!

Ant. And let my son fly the courts of princes.   [*Dies.*

Bos. Thou seem'st to have lov'd Antonio?

Serv. I brought him hither,
To have reconcil'd him to the cardinal.

Bos. I do not ask thee that.
Take him up, if thou tender thine own life,
And bear him where the lady Julia
Was wont to lodge.—Oh, my fate moves swift!
I have this cardinal in the forge already;
Now I 'll bring him to the hammer.   O direful misprision!
I will not imitate things glorious,
No more than base; I 'll be mine own example.—
On, on! and look thou represent, for silence,
The thing thou bear'st.   [*Exeunt.*

SCENE V

Enter Cardinal, with a book

Card. I am puzzled in a question about hell:
He says, in hell there 's one material fire,
And yet it shall not burn all men alike.
Lay him by.   How tedious is a guilty conscience!

When I look into the fish-ponds in my garden,
Methinks I see a thing arm'd with a rake,
That seems to strike at me.

        [Enter Bosola and Servant bearing Antonio's body.

Now, art thou come?
Thou look'st ghastly:
There sits in thy face some great determination
Mix'd with some fear.
Bos. Thus it lightens into action;
  I am come to kill thee.
Card. Ha!—Help! our guard!
Bos. Thou art deceiv'd;
  They are out of thy howling.
Card. Hold; and I will faithfully divide
  Revenues with thee.
Bos. Thy prayers and proffers
  Are both unseasonable.
Card. Raise the watch! we are betray'd!
Bos. I have confin'd your flight:
  I 'll suffer your retreat to Julia's chamber,
  But no farther.
Card. Help! we are betray'd!

    Enter, above, Pescara, Malatesti, Roderigo, and Grisolan

Mal. Listen.
Card. My dukedom for rescue!
Rod. Fie upon his counterfeiting!
Mal. Why, 'tis not the cardinal.
Rod. Yes, yes, 'tis he:
  But I 'll see him hang'd ere I 'll go down to him.
Card. Here 's a plot upon me; I am assaulted! I am lost,
  Unless some rescue!
Gris. He doth this pretty well;
  But it will not serve to laugh me out of mine honour.
Card. The sword 's at my throat!
Rod. You would not bawl so loud then.
Mal. Come, come, let 's go
  To bed: he told us thus much aforehand.
Pes. He wish'd you should not come at him; but, believe 't,
  The accent of the voice sounds not in jest:
  I 'll down to him, howsoever, and with engines
  Force ope the doors.   *[Exit above.*

Rod. Let 's follow him aloof,
   And note how the cardinal will laugh at him.
                  [*Exeunt, above, Malatesti, Roderigo, and Grisolan.*
Bos. There 's for you first,
   'Cause you shall not unbarricade the door
   To let in rescue.   [*Kills the Servant.*
Card. What cause hast thou to pursue my life?
Bos. Look there.
Card. Antonio!
Bos. Slain by my hand unwittingly.
   Pray, and be sudden: when thou kill'd'st thy sister,
   Thou took'st from Justice her most equal balance,
   And left her naught but her sword.
Card. Oh, mercy!
Bos. Now it seems thy greatness was only outward;
   For thou fall'st faster of thyself than calamity
   Can drive thee.   I 'll not waste longer time; there!
                                          [*Stabs him.*

Card. Thou hast hurt me.
Bos. Again!   [*Stabs him again.*
Card. Shall I die like a leveret,
   Without any resistance?—Help! help! help!
   I am slain!

                    Enter Ferdinand

Ferd. The alarum! give me a fresh horse;
   Rally the vaunt-guard, or the day is lost.
   Yield, yield! I give you the honour of arms,
   Shake my sword over you; will you yield?
Card. Help me; I am your brother!
Ferd. The devil!
   My brother fight upon the adverse party!
         [*He wounds the Cardinal, and, in the scuffle, gives
            Bosola his death-wound.*
   There flies your ransom.
Card. O justice!
   I suffer now for what hath former bin:
   Sorrow is held the eldest child of sin.
Ferd. Now you 're brave fellows. Cæsar's fortune was harder
   than Pompey's; Cæsar died in the arms of prosperity,
   Pompey at the feet of disgrace. You both died in the
   field. The pain 's nothing: pain many times is taken away
   with the apprehension of greater, as the toothache with

the sight of a barber that comes to pull it out: there's
philosophy for you.

Bos. Now my revenge is perfect.—Sink, thou main cause

                                     [Kills Ferdinand.

  Of my undoing! The last part of my life
  Hath done me best service.

Ferd. Give me some wet hay; I am broken-winded.
  I do account this world but a dog-kennel:
  I will vault credit and affect high pleasures
  Beyond death.

Bos. He seems to come to himself,
  Now he's so near the bottom.

Ferd. My sister, O my sister! there's the cause on't.
  Whether we fall by ambition, blood, or lust,
  Like diamonds, we are cut with our own dust.   *[Dies.*

Card. Thou hast thy payment too.

Bos. Yes, I hold my weary soul in my teeth;
  'Tis ready to part from me. I do glory
  That thou, which stood'st like a huge pyramid
  Begun upon a large and ample base,
  Shalt end in a little point, a kind of nothing.

    Enter, below, Pescara, Malatesti, Roderigo, and Grisolan

Pes. How now, my lord!

Mal. Oh, sad disaster!

Rod. How comes this?

Bos. Revenge for the Duchess of Malfi murder'd
  By the Arragonian brethren; for Antonio
  Slain by this hand; for lustful Julia
  Poison'd by this man; and lastly for myself,
  That was an actor in the main of all
  Much 'gainst mine own good nature, yet i' the end
  Neglected.

Pes. How now, my lord!

Card. Look to my brother:
  He gave us these large wounds, as we were struggling
  Here i' the rushes. And now, I pray, let me
  Be laid by and never thought of.   *[Dies.*

Pes. How fatally, it seems, he did withstand
  His own rescue!

Mal. Thou wretched thing of blood,
  How came Antonio by his death?

Bos. In a mist; I know not how:
   Such a mistake as I have often seen
   In a play.   Oh, I am gone!
   We are only like dead walls or vaulted graves,
   That, ruin'd, yield no echo.   Fare you well.
   It may be pain, but no harm, to me to die
   In so good a quarrel.   Oh, this gloomy world!
   In what a shadow, or deep pit of darkness,
   Doth womanish and fearful mankind live!
   Let worthy minds ne'er stagger in distrust
   To suffer death or shame for what is just:
   Mine is another voyage.   [*Dies.*
Pes. The noble Delio, as I came to the palace,
   Told me of Antonio's being here, and show'd me
   A pretty gentleman, his son and heir.

Enter Delio and Antonio's Son

Mal. Oh, sir, you come too late!
Delio. I heard so, and
   Was arm'd for 't, ere I came.   Let us make noble use
   Of this great ruin; and join all our force
   To establish this young hopeful gentleman
   In 's mother's right.   These wretched eminent things
   Leave no more fame behind 'em, than should one
   Fall in a frost, and leave his print in snow;
   As soon as the sun shines, it ever melts,
   Both form and matter.   I have ever thought
   Nature doth nothing so great for great men
   As when she 's pleas'd to make them lords of truth:
   Integrity of life is fame's best friend,
   Which nobly, beyond death, shall crown the end.   [*Exeunt.*

THE BROKEN HEART

To the Most Worthy Deserver of the
Noblest Titles in Honour

WILLIAM, LORD CRAVEN, BARON OF HAMPSTEAD-MARSHALL

My Lord,

The glory of a great name, acquired by a greater glory of action, hath in all ages lived the truest chronicle to his own memory. In the practice of which argument, your growth to perfection, even in youth, hath appeared so sincere, so unflattering a penman, that posterity cannot with more delight, read the merit of noble endeavours, than noble endeavours merit thanks from posterity, to be read with delight. Many nations, many eyes have been witnesses of your deserts, and loved them; be pleased, then, with the freedom of your own name, to admit *one*, amongst all, particularly into the list of such as honour a fair example of nobility. There is a kind of humble ambition, not uncommendable, when the silence of study breaks forth into discourse, coveting rather encouragement than applause; yet herein, censure commonly is too severe an auditor! without the moderation of an able patronage. I have ever been slow in courtship of greatness, not ignorant of such defects as are frequent to opinion; but the justice of your inclination to industry, emboldens my weakness of confidence to relish an experience of your mercy as many brave dangers have tasted of your courage. Your lordship strove to be known to the world when the world knew you least, by voluntary but excellent attempts; like allowance I plead of being known to your lordship (in this low presumption), by tendering, to a favourable entertainment, a devotion offered from a heart that can be as truly sensible of any least respect as ever profess the owner in my best, my readiest services, a lover of your natural love to virtue.

John Ford.

DRAMATIS PERSONÆ

AMYCLAS, King of Laconia.

ITHOCLES, a favourite.

ORGILUS, son of CROTOLON.

BASSANES, a jealous Nobleman.

ARMOSTES, Counsellor of State.

CROTOLON, another Counsellor.

PROPHILUS, friend of ITHOCLES.

NEARCHUS, Prince of Argos.

TECNICUS, a philosopher.

HEMOPHIL } Courtiers.
GRONEAS }

AMELUS, friend of NEARCHUS.

PHULAS, servant of BASSANES.

CALANTHA, daughter of AMYCLAS.

PENTHEA, sister of ITHOCLES and wife of BASSANES.

EUPHRANEA, daughter of CROTOLON, a Maid of Honour.

CHRISTALLA } Maids of Honour.
PHILEMA }

GRAUSIS, overseer of PENTHEA.

Lords, Courtiers, Officers, Attendants.

THE SCENE—SPARTA

PROLOGUE

Our scene is Sparta. He whose best of art
Hath drawn this piece, calls it *The Broken Heart*.
The title lends no expectation here
Of apish laughter, or of some lame jeer
At place or persons; no pretended clause
Of jests fit for a brothel, courts applause
From vulgar admiration: such low songs,
Turned to unchaste ears, suit not modest tongues.
The virgin-sisters then deserved fresh bays
When innocence and sweetness crowned their lays;
Then vices gasped for breath, whose whole commèrce
Was whipped to exile by unblushing verse.
This law we keep in our presentment now,
Not to take freedom more than we allow;
What may be here thought *Fiction*, when time's youth
Wanted some riper years, was known *A Truth*:
In which, if words have clothed the subject right,
You may partake a pity, with delight.

ACT I

Enter Crotolon and Orgilus

Crot. Dally not further; I will know the reason
    That speeds thee to this journey.
Org. 'Reason?' good sir,
    I can yield many.
Crot. Give me one, a good one;
    Such I expect, and ere we part must have:
    'Athens!' pray, why to Athens? you intend not
    To kick against the world, turn cynic, stoic,
    Or read the logic-lecture, or become
    An Areopagite, and judge in cases
    Touching the commonwealth; for, as I take it,
    The budding of your chin cannot prognosticate
    So grave an honour.
Org. All this I acknowledge.
Crot. You do! then, son, if books and love of knowledge
    Inflame you to this travel, here in Sparta
    You may as freely study.
Org. 'Tis not that, sir.
Crot. Not that, sir! As a father, I command thee
    To acquaint me with the truth.
Org. Thus, I obey you.
    After so many quarrels, as dissension,
    Fury, and rage had broached in blood, and sometimes
    With death to such confederates, as sided
    With now dead Thrasus and yourself, my lord;
    Our present king, Amyclas, reconciled
    Your eager swords, and sealed a gentle peace:
    Friends you professed yourselves; which to confirm,
    A resolution for a lasting league
    Betwixt your families, was entertained,
    By joining, in a Hymenean bond,

Me and the fair Penthea, only daughter
To Thrasus.

Crot. What of this?

Org. Much, much, dear sir.
A freedom of convèrse, an interchange
Of holy and chaste love, so fixed our souls
In a firm growth of union, that no time
Can eat into the pledge:—we had enjoyed
The sweets our vows expected, had not cruelty
Prevented all those triumphs we prepared for,
By Thrasus his untimely death.

Crot. Most certain.

Org. From this time sprouted up that poisonous stalk
Of aconite, whose ripened fruit hath ravished
All health, all comfort of a happy life:
For Ithocles, her brother, proud of youth,
And prouder in his power, nourished closely
The memory of former discontents,
To glory in revenge. By cunning partly,
Partly by threats, he woos at once and forces
His virtuous sister to admit a marriage
With Bassanes, a nobleman, in honour
And riches, I confess, beyond my fortunes——

Crot. All this is no sound reason to importune
My leave for thy departure.

Org. Now it follows.
Beauteous Penthea, wedded to this torture
By an insulting brother, being secretly
Compelled to yield her virgin freedom up
To him, who never can usurp her heart,
Before contracted mine; is now so yoked
To a most barbarous thraldom, misery,
Affliction, that he savours not humanity,
Whose sorrow melts not into more than pity,
In hearing but her name.

Crot. As how, pray?

Org. Bassanes,
The man that calls her wife, considers truly
What heaven of perfections he is lord of,
By thinking fair Penthea his; this thought
Begets a kind of monster-love, which love
Is nurse unto a fear so strong, and servile,
As brands all dotage with a jealousy.

All eyes who gaze upon that shrine of beauty,
He doth resolve, do homage to the miracle;
Someone, he is assured, may now or then
(If opportunity but sort) prevail:
So much, out of a self-unworthiness,
His fears transport him!—not that he finds cause
In her obedience, but his own distrust.

Crot. You spin out your discourse.

Org. My griefs are violent—
  For knowing how the maid was heretofore
  Courted by me, his jealousies grow wild
  That I should steal again into her favours,
  And undermine her virtues; which the gods
  Know, I nor dare, nor dream of: hence, from hence,
  I undertake a voluntary exile;
  First, by my absence to take off the cares
  Of jealous Bassanes; but chiefly, sir,
  To free Penthea from a hell on earth:
  Lastly, to lose the memory of something,
  Her presence makes to live in me afresh.

Crot. Enough, my Orgilus, enough.   To Athens,
  I give a full consent;—alas, good lady!—
  We shall hear from thee often?

Org. Often.

Crot. See,
  Thy sister comes to give a farewell.

Enter Euphranea

Euph. Brother!

Org. Euphranea, thus upon thy cheeks I print
  A brother's kiss; more careful of thine honour,
  Thy health, and thy well-doing, than my life.
  Before we part, in the presence of our father,
  I must prefer a suit to you.

Euph. You may style it,
  My brother, a command.

Org. That you will promise
  Never to pass to any man, however
  Worthy, your faith, till, with our father's leave,
  I give a free consent.

Crot. An easy motion!
  I 'll promise for her, Orgilus.

Org. Your pardon;
   Euphranea's oath must yield me satisfaction.
Euph. By Vesta's sacred fires, I swear.
Crot. And I,
   By great Apollo's beams, join in the vow;
   Not, without thy allowance, to bestow her
   On any living.
Org. Dear Euphranea,
   Mistake me not; far, far 'tis from my thought,
   As far from any wish of mine, to hinder
   Preferment to an honourable bed,
   Or fitting fortune; thou art young and handsome;
   And 'twere injustice,—more, a tyranny,
   Not to advance thy merit: trust me, sister,
   It shall be my first care to see thee matched
   As may become thy choice, and our contents.
   I have your oath.
Euph. You have; but mean you, brother,
   To leave us, as you say?
Crot. Ay, ay, Euphranea.
   He has just grounds direct him; I will prove
   A father and a brother to thee.
Euph. Heaven
   Does look into the secrets of all hearts:
   Gods! you have mercy with you, else——
Crot. Doubt nothing,
   Thy brother will return in safety to us.
Org. Souls sunk in sorrows never are without them;
   They change fresh airs, but bear their griefs about them.
                                                    [*Exeunt.*

SCENE II

*Flourish.   Enter Amyclas, Armostes, Prophilus, Courtiers and
Attendants*

Amyc. The Spartan gods are gracious; our humility
   Shall bend before their altars, and perfume
   Their temples with abundant sacrifice.
   See, lords, Amyclas, your old king, is entering
   Into his youth again! I shall shake off
   This silver badge of age, and change this snow
      O ⁸⁹⁹

For hairs as gay as are Apollo's locks;
Our heart leaps in new vigour.

Arm. May old time
Run back to double your long life, great sir!

Amyc. It will, it must, Armostes; thy bold nephew,
Death-braving Ithocles, brings to our gates
Triumphs and peace upon his conquering sword.
Laconia is a monarchy at length;
Hath in this latter war trod under foot
Messene's pride; Messene bows her neck
To Lacedemon's royalty.   Oh, 'twas
A glorious victory, and doth deserve
More than a chronicle; a temple, lords,
A temple to the name of Ithocles.
Where didst thou leave him, Prophilus?

Pro. At Pephon,
Most gracious sovereign; twenty of the noblest
Of the Messenians there attend your pleasure,
For such conditions as you shall propose,
In settling peace, and liberty of life.

Amyc. When comes your friend the general?

Pro. He promised
To follow with all speed convenient.

> *Enter Crotolon, Calantha, Euphranea, Christalla, and*
> *Philema with a garland*

Amyc. Our daughter! dear Calantha, the happy news,
The conquest of Messene, hath already
Enriched thy knowledge.

Cal. With the circumstance
And manner of the fight, related faithfully
By Prophilus himself—but, pray, sir, tell me,
How doth the youthful general demean
His actions in these fortunes?

Pro. Excellent princess,
Your own fair eyes may soon report a truth
Unto your judgment, with what moderation,
Calmness of nature, measure, bounds, and limits
Of thankfulness and joy, he doth digest
Such amplitude of his success, as would,
In others, moulded of a spirit less clear,
Advance them to comparison with heaven:
But Ithocles——

Cal. Your friend——
Pro. He is so, madam,
In which the period of my fate consists—
He, in this firmament of honour, stands
Like a star fixed, not moved with any thunder
Of popular applause, or sudden lightning
Of self-opinion; he hath served his country,
And thinks 'twas but his duty.
Crot. You describe
A miracle of man.
Amyc. Such, Crotolon,   [*Flourish.*
On forfeit of a king's word, thou wilt find him.
Hark, warning of his coming! all attend him.

*Enter Ithocles, ushered in by the Lords, and followed by
Hemophil and Groneas*

Amyc. Return into these arms, thy home, thy sanctuary,
Delight of Sparta, treasure of my bosom,
Mine own, own Ithocles!
Ith. Your humblest subject.
Arm. Proud of the blood I claim an interest in,
As brother to thy mother, I embrace thee,
Right noble nephew.
Ith. Sir, your love's too partial.
Crot. Our country speaks by me, who by thy valour,
Wisdom, and service, shares in this great action;
Returning thee, in part of thy due merits,
A general welcome.
Ith. You exceed in bounty.
Cal. Christalla, Philema, the chaplet. [*Takes the chaplet from
them.*] Ithocles,
Upon the wings of fame, the singular
And chosen fortune of an high attempt,
Is borne so past the view of common sight,
That I myself, with mine own hands, have wrought
To crown thy temples, this Provincial garland;
Accept, wear, and enjoy it as our gift
Deserved, not purchased.
Ith. You are a royal maid.
Amyc. She is, in all, our daughter.
Ith. Let me blush,
Acknowledging how poorly I have served,

What nothings I have done, compared with the honours
Heaped on the issue of a willing mind;
In that lay mine ability, that only:
For who is he so sluggish from his birth,
So little worthy of a name or country,
That owes not out of gratitude for life
A debt of service, in what kind soever,
Safety, or counsel of the commonwealth
Requires, for payment?

Cal. He speaks truth.

Ith. Whom heaven
Is pleased to style victorious, there, to such,
Applause runs madding, like the drunken priests
In Bacchus' sacrifices, without reason,
Voicing the leader-on a demi-god;
Whenas, indeed, each common soldier's blood
Drops down as current coin in that hard purchase,
As his, whose much more delicate condition
Hath sucked the milk of ease: judgment commands,
But resolution executes.   I use not,
Before this royal presence, these fit slights,
As in contempt of such as can direct;
My speech hath other end; not to attribute
All praise to one man's fortune, which is strengthened
By many hands: for instance, here is Prophilus,
A gentleman (I cannot flatter truth)
Of much desert; and, though in other rank,
Both Hemophil and Groneas were not missing
To wish their country's peace; for, in a word,
All there did strive their best, and 'twas our duty.

Amyc. Courtiers turn soldiers!—We vouchsafe our hand;

[*Hemophil and Groneas kiss his hand.*

Observe your great example.

Hem. With all diligence.

Gron. Obsequiously and hourly.

Amyc. Some repose
After these toils is needful.   We must think on
Conditions for the conquered; they expect them.
On!—Come, my Ithocles.

Euph. Sir, with your favour.
I need not a supporter.

Pro. Fate instructs me.

*[Exit Amyclas attended; Ithocles, Calantha, etc.—As Christalla
    and Philema are following Calantha, they are detained by
    Hemophil and Groneas.*

Chris. With me?
Phil. Indeed I dare not stay.
Hem. Sweet lady,
   Soldiers are blunt,—your lip.   *[Kisses her.*
Chris. Fye, this is rudeness;
   You went not hence such creatures.
Gron. Spirit of valour
   Is of a mounting nature.
Phil. It appears so.
   Pray [now], in earnest, how many men apiece
   Have you two been the death of?
Gron. 'Faith, not many;
   We were composed of mercy.
Hem. For our daring,
   You heard the general's approbation
   Before the king.
Chris. You '*wished* your country's peace';
   That showed your charity: where are your spoils,
   Such as the soldier fights for?
Phil. They are coming.
Chris. By the next carrier, are they not?
Gron. Sweet Philema,
   When I was in the thickest of mine enemies,
   Slashing off one man's head, another's nose,
   Another's arms and legs——
Phil. And all together.
Gron. Then I would with a sigh remember thee,
   And cry, 'Dear Philema, 'tis for thy sake
   I do these deeds of wonder!'—dost not love me
   With all thy heart now?
Phil. Now, as heretofore.
   I have not put my love to use; the principal
   Will hardly yield an interest.
Gron. By Mars,
   I 'll marry thee!
Phil. By Vulcan, you 're forsworn,
   Except my mind do alter strangely.
Gron. One word.
Chris. You lie beyond all modesty;—forbear me.

Hem. I 'll make thee mistress of a city, 'tis
   Mine own by conquest.
Chris. By petition!—sue for 't
   In *forma pauperis.*—'City?' kennel.—Gallants!
   Off with your feathers, put on aprons, gallants;
   Learn to reel, thrum, or trim a lady's dog,
   And be good quiet souls of peace, hobgoblins!
Hem. Christalla!
Chris. Practise to drill hogs, in hope
   To share in the acorns.—Soldiers! corncutters,
   But not so valiant; they oft-times draw blood,
   Which you durst never do.   When you have practis'd
   More wit, or more civility, we 'll rank you
   I' th' list of men; till then, brave things at arms,
   Dare not to speak to us,—most potent Groneas!
Phil. And Hemophil the hardy—at your services.
                              [*Exeunt Christalla and Philema.*
Gron. They scorn us as they did before we went.
Hem. Hang them, let us scorn them; and be revenged.
Gron. Shall we?
Hem. We will; and when we slight them thus,
   Instead of following them, they 'll follow us;
   It is a woman's nature.
Gron. 'Tis a scurvy one.   [*Exeunt.*

SCENE III

Enter Tecnicus, and Orgilus disguised, like one of his scholars

Tec. Tempt not the stars, young man, thou canst not play
   With the severity of fate; this change
   Of habit and disguise in outward view
   Hides not the secrets of thy soul within thee
   From their quick-piercing eyes, which dive at all times
   Down to thy thoughts: in thy aspèct I note
   A consequence of danger.
Org. Give me leave,
   Grave Tecnicus, without foredooming destiny,
   Under thy roof to ease my silent griefs,
   By applying to my hidden wounds the balm
   Of thy oraculous lectures: if my fortune
   Run such a crooked by-way as to wrest
   My steps to ruin, yet thy learned precepts

Shall call me back and set my footings straight.
I will not court the world.
Tec. Ah, Orgilus,
  Neglects in young men of delights and life,
  Run often to extremities; they care not
  For harms to others, who contemn their own.
Org. But I, most learnèd artist, am not so much
  At odds with nature, that I grudge the thrift
  Of any true deserver; nor doth malice
  Of present hopes, so check them with despair,
  As that I yield to thought of more affliction
  Than what is incident to frailty: wherefore
  Impute not this retirèd course of living
  Some little time, to any other cause
  Than what I justly render; the information
  Of an unsettled mind; as the effect
  Must clearly witness.
Tec. Spirit of truth inspire thee!
  On these conditions I conceal thy change,
  And willingly admit thee for an auditor.—
  I 'll to my study.   [*Exit.*
Org. I to contemplations,
  In these delightful walks.—Thus metamorphosed,
  I may without suspicion hearken after
  Penthea's usage, and Euphranea's faith.
  Love, thou art full of mystery! the deities
  Themselves are not secure, in searching out
  The secrets of those flames, which, hidden, waste
  A breast, made tributary to the laws
  Of beauty; physic yet hath never found
  A remedy to cure a lover's wound.—
  Ha! who are those that cross yon private walk
  Into the shadowing grove, in amorous foldings?

Prophilus and Euphranea pass by, arm in arm, and whispering

  My sister; oh, my sister! 'tis Euphranea
  With Prophilus; supported too! I would
  It were an apparition! Prophilus
  Is Ithocles his friend: it strangely puzzles me.—
                          [*Re-enter Prophilus and Euphranea.*
  Again! help me my book; this scholar's habit
  Must stand my privilege; my mind is busy,
  Mine eyes and ears are open. [*Walks aside, pretending to read.*

Pro. Do not waste
    The span of this stolen time, lent by the gods
    For precious use, in niceness.   Bright Euphranea,
    Should I repeat old vows, or study new,
    For purchase of belief to my desires.—
Org. Desires!
Pro. My service, my integrity.—
Org. That 's better.
Pro. I should but repeat a lesson
    Oft conn'd without a prompter, but thine eyes:
    My love is honourable.—
Org. So was mine
    To my Penthea; chastely honourable.
Pro. Nor wants there more addition to my wish
    Of happiness, than having thee a wife;
    Already sure of Ithocles, a friend
    Firm and unalterable.
Org. But a brother
    More cruel than the grave.
Euph. What can you look for
    In answer to your noble protestations,
    From an unskilful maid, but language suited
    To a divided mind?
Org. Hold out, Euphranea!
Euph. Know, Prophilus, I never undervalued,
    From the first time you mention'd worthy love,
    Your merit, means, or person; it had been
    A fault of judgment in me, and a dullness
    In my affections, not to weigh and thank
    My better stars, that offered me the grace
    Of so much blissfulness: for, to speak truth,
    The law of my desires kept equal pace
    With yours; nor have I left that resolution:
    But only, in a word, whatever choice
    Lives nearest in my heart, must first procure
    Consent, both from my father and my brother,
    Ere he can own me his.
Org. She is forsworn else.
Pro. Leave me that task.
Euph. My brother, ere he parted
    To Athens, had my oath.
Org. Yes, yes, he had sure.

Pro. I doubt not, with the means the court supplies,
   But to prevail at pleasure.
Org. Very likely!
Pro. Meantime, best, dearest, I may build my hopes
   On the foundation of thy constant sufferance,
   In any opposition.
Euph. Death shall sooner
   Divorce life, and the joys I have in living,
   Than my chaste vows from truth.
Pro. On thy fair hand
   I seal the like.
Org. There is no faith in woman.
   Passion, oh, be contained!—my very heart-strings
   Are on the tenters.
Euph. We are overheard.
   Cupid protect us! 'twas a stirring, sir,
   Of someone near.
Pro. Your fears are needless, lady;
   None have access into these private pleasures,
   Except some near in court, or bosom student
   From Tecnicus his oratory; granted
   By special favour lately from the king
   Unto the grave philosopher.
Euph. Methinks
   I hear one talking to himself—I see him.
Pro. 'Tis a poor scholar; as I told you, lady.
Org. I am discovered.—Say it; is it possible,
               [*Half aloud to himself, as if studying.*
   With a smooth tongue, a leering countenance,
   Flattery, or force of reason—I come to you, sir—
   To turn or to appease the raging sea?
   Answer to that.—Your art!—what art? to catch
   And hold fast in a net the sun's small atoms?
   No, no; they 'll out; you may as easily
   Outrun a cloud driven by a northern blast,
   As—fiddle-faddle so! peace, or speak sense.
Euph. Call you this thing a scholar? 'las, he 's lunatic.
Pro. Observe him, sweet; 'tis but his recreation.
Org. But you will hear a little? You are so tetchy,
   You keep no rule in argument; philosophy
   Works not upon impossibilities,
   But natural conclusions.—Mew!—*absurd!*
   The metaphysics are but speculations

Of the celestial bodies, or such accidents
As not mixed perfectly, in the air engendered,
Appear to us unnatural; that 's all.
Prove it;—yet, with a reverence to your gravity,
I 'll balk illiterate sauciness, submitting
My sole opinion to the touch of writers.
Pro. Now let us fall in with him.   [*They come forward.*
Org. Ha, ha, ha!
  These apish boys, when they but taste the grammates,
  And principles of theory, imagine
  They can oppose their teachers.   Confidence
  Leads many into errors.
Pro. By your leave, sir.
Euph. Are you a scholar, friend?
Org. I am, gay creature,
  With pardon of your deities, a mushroom
  On whom the dew of heaven drops now and then;
  The sun shines on me too, I thank his beams!
  Sometimes I feel their warmth; and eat and sleep.
Pro. Does Tecnicus read to thee?
Org. Yes, forsooth,
  He is my master surely; yonder door
  Opens upon his study.
Pro. Happy creatures!
  Such people toil not, sweet, in heats of state,
  Nor sink in thaws of greatness: their affections
  Keep order with the limits of their modesty;
  Their love is love of virtue.—What 's thy name?
Org. Aplotes, sumptuous master, a poor wretch.
Euph. Dost thou want anything?
Org. Books, Venus, books.
Pro. Lady, a new conceit comes in my thought,
  And most available for both our comforts.
Euph. My lord,——
Pro. While I endeavour to deserve
  Your father's blessing to our loves, this scholar
  May daily at some certain hours attend,
  What notice I can write of my success,
  Here, in this grove, and give it to your hands;
  The like from you to me: so can we never,
  Barr'd of our mutual speech, want sure intelligence;
  And thus our hearts may talk when our tongues cannot.
Euph. Occasion is most favourable; use it.

Pro. Aplotes, wilt thou wait us twice a day,
  At nine i' the morning, and at four at night,
  Here, in this bower, to convey such letters
  As each shall send to other? Do it willingly,
  Safely, and secretly, and I will furnish
  Thy study, or what else thou canst desire.

Org. Jove, make me thankful, thankful, I beseech thee,
  Propitious Jove! I will prove sure and trusty:
  You will not fail me books?

Pro. Nor aught besides,
  Thy heart can wish.   This lady's name 's Euphranea,
  Mine Prophilus.

Org. I have a pretty memory;
  It must prove my best friend—I will not miss
  One minute of the hours appointed.

Pro. Write
  The books thou would'st have bought thee, in a note,
  Or take thyself some money.

Org. No, no money:
  Money to scholars is a spirit invisible,
  We dare not finger it; or books, or nothing.

Pro. Books of what sort thou wilt: do not forget
  Our names.

Org. I warrant ye, I warrant ye.

Pro. Smile, Hymen, on the growth of our desires;
  We 'll feed thy torches with eternal fires!

                    [*Exeunt Prophilus and Euphranea.*

Org. Put out thy torches, Hymen, or their light
  Shall meet a darkness of eternal night!
  Inspire me, Mercury, with swift deceits.
  Ingenious Fate has leapt into mine arms,
  Beyond the compass of my brains.—Mortality
  Creeps on the dung of earth, and cannot reach
  The riddles which are purposed by the gods.
  Great arts best write themselves in their own stories;
  They die too basely, who outlive their glories.   [*Exit.*

ACT II

SCENE I

Enter Bassanes and Phulas

Bass. I 'll have that window next the street dammed up;
　　It gives too full a prospect to temptation,
　　And courts a gazer's glances: there 's a lust
　　Committed by the eye, that sweats and travails,
　　Plots, wakes, contrives, till the deformed bear-whelp,
　　Adultery, be licked into the act,
　　The very act:—that light shall be dammed up;
　　D' ye hear, sir?
Phu. I do hear, my lord; a mason
　　Shall be provided suddenly.
Bass. Some rogue,
　　Some rogue of your confederacy, (factor
　　For slaves and strumpets!) to convey close packets
　　From this spruce springal, and the t' other youngster;
　　That gaudy earwig, or my lord your patron,
　　Whose pensioner you are.—I 'll tear thy throat out,
　　Son of a cat, ill-looking hounds-head, rip up
　　Thy ulcerous maw, if I but scent a paper,
　　A scroll, but half as big as what can cover
　　A wart upon thy nose, a spot, a pimple,
　　Directed to my lady; it may prove
　　A mystical preparative to lewdness.
Phu. Care shall be had.—I will turn every thread
　　About me to an eye.—Here 's a sweet life!   [*Aside.*
Bass. The city housewives, cunning in the traffic
　　Of chamber merchandise, set all at price
　　By wholesale; yet they wipe their mouths and simper,
　　Coll, kiss, and cry 'sweetheart', and stroke the head
　　Which they have branched; and all is well again!
　　Dull clods of dirt, who dare not feel the rubs
　　Stuck on the forehead.
Phu. 'Tis a villainous world;
　　One cannot hold his own in 't.
Bass. Dames at court
　　Who flaunt in riots, run another bias:
　　Their pleasure heaves the patient ass that suffers

Upon the stilts of office, titles, incomes;
Promotion justifies the shame, and sues for 't.
Poor honour! thou art stabbed, and bleed'st to death
By such unlawful hire.   The country mistress
Is yet more wary, and in blushes hides
Whatever trespass draws her troth to guilt;
But all are false: on this truth I am bold,
No woman but can fall, and doth, or would.—
Now, for the newest news about the city;
What blab the voices, sirrah?
Phu. Oh, my lord,
The rarest, quaintest, strangest, tickling news,
That ever——
Bass. Hey-day! up and ride me, rascal!
What is 't?
Phu. Forsooth, they say, the king has mew'd
All his grey beard, instead of which is budded
Another of a pure carnation colour,
Speckled with green and russet.
Bass. Ignorant block!
Phu. Yes, truly; and 'tis talk'd about the streets,
That since Lord Ithocles came home, the lions
Never left roaring, at which noise the bears
Have danced their very hearts out.
Bass. Dance out thine too.
Phu. Besides, Lord Orgilus is fled to Athens
Upon a fiery dragon, and 'tis thought
He never can return.
Bass. Grant it, Apollo!
Phu. Moreover, please your lordship, 'tis reported
For certain, that whoever is found jealous
Without apparent proof that 's wife is wanton,
Shall be divorced;—but this is but she-news,
I had it from a midwife.   I have more yet.
Bass. Antic, no more! idiots and stupid fools
Grate my calamities.   Why to be fair,
Should yield presumption of a faulty soul——
Look to the doors.
Phu. The horn of plenty crest him!   [*Aside, and exit.*
Bass. Swarms of confusion huddle in my thoughts
In rare distemper.—Beauty! oh, it is
An unmatched blessing, or a horrid curse.
She comes, she comes! so shoots the morning forth,

Spangled with pearls of transparent dew.—
The way to poverty is to be rich;
As I in her am wealthy; but for her,
In all contents, a bankrupt.   [*Enter Penthea and Grausis.*
Loved Penthea!
How fares my heart's best joy?

Grau. In sooth not well,
   She is so over-sad.

Bass. Leave chattering, magpie.—
   Thy brother is returned, sweet, safe, and honoured
   With a triumphant victory; thou shalt visit him;
   We will to court, where, if it be thy pleasure,
   Thou shalt appear in such a ravishing lustre
   Of jewels above value, that the dames
   Who brave it there, in rage to be outshined,
   Shall hide them in their closets, and unseen
   Fret in their tears; whilst every wondering eye
   Shall crave none other brightness but thy presence.
   Choose thine own recreations; be a queen
   Of what delights thou fanciest best, what company,
   What place, what times; do anything, do all things
   Youth can command, so thou wilt chase these clouds
   From the pure firmament of thy fair looks.

Grau. Now, 'tis well said, my lord.   What, lady! laugh,
   Be merry; time is precious.

Bass. Furies whip thee!   [*Aside.*

Pen. Alas, my lord! this language to your handmaid
   Sounds as would music to the deaf; I need
   No braveries, nor cost of art, to draw
   The whiteness of my name into offence:
   Let such, if any such there are, who covet
   A curiosity of admiration,
   By laying out their plenty to full view,
   Appear in gaudy outsides; my attires
   Shall suit the inward fashion of my mind;
   From which, if your opinion, nobly placed,
   Change not the livery your words bestow,
   My fortunes with my hopes are at the highest.

Bass. This house, methinks, stands somewhat too much inward,
   It is too melancholy; we 'll remove
   Nearer the court: or what thinks my Penthea
   Of the delightful island we command?
   Rule me as thou canst wish.

Pen. I am no mistress:
    Whither you please, I must attend; all ways
    Are alike pleasant to me.
Grau. 'Island!' prison;
    A prison is as gaysome: we 'll no islands;
    Marry, out upon 'em! whom shall we see there?
    Sea-gulls, and porpoises, and water-rats,
    And crabs, and mews, and dog-fish; goodly gear
    For a young lady's dealings,—or an old one's!
    On no terms, islands; I 'll be stewed first.
Bass. [*Aside to Grausis.*] Grausis,
    You are a juggling bawd.—This sadness, sweetest,
    Becomes not youthful blood;—I 'll have you pounded—
    For my sake put on a more cheerful mirth;
    Thou 'lt mar thy cheeks, and make me old in griefs.
    Damnable bitch-fox!   [*To Grausis.*
Grau. I am thick of hearing,
    Still, when the wind blows southerly.—What think you,
    If your fresh lady breed young bones, my lord!
    Would not a chopping boy do you good at heart?
    But, as you said——
Bass. I 'll spit thee on a stake,
    Or chop thee into collops!   [*Aside to Grausis.*
Grau. Pray, speak louder.
    Sure, sure the wind blows south still.
Pen. Thou prat'st madly.
Bass. 'Tis very hot; I sweat extremely.—Now?

Enter Phulas

Phu. A herd of lords, sir.
Bass. Ha!
Phu. A flock of ladies.
Bass. Where?
Phu. Shoals of horses.
Bass. Peasant, how?
Phu. Caroches.
    In drifts—the one enter, the other stand without, sir,
    And now I vanish.   [*Exit.*

Enter Prophilus, Hemophil, Groneas, Christalla and Philema

Pro. Noble Bassanes!
Bass. Most welcome, Prophilus: ladies, gentlemen,
    To all, my heart is open; you all honour me.—

(A tympany swells in my head already)   [*Aside.*
Honour me bountifully.—How they flutter,
Wagtails and jays together!   [*Aside.*

Pro. From your brother,
  By virtue of your love to him, I require
  Your instant presence, fairest.

Pen. He is well, sir?

Pro. The gods preserve him ever! Yet, dear beauty,
  I find some alteration in him lately,
  Since his return to Sparta.—My good lord,
  I pray, use no delay.

Bass. We had not needed
  An invitation, if his sister's health
  Had not fallen into question.—Haste, Penthea,
  Slack not a minute; lead the way, good Prophilus,
  I 'll follow step by step.

Pro. Your arm, fair madam.
             [*Exeunt all but Bassanes and Grausis.*

Bass. One word with your old bawdship: thou hadst better
  Railed at the saints thou worshipp'st than have thwarted
  My will; I 'll use thee cursedly.

Grau. You dote,
  You are beside yourself.   A politician
  In jealousy? no, you 're too gross, too vulgar.
  Pish, teach not me my trade; I know my cue:
  My crossing you sinks me into her trust,
  By which I shall know all; my trade 's a sure one.

Bass. Forgive me, Grausis, 'twas consideration
  I relished not; but have a care now.

Grau. Fear not,
  I am no new-come-to 't.

Bass. Thy life 's upon it,
  And so is mine.   My agonies are infinite.   [*Exeunt.*

Scene II

Enter Ithocles

Ith. Ambition! 'tis of viper's breed: it gnaws
  A passage through the womb that gave it motion.
  Ambition, like a seeled dove, mounts upward,
  Higher and higher still, to perch on clouds,

But tumbles headlong down with heavier ruin.
So squibs and crackers fly into the air,
Then, only breaking with a noise, they vanish
In stench and smoke.   Morality, applied
To timely practice, keeps the soul in tune,
At whose sweet music all our actions dance:
But this is formed of books, and school-tradition;
It physics not the sickness of a mind
Broken with griefs: strong fevers are not eased
With counsel, but with best receipts, and means:
Means, speedy means, and certain; that 's the cure.

Enter Armostes and Crotolon

Arm. You stick, Lord Crotolon, upon a point
　　Too nice and too unnecessary; Prophilus
　　Is every way desertful.   I am confident
　　Your wisdom is too ripe to need instruction
　　From your son's tutelage.
Crot. Yet not so ripe,
　　My Lord Armostes, that it dares to dote
　　Upon the painted meat of smooth persuasion,
　　Which tempts me to a breach of faith.
Ith. Not yet
　　Resolved, my lord? Why, if your son's consent
　　Be so available, we 'll write to Athens
　　For his repair to Sparta: the king's hand
　　Will join with our desires; he has been moved to 't.
Arm. Yes, and the king himself importuned Crotolon
　　For a dispatch.
Crot. Kings may command; their wills
　　Are laws not to be questioned.
Ith. By this marriage
　　You knit a union so devout, so hearty,
　　Between your loves to me, and mine to yours,
　　As if mine own blood had an interest in it;
　　For Prophilus is mine, and I am his.
Crot. My lord, my lord!
Ith. What, good sir? speak your thought.
Crot. Had this sincerity been real once,
　　My Orgilus had not been now unwived,
　　Nor your lost sister buried in a bride-bed:
　　Your uncle here, Armostes, knows this truth;
　　　p 899

For had your father Thrasus lived—but peace
Dwell in his grave! I have done.

Arm. You are bold and bitter.

Ith. He presses home the injury; it smarts.—   [*Aside.*
No reprehensions, uncle; I deserve them.
Yet, gentle sir, consider what the heat
Of an unsteady youth, a giddy brain,
Green indiscretion, flattery of greatness,
Rawness of judgment, wilfulness in folly,
Thoughts vagrant as the wind, and as uncertain,
Might lead a boy in years to:—'twas a fault,
A capital fault; for then I could not dive
Into the secrets of commanding love;
Since when experience, by the extremes in others,
Hath forced me to collect—and, trust me, Crotolon,
I will redeem those wrongs with any service
Your satisfaction can require for current.

Arm. The acknowledgment is satisfaction:
What would you more?

Crot. I am conquered: if Euphranea
Herself admit the motion, let it be so;
I doubt not my son's liking.

Ith. Use my fortunes,
Life, power, sword and heart, all are your own.

Arm. The princess, with your sister.

*Enter Bassanes, Prophilus, Calantha, Penthea, Euphranea,
Christalla, Philema, and Grausis*

Cal. I present you
A stranger here in court, my lord; for did not
Desire of seeing you draw her abroad,
We had not been made happy in her company.

Ith. You are a gracious princess.—Sister, wedlock
Holds too severe a passion in your nature,
Which can engross all duty to your husband,
Without attendance on so dear a mistress.
'Tis not my brother's pleasure, I presume,   [*To Bassanes.*
T' immure her in a chamber.

Bass. 'Tis her will;
She governs her own hours.   Noble Ithocles,
We thank the gods for your success and welfare:
Our lady has of late been indisposed,
Else we had waited on you with the first.

Ith. How does Penthea now?
Pen. You best know, brother,
  From whom my health and comforts are derived.
Bass. [*Aside.*] I like the answer well; 'tis sad and modest.
  There may be tricks yet, tricks—— Have an eye, Grausis!
Cal. Now, Crotolon, the suit we joined in must not
  Fall by too long demur.
Crot. 'Tis granted, princess,
  For my part.
Arm. With condition, that his son
  Favour the contract.
Cal. Such delay is easy.
  The joys of marriage make thee, Prophilus,
  A proud deserver of Euphranea's love,
  And her of thy desert!
Pro. Most sweetly gracious!
Bass. The joys of marriage are the heaven on earth,
  Life's paradise, great princess, the soul's quiet,
  Sinews of concord, earthly immortality,
  Eternity of pleasures;—no restoratives
  Like to a constant woman!—(but where is she?
  'Twould puzzle all the gods, but to create
  Such a new monster) [*Aside.*]—I can speak by proof,
  For the rest in Elysium; 'tis my happiness.
Crot. Euphranea, how are you resolved, speak freely,
  In your affections to this gentleman?
Euph. Nor more, nor less than as his love assures me:
  Which (if your liking with my brother's warrants)
  I cannot but approve in all points worthy.
Crot. So, so! I know your answer.   [*To Prophilus.*
Ith. 'T had been pity,
  To sunder hearts so equally consented.

Enter Hemophil

Hem. The king, Lord Ithocles, commands your presence;
  And, fairest princess, yours.
Cal. We will attend him.

Enter Groneas

Gron. Where are the lords? all must unto the king
  Without delay; the Prince of Argos——
Cal. Well, sir?
Gron. Is coming to the court, sweet lady.

Cal. How!

   The Prince of Argos?

Gron. 'Twas my fortune, madam,

   T' enjoy the honour of these happy tidings.

Ith. Penthea!

Pen. Brother.

Ith. Let me an hour hence

   Meet you alone, within the palace grove,

   I have some secret with you.—Prithee, friend,

   Conduct her thither, and have special care

   The walks be cleared of any to disturb us.

Pro. I shall.

Bass. How 's that?

Ith. Alone, pray be alone.—

   I am your creature, princess.—On, my lords.

                        [Exeunt all but Bassanes.

Bass. Alone? alone? what means that word *alone?*

   Why might not I be there?—hum!—he 's her brother.

   Brothers and sisters are but flesh and blood,

   And this same whoreson court-ease is temptation

   To a rebellion in the veins;—besides,

   His fine friend Prophilus must be her guardian:

   Why may not he dispatch a business nimbly

   Before the other come?—or—pandering, pandering

   For one another—(be 't to sister, mother,

   Wife, cousin, anything,) 'mongst youths of metal

   Is in request; it is so—stubborn fate!

   But if I be a cuckold, and can know it,

   I will be fell, and fell.

Re-enter Groneas

Gron. My lord, you are called for.

Bass. Most heartily I thank you: where 's my wife, pray?

Gron. Retired amongst the ladies.

Bass. Still I thank you.

   There 's an old waiter with her, saw you her too?

Gron. She sits i' th' presence-lobby fast asleep, sir.

Bass. Asleep? asleep, sir!

Gron. Is your lordship troubled?

   You will not to the king?

Bass. Your humblest vassal.

Gron. Your servant, my good lord.

Bass. I wait your footsteps.   *[Exeunt.*

SCENE III

Enter Prophilus and Penthea

Pro. In this walk, lady, will your brother find you;
    And, with your favour, give me leave a little
    To work a preparation: in his fashion
    I have observed of late some kind of slackness
    To such alacrity as nature [once]
    And custom took delight in; sadness grows
    Upon his recreations, which he hoards
    In such a willing silence, that to question
    The grounds will argue [little] skill in friendship,
    And less good manners.
Pen. Sir, I am not inquisitive
    Of secrecies, without an invitation.
Pro. With pardon, lady, not a syllable
    Of mine implies so rude a sense; the drift——

                                     [*Enter Orgilus, as before.*
    Do thy best   [*To Orgilus.*
    To make this lady merry for an hour.
Org. Your will shall be a law, sir.   [*Exit Prophilus.*
Pen. Prithee, leave me,
    I have some private thoughts I would account with;
    Use thou thine own.
Org. Speak on, fair nymph, our souls
    Can dance as well to music of the spheres,
    As any 's who have feasted with the gods.
Pen. Your school-terms are too troublesome.
Org. What heaven
    Refines mortality from dross of earth,
    But such as uncompounded beauty hallows
    With glorified perfection!
Pen. Set thy wits
    In a less wild proportion.
Org. Time can never
    On the white table of unguilty faith
    Write counterfeit dishonour; turn those eyes
    (The arrows of pure love) upon that fire,
    Which once rose to a flame, perfumed with vows,
    As sweetly scented as the incense smoking
    On Vesta's altars, . . .
    . . . the holiest odours, virgin's tears,

    . . . sprinkled, like dews, to feed them
    And to increase their fervour.

Pen. Be not frantic.

Org. All pleasures are but mere imagination,
    Feeding the hungry appetite with steam,
    And sight of banquet, whilst the body pines,
    Not relishing the real taste of food:
    Such is the leanness of a heart, divided
    From intercourse of troth-contracted loves;
    No horror should deface that precious figure
    Seal'd with the lively stamp of equal souls.

Pen. Away! some fury hath bewitch'd thy tongue:
    The breath of ignorance that flies from thence,
    Ripens a knowledge in me of afflictions,
    Above all sufferance.—Thing of talk, begone,
    Begone, without reply!

Org. Be just, Penthea,
    In thy commands; when thou send'st forth a doom
    Of banishment, know first on whom it lights.
    Thus I take off the shroud, in which my cares
    Are folded up from view of common eyes.

                     [Throws off his scholar's dress.

    What is thy sentence next?

Pen. Rash man! thou lay'st
    A blemish on mine honour, with the hazard
    Of thy too desperate life; yet I profess,
    By all the laws of ceremonious wedlock,
    I have not given admittance to one thought
    Of female change, since cruelty enforced
    Divorce betwixt my body and my heart.
    Why would you fall from goodness thus?

Org. Oh, rather
    Examine me, how I could live to say
    I have been much, much wronged.   'Tis for thy sake
    I put on this imposture; dear Penthea,
    If thy soft bosom be not turned to marble,
    Thou 'lt pity our calamities; my interest
    Confirms me, thou art mine still.

Pen. Lend your hand;
    With both of mine I clasp it thus, thus kiss it,
    Thus kneel before ye.   *[Penthea kneels.*

Org. You instruct my duty.   *[Orgilus kneels.*

Pen. We may stand up. [*They rise.*] Have you aught else to
    urge
  Of new demand? as for the old, forget it;
  'Tis buried in an everlasting silence,
  And shall be, shall be ever: what more would you?
Org. I would possess my wife; the equity
  Of very reason bids me.
Pen. Is that all?
Org. Why, 'tis the all of me, myself.
Pen. Remove
  Your steps some distance from me; at this space
  A few words I dare change; but first put on
  Your borrow'd shape.
Org. You are obey'd; 'tis done.   [*He resumes his disguise.*
Pen. How, Orgilus, by promise, I was thine,
  The heavens do witness; they can witness too
  A rape done on my truth: how I do love thee
  Yet, Orgilus, and yet, must best appear
  In tendering thy freedom; for I find
  The constant preservation of thy merit,
  By thy not daring to attempt my fame
  With injury of any loose conceit,
  Which might give deeper wounds to discontents.
  Continue this fair race; then, though I cannot
  Add to thy comfort, yet I shall more often
  Remember from what fortune I am fallen,
  And pity mine own ruin. Live, live happy,
  Happy in thy next choice, that thou may'st people
  This barren age with virtues in thy issue!
  And, oh, when thou art married, think on me
  With mercy, not contempt; I hope thy wife,
  Hearing my story, will not scorn my fall.—
  Now let us part.
Org. Part! yet advise thee better:
  Penthea is the wife to Orgilus,
  And ever shall be.
Pen. Never shall, nor will.
Org. How!
Pen. Hear me; in a word I'll tell thee why.
  The virgin-dowry which my birth bestow'd,
  Is ravished by another; my true love
  Abhors to think, that Orgilus deserved
  No better favours than a second bed.

Org. I must not take this reason.

Pen.   To confirm it;
Should I outlive my bondage, let me meet
Another worse than this, and less desired,
If, of all men alive, thou should'st but touch
My lip, or hand again!

Org.   Penthea, now
I tell you, you grow wanton in my sufferance;
Come, sweet, thou art mine.

Pen.   Uncivil sir, forbear,
Or I can turn affection into vengeance;
Your reputation, if you value any,
Lies bleeding at my feet.   Unworthy man,
If ever henceforth thou appear in language,
Message, or letter, to betray my frailty,
I 'll call thy former protestations lust,
And curse my stars for forfeit of my judgment.
Go thou, fit only for disguise, and walks,
To hide thy shame; this once I spare thy life.
I laugh at mine own confidence; my sorrows
By thee are made inferior to my fortunes:
If ever thou didst harbour worthy love,
Dare not to answer.   My good Genius guide me,
That I may never see thee more!—Go from me!

Org. I 'll tear my veil of politic French off,
And stand up like a man resolved to do:—
Action, not words, shall show me.—Oh, Penthea!   [*Exit.*

Pen. He sighed my name sure, as he parted from me;
I fear I was too rough.   Alas, poor gentleman!
He look'd not like the ruins of his youth,
But like the ruins of those ruins.   Honour,
How much we fight with weakness to preserve thee!

                                        [*Walks aside.*

Enter Bassanes and Grausis

Bass. Fie on thee! damn thee, rotten maggot, damn thee!
Sleep, sleep at court? and now?   Aches, convulsions,
Imposthumes, rheums, gouts, palsies, clog thy bones
A dozen years more yet!

Grau. Now you are in humours.

Bass. She 's by herself, there 's hope of that; she 's sad too;
She 's in strong contemplation; yes, and fixed:
The signs are wholesome.

Grau. Very wholesome, truly.

Bass. Hold your chops, nightmare!—Lady, come; your brother
   Is carried to his closet; you must thither.

Pen. Not well, my lord?

Bass. A sudden fit, 'twill off;
   Some surfeit of disorder.—How dost, dearest?

Pen. Your news is none o' th' best.

Enter Prophilus

Pro. The chief of men.
   The excellentest Ithocles, desires
   Your presence, madam.

Bass. We are hasting to him.

Pen. In vain we labour in this course of life
   To piece our journey out at length, or crave
   Respite of breath; our home is in the grave.

Bass. Perfect philosophy!

Pen. Then let us care
   To live so, that our reckonings may fall even,
   When we 're to make account.

Pro. He cannot fear
   Who builds on noble grounds: sickness or pain
   Is the deserver's exercise; and such
   Your virtuous brother to the world is known.
   Speak comfort to him, lady, be all gentle;
   Stars fall but in the grossness of our sight,
   A good man dying, th' earth doth lose a light.   [*Exeunt.*

ACT III

SCENE I

Enter Tecnicus, and Orgilus, in his usual dress

Tec. Be well advised; let not a resolution
  Of giddy rashness choke the breath of reason.
Org. It shall not, most sage master.
Tec. I am jealous;
  For if the borrow'd shape so late put on,
  Inferred a consequence, we must conclude
  Some violent design of sudden nature
  Hath shook that shadow off, to fly upon
  A new-hatch'd execution. Orgilus,
  Take heed thou hast not, under our integrity,
  Shrouded unlawful plots; our mortal eyes
  Pierce not the secrets of your heart, the gods
  Are only privy to them.
Org. Learned Tecnicus,
  Such doubts are causeless; and, to clear the truth
  From misconceit,—the present state commands me.
  The Prince of Argos comes himself in person
  In quest of great Calantha for his bride,
  Our kingdom's heir; besides, mine only sister,
  Euphranea, is disposed to Prophilus:
  Lastly, the king is sending letters for me
  To Athens, for my quick repair to court;
  Please to accept these reasons.
Tec. Just ones, Orgilus,
  Not to be contradicted: yet, beware
  Of an unsure foundation; no fair colours
  Can fortify a building faintly jointed.
  I have observ'd a growth in thy aspèct
  Of dangerous extent, sudden, and—look to 't—
  I might add, certain——
Org. My aspect! could art
  Run through mine inmost thoughts, it should not sift
  An inclination there, more than what suited
  With justice of mine honour.
Tec. I believe it.
  But know then, Orgilus, what honour is:

Honour consists not in a bare opinion
By doing any act that feeds content,
Brave in appearance, 'cause we think it brave;
Such honour comes by accident, not nature,
Proceeding from the vices of our passion,
Which makes our reason drunk: but real honour
Is the reward of virtue, and acquired
By justice, or by valour which, for basis,
Hath justice to uphold it.   He then fails
In honour, who, for lucre or revenge,
Commits thefts, murther, treasons, and adulteries,
With such like, by intrenching on just laws,
Whose sovereignty is best preserv'd by Justice.
Thus, as you see how honour must be grounded
On knowledge, not opinion, (for opinion
Relies on probability and accident,
But knowledge on necessity and truth,)
I leave thee to the fit consideration
Of what becomes the grace of real honour,
Wishing success to all thy virtuous meanings.
Org. The gods increase thy wisdom, reverend oracle,
    And in thy precepts make me ever thrifty!   [*Exit.*
Tec. I thank thy wish.—Much mystery of fate
    Lies hid in that man's fortunes; curiosity
    May lead his actions into rare attempts:
    But let the gods be moderators still;
    No human power can prevent their will.
                              [*Enter Armostes, with a casket.*
    From whence come you?
Arm. From King Amyclas,—pardon
    My interruption of your studies.—Here,
    In this seal'd box, he sends a treasure [to you],
    Dear to him as his crown; he prays your Gravity,
    You would examine, ponder, sift, and bolt
    The pith and circumstance of every tittle
    The scroll within contains.
Tec. What is 't, Armostes?
Arm. It is the health of Sparta, the king's life,
    Sinews and safety of the commonwealth;
    The sum of what the oracle delivered,
    When last he visited the prophetic temple
    At Delphos: what his reasons are, for which,
    After so long a silence, he requires

Your counsel now, grave man, his majesty
Will soon himself acquaint you with.
Tec. Apollo   [*He takes the casket.*
Inspire my intellect!—The Prince of Argos
Is entertain'd?
Arm. He is; and has demanded
Our princess for his wife; which I conceive
One special cause the king importunes you
For resolution of the oracle.
Tec. My duty to the king, good peace to Sparta,
And fair day to Armostes!
Arm. Like to Tecnicus.   [*Exeunt.*

Scene II

*Soft Music:—A Song within, during which Prophilus, Bassanes,
    Penthea, and Grausis pass over the stage. Bassanes and
    Grausis re-enter softly, and listen in different places.*

Song

Can you paint a thought? or number
Every fancy in a slumber?
Can you count soft minutes roving
From a dial's point by moving?
Can you grasp a sigh? or, lastly,
Rob a virgin's honour chastely?

No, oh no! yet you may
    Sooner do both that and this,
    This and that, and never miss,
Than by any praise display
    Beauty's beauty; such a glory,
    As beyond all fate, all story,
        All arms, all arts,
        All loves, all hearts,
    Greater than those, or they,
    Do, shall, and must obey.

Bass. All silent, calm, secure.—Grausis, no creaking,
No noise; dost [thou] hear nothing?
Grau. Not a mouse,
    Or whisper of the wind.

Bass. The floor is matted;
    The bed-posts sure as steel or marble.—Soldiers
    Should not affect, methinks, strains so effeminate;
    Sounds of such delicacy are but fawnings
    Upon the sloth of luxury, they heighten
    Cinders of covert lust up to a flame.
Grau. What do you mean, my lord?—speak low; that gabbling
    Of yours will but undo us.
Bass. Chamber-combats
    Are felt, not heard!
Pro. [*Within.*] He wakes.
Bass. What's that?
Ith. [*Within.*] Who's there?
    Sister?—All quit the room else.
Bass. 'Tis consented!

Enter Prophilus

Pro. Lord Bassanes, your brother would be private,
    We must forbear; his sleep hath newly left him.
    Please you, withdraw!
Bass. By any means; 'tis fit.
Pro. Pray, gentlewoman, walk too.
Grau. Yes, I will, sir.   [*Exeunt.*

*The Scene opens: Ithocles is discovered in a chair, and
Penthea beside him*

Ith. Sit nearer, sister, to me; nearer yet:
    We had one father, in one womb took life,
    Were brought up twins together, yet have lived
    At distance, like two strangers; I could wish
    That the first pillow whereon I was cradled,
    Had prov'd to me a grave.
Pen. You had been happy:
    Then had you never known that sin of life,
    Which blots all following glories with a vengeance,
    For forfeiting the last will of the dead,
    From whom you had your being.
Ith. Sad Penthea,
    Thou canst not be too cruel; my rash spleen
    Hath with a violent hand plucked from thy bosom
    A love-blest heart, to grind it into dust;
    For which mine's now a-breaking.

Pen. Not yet, heaven.
  I do beseech thee! first, let some wild fires
  Scorch, not consume it! may the heat be cherished
  With desires infinite, but hopes impossible!
Ith. Wronged soul, thy prayers are heard.
Pen. Here, lo, I breathe,
  A miserable creature, led to ruin
  By an unnatural brother!
Ith. I consume
  In languishing affections for that trespass;
  Yet cannot die.
Pen. The handmaid to the wages
  Of country toil, drinks the untroubled streams
  With leaping kids, and with the bleating lambs,
  And so allays her thirst secure; whilst I
  Quench my hot sighs with fleetings of my tears.
Ith. The labourer doth eat his coarsest bread,
  Earned with his sweat, and lays him down to sleep;
  While every bit I touch turns in digestion
  To gall, as bitter as Penthea's curse.
  Put me to any penance for my tyranny;
  And I will call thee merciful.
Pen. Pray kill me,
  Rid me from living with a jealous husband;
  Then we will join in friendship, be again
  Brother and sister.—Kill me, pray; nay, will you?
Ith. How doth thy lord esteem thee?
Pen. Such an one
  As only you have made me; a faith-breaker,
  A spotted whore;—forgive me, I am one—
  In act, not in desires, the gods must witness.
Ith. Thou doth bely thy friend.
Pen. I do not, Ithocles;
  For she that's wife to Orgilus, and lives
  In known adultery with Bassanes,
  Is, at the best, a whore. Wilt kill me now?
  The ashes of our parents will assume
  Some dreadful figure, and appear to charge
  Thy bloody guilt, that hast betrayed their name
  To infamy, in this reproachful match.
Ith. After my victories abroad, at home
  I meet despair; ingratitude of nature
  Hath made my actions monstrous: thou shalt stand

A deity, my sister, and be worshipped
For thy resolved martyrdom; wronged maids
And married wives shall to thy hallowed shrine
Offer their orisons, and sacrifice
Pure turtles, crowned with myrtle; if thy pity
Unto a yielding brother's pressure, lend
One finger but to ease it.

Pen. Oh, no more!

Ith. Death waits to waft me to the Stygian banks,
And free me from this chaos of my bondage;
And till thou wilt forgive, I must endure.

Pen. Who is the saint you serve?

Ith. Friendship, or [nearness]
Of birth to any but my sister, durst not
Have mov'd this question; 'tis a secret, sister,
I dare not murmur to myself.

Pen. Let me,
By your new protestations I conjure you,
Partake her name.

Ith. Her name?—'tis—'tis—I dare not.

Pen. All your respects are forged.

Ith. They are not.—Peace!
Calantha is—the princess—the king's daughter—
Sole heir of Sparta.—Me, most miserable!
Do I now love thee? for my injuries
Revenge thyself with bravery, and gossip
My treasons to the king's ears, do;—Calantha
Knows it not yet, nor Prophilus, my nearest.

Pen. Suppose you were contracted to her, would it not
Split even your very soul to see her father
Snatch her out of your arms against her will,
And force her on the Prince of Argos?

Ith. Trouble not
The fountains of mine eyes with thine own story;
I sweat in blood for 't.

Pen. We are reconciled.
Alas, sir, being children, but two branches
Of one stock, 'tis not fit we should divide;
Have comfort, you may find it.

Ith. Yes, in thee;
Only in thee, Penthea mine.

Pen. If sorrows

Have not too much dulled my infected brain,
I 'll cheer invention, for an active strain.
Ith. Mad man!—Why have I wrong'd a maid so excellent?

*Bassanes rushes in with a poniard, followed by Prophilus, Groneas,
Hemophil, and Grausis*

Bass. I can forbear no longer; more, I will not:
Keep off your hands, or fall upon my point.—
Patience is tired,—for, like a slow-paced ass,
You ride my easy nature, and proclaim
My sloth to vengeance a reproach, and property.
Ith. The meaning of this rudeness?
Pro. He 's distracted.
Pen. Oh, my grieved lord!
Grau. Sweet lady, come not near him:
He holds his perilous weapon in his hand
To prick he cares not whom, nor where,—see! see! see!
Bass. My birth is noble: through the popular blast
Of vanity, as giddy as thy youth,
Hath reared thy name up to bestride a cloud,
Or progress in the chariot of the sun;
I am no clod of trade, to lackey pride,
Nor, like your slave of expectation, wait
The baudy hinges of your doors, or whistle
For mystical conveyance to your bed-sports.
Gron. Fine humours! they become him.
Hem. How he stares,
Struts, puffs, and sweats! most admirable lunacy!
Ith. But that I may conceive the spirit of wine
Has took possession of your soberer custom,
I 'd say you were unmannerly.
Pen. Dear brother!
Bass. Unmannerly!—mew, kitling!—smooth formality
Is usher to the rankness of the blood,
But impudence bears up the train.   Indeed, sir,
Your fiery metal, or your springal blaze
Of huge renown, is no sufficient royalty
To print upon my forehead the scorn, 'cuckold'.
Ith. His jealousy hath robbed him of his wits;
He talks he knows not what.
Bass. Yes, and he knows
To whom he talks! to one that franks his lust
In swine-security of bestial incest.

Ith. Ha, devil!

Bass. I will haloo 't; though I blush more
   To name the filthiness, than thou to act it.

Ith. Monster!   [*Draws his sword.*

Pro. Sir, by our friendship——

Pen. By our bloods!
   Oh, brother, will you quite undo us both?

Grau. Out on him!
   These are his megrims, firks, and melancholies.

Hem. Well said, old touch-hole.

Gron. Kick him out at doors.

Pen. With favour, let me speak.—My lord, what slackness
   In my obedience hath deserved this rage?
   Except humility and silent duty
   Hath drawn on your unquiet, my simplicity
   Ne'er studied your vexation.

Bass. Light of beauty,
   Deal not ungently with a desperate wound!
   No breach of reason dares make war with her
   Whose looks are sovereignty, whose breath is balm:
   Oh, that I could preserve thee in fruition
   As in devotion!

Pen. Sir, may every evil,
   Lock'd in Pandora's box, shower, in your presence,
   On my unhappy head, if, since you made me
   A partner in your bed, I have been faulty
   In one unseemly thought, against your honour.

Ith. Purge not his griefs, Penthea.

Bass. Yes, say on,
   Excellent creature!—Good, be not a hindrance
   To peace, and praise of virtue. [*To Ithocles.*]—Oh, my senses
   Are charm'd with sounds celestial.—On, dear, on:
   I never gave you one ill word: say, did I?
   Indeed I did not!

Pen. Nor, by Juno's forehead,
   Was I e'er guilty of a wanton error!

Bass. A goddess! let me kneel.

Grau. Alas, kind animal!

Ith. No! but for penance.

Bass. Noble sir, what is it?
   With gladness I embrace it; yet, pray let not
   My rashness teach you to be too unmerciful.

Ith. When you shall show good proof, that manly wisdom,

Q 899

Not oversway'd by passion or opinion,
Knows how to lead [your] judgment, then this lady,
Your wife, my sister, shall return in safety
Home to be guided by you; but, till first
I can out of clear evidence, approve it,
She shall be my care.

Bass. Rip my bosom up,
I 'll stand the execution with a constancy;
This torture is insufferable.

Ith. Well, sir,
I dare not trust her to your fury.

Bass. But
Penthea says not so.

Pen. She needs no tongue
To plead excuse, who never purposed wrong.
                              [*Exit with Ithocles and Prophilus.*

Hem. Virgin of reverence and antiquity,
Stay you behind!   [*To Grausis, who is followed by Penthea.*

Gron. The court wants not your diligence.
                              [*Exeunt Hemophil and Groneas.*

Grau. What will you do, my lord? my lady 's gone;
I am denied to follow.

Bass. I may see her,
Or speak to her once more?

Grau. And feel her too, man;
Be of good cheer, she 's your own flesh and bone.

Bass. Diseases desperate must find cures alike;
She swore she has been true.

Grau. True, on my modesty.

Bass. Let him want truth who credits not her vows!
Much wrong I did her, but her brother infinite;
Rumour will voice me the contempt of manhood.
Should I run on thus? some way I must try
To outdo art, and jealousy decry.
                              [*Exeunt.*

SCENE III

*Flourish.   Enter Amyclas, Nearchus leading Calantha, Armostes,
Crotolon, Euphranea, Christalla, Philema, and Amelus*

Amyc. Cousin of Argos, what the heavens have pleas'd,
  In their unchanging counsels, to conclude
  For both our kingdoms' weal, we must submit to:
  Nor can we be unthankful to their bounties,
  Who, when we were ev'n creeping to our graves,
  Sent us a daughter, in whose birth, our hope
  Continues of succession.   As you are
  In title next, being grandchild to our aunt,
  So we in heart desire you may sit nearest
  Calantha's love; since we have ever vowed
  Not to enforce affection by our will,
  But by her own choice to confirm it gladly.
Near. You speak the nature of a right just father.
  I come not hither roughly to demand
  My cousin's thraldom, but to free mine own:
  Report of great Calantha's beauty, virtue,
  Sweetness and singular perfections, courted
  All ears to credit what I find was published
  By constant truth; from which, if any service
  Of my desert can purchase fair construction,
  This lady must command it.
Cal. Princely sir,
  So well you know how to profess observance,
  That you instruct your hearers to become
  Practitioners in duty; of which number
  I 'll study to be chief.
Near.   Chief, glorious virgin,
  In my devotion, as in all men's wonder.
Amyc. Excellent cousin, we deny no liberty:
  Use thine own opportunities.—Armostes,
  We must consult with the philosophers;
  The business is of weight.
Arm.   Sir, at your pleasure.
Amyc. You told me, Crotolon, your son 's returned
  From Athens: wherefore comes he not to court,
  As we commanded?
Crot.   He shall soon attend
  Your royal will, great sir.

Amyc. The marriage
    Between young Prophilus and Euphranea,
    Tastes of too much delay.
Crot. My lord——
Amyc. Some pleasures
    At celebration of it, would give life
    To the entertainment of the prince our kinsman;
    Our court wears gravity more than we relish.
Arm. Yet the heavens smile on all your high attempts,
    Without a cloud.
Crot. So may the gods protect us!
Cal. A prince, a subject?
Near. Yes, to beauty's sceptre;
    As all hearts kneel, so mine.
Cal. You are too courtly.

Enter Ithocles, Orgilus, and Prophilus

Ith. Your safe return to Sparta is most welcome:
    I joy to meet you here, and, as occasion
    Shall grant us privacy, will yield you reasons
    Why I should covet to deserve the title
    Of your respected friend; for, without compliment,
    Believe it, Orgilus, 'tis my ambition.
Org. Your lordship may command me, your poor servant.
Ith. So amorously close!—so soon—my heart!   [*Aside.*
Pro. What sudden change is next?
Ith. Life to the king!
    To whom I here present this noble gentleman,
    New come from Athens; royal sir, vouchsafe
    Your gracious hand in favour of his merit.
                [*The King gives Orgilus his hand to kiss.*
Crot. My son preferred by Ithocles!   [*Aside.*
Amyc. Our bounties
    Shall open to thee, Orgilus; for instance,
    (Hark, in thine ear)—if, out of those inventions,
    Which flow in Athens, thou hast there engrossed
    Some rarity of wit, to grace the nuptials
    Of thy fair sister, and renown our court
    In th' eyes of this young prince, we shall be debtor
    To thy conceit: think on 't.
Org. Your highness honours me.
Near. My tongue and heart are twins.
Cal. A noble birth,

Becoming such a father.—Worthy Orgilus,
You are a guest most wish'd for.
Org. May my duty
Still rise in your opinion, sacred princess!
Ith. Euphranea's brother, sir; a gentleman
Well worthy of your knowledge.
Near. We embrace him,
Proud of so dear acquaintance.
Amyc. All prepare
For revels and disport; the joys of Hymen,
Like Phœbus in his lustre, put to flight
All mists of dullness; crown the hours with gladness:
No sounds but music, no discourse but mirth!
Cal. Thine arm, I prithee, Ithocles.—Nay, good
My lord, keep on your way, I am provided.
Near. I dare not disobey.
Ith. Most heavenly lady!   [*Exeunt omnes.*

SCENE IV

Enter Crotolon and Orgilus

Crot. The king hath spoke his mind.
Org. His will he hath;
But were it lawful to hold plea against
The power of greatness, not the reason, haply
Such undershrubs as subjects, sometimes might
Borrow of nature, justice, to inform
That licence sovereignty holds, without check,
Over a meek obedience.
Crot. How resolve you
Touching your sister's marriage? Prophilus
Is a deserving and a hopeful youth.
Org. I envy not his merit, but applaud it;
Could wish him thrift in all his best desires.
And, with a willingness, inleague our blood
With his, for purchase of full growth in friendship.
He never touched on any wrong that maliced
The honour of our house, nor stirr'd our peace;
Yet, with your favour, let me not forget
Under whose wing he gathers warmth and comfort,
Whose creature he is bound, made, and must live so.

Crot. Son, son, I find in thee a harsh condition,
    No courtesy can win it; 'tis too rancorous.
Org. Good sir, be not severe in your construction;
    I am no stranger to such easy calms
    As sit in tender bosoms: lordly Ithocles
    Hath graced my entertainment in abundance;
    Too humbly hath descended from that height
    Of arrogance and spleen which wrought the rape
    On grieved Penthea's purity; his scorn
    Of my untoward fortunes is reclaimed
    Unto a courtship, almost to a fawning:—
    I 'll kiss his foot, since you will have it so.
Crot. Since I will have it so! friend, I will have it so,
    Without our ruin by your politic plots,
    Or wolf of hatred snarling in your breast.
    You have a spirit, sir, have you? a familiar
    That posts i' th' air for your intelligence?
    Some such hobgoblin hurried you from Athens,
    For yet you come unsent for.
Org. If unwelcome,
    I might have found a grave there.
Crot. Sure your business
    Was soon dispatched, or your mind altered quickly.
Org. 'Twas care, sir, of my health, cut short my journey;
    For there, a general infection
    Threatens a desolation.
Crot. And I fear
    Thou hast brought back a worse infection with thee,
    Infection of thy mind; which, as thou say'st,
    Threatens the desolation of our family.
Org. Forbid it, our dear Genius! I will rather
    Be made a sacrifice on Thrasus' monument,
    Or kneel to Ithocles his son in dust,
    Than woo a father's curse: my sister's marriage
    With Prophilus is from my heart confirmed;
    May I live hated, may I die despised,
    If I omit to further it in all
    That can concern me!
Crot. I have been too rough.
    My duty to my king made me so earnest;
    Excuse it, Orgilus.
Org. Dear sir!

Enter Prophilus, Euphranea, Ithocles, Groneas, and Hemophil

Crot. Here comes
  Euphranea, with Prophilus and Ithocles.
Org. Most honoured!—ever famous!
Ith. Your true friend!
  On earth not any truer.—With smooth eyes
  Look on this worthy couple; your consent
  Can only make them one.
Org. They have it.—Sister,
  Thou pawn'd'st to me an oath, of which engagement
  I never will release thee, if thou aim'st
  At any other choice than this.
Euph. Dear brother,
  To him, or none.
Crot. To which my blessing 's added.
Org. Which, till a greater ceremony perfect,—
  Euphranea, lend thy hand;—here, take her, Prophilus,
  Live long a happy man and wife; and further,
  That these in presence may conclude an omen,
  Thus for a bridal song I close my wishes:

> 'Comforts lasting, loves increasing,
> Like soft hours never ceasing;
> Plenty's pleasure, peace complying,
> Without jars, or tongues envying;
> Hearts by holy union wedded,
> More than theirs by custom bedded;
> Fruitful issues; life so graced,
> Not by age to be defaced;
> Budding, as the year ensu'th,
> Every spring another youth:
> All what thought can add beside,
> Crown this Bridegroom and this Bride!'

Pro. You have sealed joy close to my soul.—Euphranea,
  Now I may call thee mine.
Ith. I but exchange
  One good friend for another.
Org. If these gallants
  Will please to grace a poor invention
  By joining with me in some slight device,
  I 'll venture on a strain my younger days
  Have studied for delight.

Hem. With thankful willingness
  I offer my attendance.
Gron. No endeavour
  Of mine shall fail to show itself.
Ith. We will
  All join to wait on thy directions, Orgilus.
Org. Oh, my good lord, your favours flow towards
  A too unworthy worm;—but, as you please,
  I am what you will shape me.
Ith. A fast friend.
Crot. I thank thee, son, for this acknowledgment,
  It is a sight of gladness.
Org. But my duty.   *[Exeunt omnes.*

Scene V

Enter Calantha, Penthea, Christalla, and Philema

Cal. Whoe'er would speak with us, deny his entrance;
  Be careful of our charge.
Chris. We shall, madam.
Cal. Except the king himself, give none admittance;
  Not any.
Phil. Madam, it shall be our care.
        [Exeunt Christalla and Philema.
Cal. Being alone, Penthea, you have, granted,
  The opportunity you sought, and might
  At all time have commanded.
Pen. 'Tis a benefit
  Which I shall owe your goodness even in death for:
  My glass of life, sweet princess, hath few minutes
  Remaining to run down; the sands are spent;
  For by an inward messenger I feel
  The summons of departure short and certain.
Cal. You feed too much your melancholy.
Pen. Glories
  Of human greatness are but pleasing dreams,
  Of shadows soon decaying; on the stage
  Of my mortality, my youth hath acted
  Some scenes of vanity, drawn out at length
  By varied pleasures, sweeten'd in the mixture,

But tragical in issue: beauty, pomp,
With every sensuality our giddiness
Doth frame an idol, are unconstant friends,
When any troubled passion makes assault
On the unguarded castle of the mind.

Cal. Contemn not your condition, for the proof
Of bare opinion only: to what end
Reach all these moral texts?

Pen. To place before you
A perfect mirror, wherein you may see
How weary I am of a lingering life,
Who count the best a misery.

Cal. Indeed
You have no little cause; yet none so great
As to distrust a remedy.

Pen. That remedy
Must be a winding-sheet, a fold of lead,
And some untrod-on corner in the earth.—
Not to detain your expectation, princess,
I have an humble suit.

Cal. Speak; I enjoy it.

Pen. Vouchsafe, then, to be my executrix,
And take that trouble on you, to dispose
Such legacies as I bequeath, impartially;
I have not much to give, the pains are easy;
Heav'n will reward your piety, and thank it
When I am dead; for sure I must not live;
I hope I cannot.

Cal. Now, beshrew thy sadness,
Thou turn'st me too much woman.   [*Weeps.*

Pen. Her fair eyes
Melt into passion.   [*Aside.*]—Then I have assurance
Encouraging my boldness.   In this paper
My will was charactered; which you, with pardon,
Shall now know from mine own mouth.

Cal. Talk on, prithee;
It is a pretty earnest.

Pen. I have left me
But three poor jewels to bequeath.   The first is
My Youth; for though I am much old in griefs,
In years I am a child.

Cal. To whom that?

Pen. To virgin-wives, such as abuse not wedlock

By freedom of desires; but covet chiefly
The pledges of chaste beds for ties of love,
Rather than ranging of their blood: and next
To married maids, such as prefer the number
Of honourable issue in their virtues
Before the flattery of delights by marriage;
May those be ever young!

Cal. A second jewel
You mean to part with?

Pen. 'Tis my Fame; I trust,
By scandal yet untouched: this I bequeath
To Memory, and Time's old daughter, Truth.
If ever my unhappy name find mention,
When I am fallen to dust, may it deserve
Beseeming charity without dishonour!

Cal. How handsomely thou playest with harmless sport
Of mere imagination! speak the last;
I strangely like thy will.

Pen. This jewel, madam,
Is dearly precious to me; you must use
The best of your discretion to employ
This gift as I intend it.

Cal. Do not doubt me.

Pen. 'Tis long agone since first I lost my heart:
Long have I lived without it, else for certain,
I should have given that too; but instead
Of it, to great Calantha, Sparta's heir,
By service bound, and by affection vowed,
I do bequeath, in holiest rites of love,
Mine only brother, Ithocles.

Cal. What said'st thou?

Pen. Impute not, heaven-blest lady, to ambition
A faith as humbly perfect, as the prayers
Of a devoted suppliant can endow it:
Look on him, princess, with an eye of pity;
How like the ghost of what he late appeared,
He moves before you!

Cal. Shall I answer here,
Or lend my ear too grossly?

Pen. First his heart
Shall fall in cinders, scorched by your disdain,
Ere he will dare, poor man, to ope an eye
On these divine looks, but with low-bent thoughts

Accusing such presumption; as for words,
He dares not utter any but of service:
Yet this lost creature loves you.—Be a princess
In sweetness as in blood; give him his doom,
Or raise him up to comfort.
Cal. What new change
Appears in my behaviour, that thou dar'st
Tempt my displeasure?
Pen. I must leave the world
To revel [in] Elysium, and 'tis just
To wish my brother some advantage here;
Yet by my best hopes, Ithocles is ignorant
Of this pursuit: but if you please to kill him,
Lend him one angry look, or one harsh word,
And you shall soon conclude how strong a power
Your absolute authority holds over
His life and end.
Cal. You have forgot, Penthea,
How still I have a father.
Pen. But remember
I am a sister, though to me this brother
Hath been, you know, unkind; oh, most unkind!
Cal. Christalla, Philema, where are you?—Lady,
Your check lies in my silence.

Enter Christalla and Philema

Both. Madam, here.
Cal. I think you sleep, you drones: wait on Penthea
Unto her lodging.—Ithocles? wrong'd lady!   [*Aside.*
Pen. My reckonings are made even; death or fate
Can now nor strike too soon, nor force too late.   [*Exeunt.*

ACT IV

Scene I

Enter Ithocles and Armostes

Ith. Forbear your inquisition; curiosity
　　Is of too subtle and too searching nature:
　　In fear of love too quick; too slow credit.—
　　I am not what you doubt me.
Arm. Nephew, be then
　　As I would wish;—all is not right.—Good Heaven
　　Confirm your resolutions for dependence
　　On worthy ends, which may advance your quiet!
Ith. I did the noble Orgilus much injury,
　　But grieved Penthea more; I now repent it,
　　Now, uncle, now; this Now is now too late.
　　So provident is folly in sad issue,
　　The afterwit, like bankrupt's debts, stands tallied,
　　Without all possibilities of payment.
　　Sure he 's an honest, very honest gentleman;
　　A man of single meaning.
Arm. I believe it:
　　Yet, nephew, 'tis the tongue informs our ears;
　　Our eyes can never pierce into the thoughts,
　　For they are lodged too inward:—but I question
　　No truth in Orgilus.—The princess, sir.
Ith. The princess? ha!
Arm. With her the Prince of Argos.

Enter Nearchus, leading Calantha; Amelus, Christalla, Philema

Near. Great fair one, grace my hopes with any instance
　　Of livery, from the allowance of your favour;
　　This little spark——　　*[Attempts to take a ring from her finger.*
Cal. A toy!
Near. Love feasts on toys,
　　For Cupid is a child;—vouchsafe this bounty:
　　It cannot be denied.
Cal. You shall not value,
　　Sweet cousin, at a price, what I count cheap;
　　So cheap, that let him take it, who dare stoop for 't,

And give it, at next meeting, to a mistress:
She 'll thank him for 't, perhaps.
     [Casts the ring before Ithocles, who takes it up.
Ame. The ring, sir, is
 The princess's; I could have took it up.
Ith. Learn manners, prithee.—To the blessed owner,
 Upon my knees——   *[Kneels and offers it to Calantha.*
Near. You are saucy.
Cal. This is pretty!
 I am, belike, 'a mistress'—wondrous pretty!
 Let the man keep his fortune, since he found it;
 He 's worthy on 't.—On, cousin!
   [Exeunt Nearchus, Calantha, Christalla, and Philema.
Ith. [*To Amelus.*] Follow, spaniel;
 I 'll force you to a fawning else.
Ame. You dare not.   *[Exit.*
Arm. My lord, you were too forward.
Ith. Look ye, uncle,
 Some such there are, whose liberal contents
 Swarm without care in every sort of plenty;
 Who, after full repasts, can lay them down
 To sleep; and they sleep, uncle: in which silence
 Their very dreams present 'em choice of pleasures,
 Pleasures (observe me, uncle) of rare object:
 Here heaps of gold, there increments of honours,
 Now change of garments, then the votes of people;
 Anon varieties of beauty, courting,
 In flatteries of the night, exchange of dalliance;
 Yet these are still but dreams. Give me felicity
 Of which my senses waking are partakers
 A real, visible, material happiness;
 And then, too, when I stagger in expectance
 Of the least comfort that can cherish life—
 I saw it, sir, I saw it; for it came
 From her own hand.
Arm. The princess threw it to you.
Ith. True; and she said—well I remember what—
 Her cousin prince would beg it.
Arm. Yes, and parted
 In anger at your taking on 't.
Ith. Penthea,
 Oh, thou hast pleaded with a powerful language!

I want a fee to gratify thy merit;
But I will do——

Arm. What is 't you say?

Ith. 'In anger'?
In anger let him part; for could his breath,
Like whirlwinds, toss such servile slaves, as lick
The dust his footsteps print, into a vapour,
It durst not stir a hair of mine; it should not;
I 'd rend it up by th' roots first.   To be anything
Calantha smiles on, is to be a blessing
More sacred than a petty prince of Argos
Can wish to equal, or in worth or title.

Arm. Contain yourself, my lord; Ixion, aiming
To embrace Juno, bosom'd but a cloud,
And begat Centaurs; 'tis an useful moral;
Ambition, hatch'd in clouds of mere opinion,
Proves but in birth a prodigy.

Ith. I thank you;
Yet, with your licence, I should seem uncharitable
To gentler fate, if relishing the dainties
Of a soul's settled peace, I were so feeble
Not to digest it.

Arm. He deserves small trust,
Who is not privy-counsellor to himself.

Re-enter Nearchus, Orgilus, and Amelus

Near. Brave me?

Org. Your excellence mistakes his temper,
For Ithocles, in fashion of his mind,
Is beautiful, soft, gentle, the clear mirror
Of absolute perfection!

Ame. Was 't your modesty
Term'd any of the prince's servants 'spaniel'?
Your nurse sure taught you other language.

Ith. Language!

Near. A gallant man at arms is here; a doctor
In feats of chivalry; blunt and rough-spoken,
Vouchsafing not the fustian of civility,
Which [less] rash spirits style good manners.

Ith. Manners?

Org. No more, illustrious sir, 'tis matchless Ithocles.

Near. You might have understood who I am.

Ith. Yes,

I did,—else—but the presence calm'd the affront—
You are cousin to the princess.

Near. To the king too;
A certain instrument that lent supportance
To your Colossic greatness—to that king too,
You might have added.

Ith. There is more divinity
In beauty than in majesty.

Arm. Oh, fie, fie!

Near. This odd youth's pride turns heretic in loyalty.
Sirrah! low mushrooms never rival cedars.

[*Exeunt Nearchus and Amelus.*

Ith. Come back;—what pitiful dull thing am I
So to be tamely scolded at! come back.—
Let him come back, and echo once again
That scornful sound of *mushroom*! painted colts
(Like heralds' coats, gilt o'er with crowns and sceptres)
May bait a muzzled lion.

Arm. Cousin, cousin,
Thy tongue is not thy friend.

Org. In point of honour,
Discretion knows no bounds. Amelus told me
'Twas all about a little ring.

Ith. A ring
The princess threw away, and I took up—
Admit she threw 't to me, what arm of brass
Can snatch it hence? No; could he grind the hoop
To powder, he might sooner reach my heart,
Than steal and wear one with dust on 't.—Orgilus,
I am extremely wronged.

Org. A lady's form is not to be so slighted.

Ith. Slighted!

Arm. Quiet
These vain unruly passions, which will render you
Into a madness.

Org. Griefs will have their vent.

Enter Tecnicus, with a scroll

Arm. Welcome; thou com'st in season, reverend man,
To pour the balsam of a suppling patience
Into the festering wound of ill-spent fury.

Org. What makes he here?   [*Aside.*

Tec. The hurts are yet more mortal,

Which shortly will prove deadly.   To the king,
Armostes, see in safety thou deliver
This seal'd-up counsel; bid him with a constancy
Peruse the secrets of the gods.—O Sparta,
O Lacedemon! double named, but one
In fate!—when kingdoms reel, (mark well my saw)
Their heads must needs be giddy: tell the king,
That henceforth he no more must inquire after
My aged head; Apollo wills it so:
I am for Delphos.

Arm. Not without some conference
With our great master?

Tec. Never more to see him;
A greater prince commands me.—Ithocles,
'When Youth is ripe, and Age from time doth part,
The lifeless Trunk shall wed the Broken Heart.'

Ith. What 's this, if understood?

Tec. List, Orgilus:
Remember what I told thee long before,
These tears shall be my witness.

Arm. 'Las good man!

Tec. [*Aside to Orgilus.*] Let craft with courtesy a while confer,
Revenge proves its own executioner.

Org. Dark sentences are for Apollo's priests;
I am not Œdipus.

Tec. My hour is come;
Cheer up the king; farewell to all.—O Sparta,
O Lacedemon!   [*Exit.*

Arm. If prophetic fire
Have warmed this old man's bosom, we might construe
His words to fatal sense.

Ith. Leave to the powers
Above us, the effect of their decrees;
My burden lies within me: servile fears
Prevent no great effects.—Divine Calantha!

Arm. The gods be still propitious. [*Exeunt Ithocles and Armostes.*

Org. Something oddly
The bookman prated, yet he talk'd it weeping;

'Let craft with courtesy a while confer,
Revenge proves its own executioner.'

Con it again;—for what? It shall not puzzle me;
'Tis dotage of a withered brain.—Penthea

Forbade me not her presence; I may see her,
And gaze my fill.   Why see her then I may,
When, if I faint to speak—I must be silent.   [*Exit.*

SCENE II

Enter Bassanes, Grausis, and Phulas

Bass. Pray, use your recreations, all the service
I will expect is quietness amongst ye;
Take liberty at home, abroad, at all times,
And in your charities appease the gods
Whom I, with my distractions, have offended.
Grau. Fair blessings on thy heart!
Phu. Here's a rare change!
My lord, to cure the itch, is surely gelded;
The cuckold in conceit, hath cast his horns.   [*Aside.*
Bass. Betake you to your several occasions;
And, wherein I have heretofore been faulty,
Let your constructions mildly pass it over;
Henceforth I'll study reformation,—more,
I have not for employment.
Grau. Oh, sweet man!
Thou art the very honeycomb of honesty.
Phu. The garland of good will.—Old lady, hold up
Thy reverend snout, and trot behind me softly,
As it becomes a mule of ancient carriage.
                    [*Exeunt Grausis and Phulas.*
Bass. Beasts, only capable of sense, enjoy
The benefit of food and ease with thankfulness:
Such silly creatures, with a grudging, kick not
Against the portion nature hath bestowed;
But men, endowed with reason, and the use
Of reason, to distinguish from the chaff
Of abject scarcity, the quintessence,
Soul, and elixir of the earth's abundance,
The treasures of the sea, the air, nay heaven,
Repining at these glories of creation,
Are verier beasts than beasts; and of those beasts
The worst am I.   I, who was made a monarch
Of what a heart could wish for, a chaste wife,
Endeavoured, what in me lay, to pull down

R 899

That temple built for adoration only,
And level 't in the dust of causeless scandal:—
But, to redeem a sacrilege so impious,
Humility shall pour before the deities
I have incensed, a largess of more patience
Than their displeased altars can require.
No tempests of commotion shall disquiet
The calms of my composure.

Enter Orgilus

Org. I have found thee,
　　Thou patron of more horrors than the bulk
　　Of manhood, hooped about with ribs of iron,
　　Can cram within thy breast: Penthea, Bassanes,
　　Cursed by thy jealousies, more, by thy dotage,
　　Is left a prey to words.
Bass. Exercise
　　Your trials for addition to my penance;
　　I am resolv'd.
Org. Play not with misery
　　Past cure: some angry minister of fate hath
　　Deposed the empress of her soul, her reason,
　　From its most proper throne; but—what 's the miracle
　　More new, I, I have seen it, and yet live!
Bass. You may delude my senses, not my judgment;
　　'Tis anchored into a firm resolution;
　　Dalliance of mirth or wit can ne'er unfix it:
　　Practise yet further.
Org. May thy death of love to her,
　　Damn all thy comforts to a lasting fast
　　From every joy of life! thou barren rock,
　　By thee we have been split in ken of harbour.

Enter Penthea, with her hair loose, Ithocles, Philema, and Christalla

Ith. Sister, look up, your Ithocles, your brother
　　Speaks to you; why d' you weep? dear, turn not from me.—
　　Here is a killing sight; lo, Bassanes,
　　A lamentable object!
Org. Man, dost see it?
　　Sports are more gamesome; am I yet in merriment?
　　Why dost not laugh?
Bass. Divine and best of ladies,
　　Please to forget my outrage; mercy ever

Cannot but lodge under a roof so excellent:
I have cast off that cruelty of frenzy
Which once appeared imposture, and then juggled
To cheat my sleeps of rest.
Org. Was I in earnest?
Pen. Sure, if we were all sirens, we should sing pitifully,
And 'twere a comely music, when in parts
One sung another's knell; the turtle sighs
When he hath lost his mate; and yet some say
He must be dead first: 'tis a fine deceit
To pass away in a dream! indeed, I 've slept
With mine eyes open, a great while.   No falsehood
Equals a broken faith; there 's not a hair
Sticks on my head but, like a leaden plummet,
It sinks me to the grave: I must creep thither;
The journey is not long.
Ith. But thou, Penthea,
Hast many years, I hope, to number yet,
Ere thou canst travel that way.
Bass. Let the sun first
Be wrapped up in an everlasting darkness,
Before the light of nature, chiefly formed
For the whole world's delight, feel an eclipse
So universal!
Org. Wisdom, look ye,
Begins to rave!—art thou mad too, antiquity?
Pen. Since I was first a wife, I might have been
Mother to many pretty prattling babes;
They would have smiled when I smiled; and, for certain
I should have cried when they cried:—truly, brother,
My father would have picked me out a husband,
And then my little ones had been no bastards;
But 'tis too late for me to marry now,
I am past child-bearing; 'tis not my fault.
Bass. Fall on me, if there be a burning Etna,
And bury me in flames! sweats, hot as sulphur,
Boil through my pores:—affliction hath in store
No torture like to this.
Org. Behold a patience!
Lay by thy whining grey dissimulation,
Do something worth a chronicle; show justice
Upon the author of this mischief; dig out
The jealousies that hatched this thraldom first

With thine own poniard: every antic rapture
Can roar as thine does.

Ith. Orgilus, forbear.

Bass. Disturb him not; it is a talking motion
Provided for my torment.   What a fool am I
To bawdy passion! ere I 'll speak a word,
I will look on and burst.

Pen. I loved you once.   [*To Orgilus.*

Org. Thou didst, wronged creature: in despite of malice,
For it I 'll love thee ever.

Pen. Spare your hand;
Believe me, I 'll not hurt it.

Org. My heart too.

Pen. Complain not though I wring it hard: I 'll kiss it;
Oh, 'tis a fine soft palm!—hark, in thine ear;
Like whom do I look, prithee?—nay, no whispering,
Goodness! we had been happy; too much happiness
Will make folk proud, they say—but that is he—
                              [*Pointing to Ithocles.*
And yet he paid for 't home; alas! his heart
Is crept into the cabinet of the princess;
We shall have points and bride-laces.   Remember,
When we last gathered roses in the garden,
I found my wits; but truly you lost yours,
That 's he, and still 'tis he.   [*Again pointing to Ithocles.*

Ith. Poor soul, how idly
Her fancies guide her tongue!

Bass. Keep in, vexation,
And break not into clamour.   [*Aside.*

Org. She has tutored me;
Some powerful inspiration checks my laziness:
Now let me kiss your hand, grieved beauty.

Pen. Kiss it.—
Alack, alack, his lips be wondrous cold;
Dear soul, he has lost his colour: have you seen
A straying heart? all crannies! every drop
Of blood is turned to an amethyst,
Which married bachelors hang in their ears.

Org. Peace usher her into Elysium!
If this be madness, madness is an oracle.   [*Exit.*

Ith. Christalla, Philema, when slept my sister,
Her ravings are so wild?

Chris. Sir, not these ten days.

Phil. We watch by her continually; besides,
  We cannot any way pray her to eat.

Bass. Oh,—misery of miseries!

Pen. Take comfort,
  You may live well, and die a good old man:
  By yea and nay, an oath not to be broken,
  If you had joined our hands once in the temple,
  ('Twas since my father died, for had he lived
  He would have done 't) I must have called you father.—
  Oh, my wrecked honour! ruined by those tyrants,
  A cruel brother, and a desperate dotage.
  There is no peace left for a ravished wife
  Widowed by lawless marriage; to all memory,
  Penthea, poor Penthea's name is strumpeted:
  But since her blood was seasoned by the forfeit
  Of noble shame, with mixtures of pollution,
  Her blood—'tis just—be henceforth never heightened
  With taste of sustenance! starve; let that fullness
  Whose pleurisy hath fever'd faith and modesty——
  Forgive me; oh! I faint. [*Falls into the arms of her attendants.*

Arm. Be not so wilful,
  Sweet niece, to work thine own destruction.

Ith. Nature
  Will call her daughter, monster!—what! not eat?
  Refuse the only ordinary means
  Which are ordained for life? be not, my sister,
  A murtheress to thyself.—Hear'st thou this, Bassanes?

Bass. Foh! I am busy; for I have not thoughts
  Enough to think: all shall be well anon.
  'Tis tumbling in my head; there is a mastery
  In art, to fatten and keep smooth the outside;
  Yes, and to comfort up the vital spirits
  Without the help of food, fumes or perfumes,—
  Perfumes or fumes. Let her alone; I 'll search out
  The trick on 't.   [*Aside.*

Pen. Lead me gently; heavens reward ye.
  Griefs are sure friends; they leave, without control,
  Nor cure nor comforts for a leprous soul.

            [*Exit, supported by Christalla and Philema.*

Bass. I grant ye; and will put in practice instantly
  What you shall still admire: 'tis wonderful,
  'Tis super-singular, not to be match'd;

Yet, when I 've done 't, I 've done 't: ye shall all thank me.

[*Exit.*

Arm. The sight is full of terror.

Ith. On my soul
  Lies such an infinite clog of massy dullness,
  As that I have not sense enough to feel it.—
  See, uncle, the angry thing returns again,
  Shall 's welcome him with thunder? we are haunted,
  And must use exorcism to conjure down
  This spirit of malevolence.

Enter Nearchus and Amelus

Arm. Mildly, nephew.

Near. I come not, sir, to chide your late disorder;
  Admitting that th' inurement to a roughness
  In soldiers of your years and fortunes, chiefly,
  So lately prosperous, hath not yet shook off
  The custom of the war, in hours of leisure;
  Nor shall you need excuse, since you 're to render
  Account to that fair excellence, the princess,
  Who in her private gallery expects it
  From your own mouth alone: I am a messenger
  But to her pleasure.

Ith. Excellent Nearchus,
  Be prince still of my services, and conquer,
  Without the combat of dispute; I honour you.

Near. The king is on a sudden indisposed,
  Physicians are call'd for; 'twere fit, Armostes,
  You should be near him.

Arm. Sir, I kiss your hands. [*Exeunt Ithocles and Armostes.*

Near. Amelus, I perceive Calantha's bosom
  Is warm'd with other fires than such as can
  Take strength from any fuel of the love
  I might address to her; young Ithocles,
  Or ever I mistake, is lord ascendant
  Of her devotions; one, to speak him truly,
  In every disposition nobly fashioned.

Ame. But can your highness brook to be so rivalled,
  Considering th' inequality of the persons?

Near. I can, Amelus; for affections, injured
  By tyranny, or rigour of compulsion,
  Like tempest-threatened trees unfirmly rooted,
  Ne'er spring to timely growth: observe, for instance,

Life-spent Penthea, and unhappy Orgilus.
Ame. How does your grace determine?
Near. To be jealous
  In public, of what privately I 'll further;
  And, though they shall not know, yet they shall find it.

                                [Exeunt.

SCENE III

Enter the King, led by Hemophil and Groneas, followed by Armostes,
  with a box, Crotolon, and Prophilus. The King is placed in
  a chair.

Amyc. Our daughter is not near?
Arm. She is retired, sir,
  Into her gallery.
Amyc. Where 's the prince our cousin?
Pro. New walk'd into the grove, my lord.
Amyc. All leave us
  Except Armostes, and you, Crotolon;
  We would be private.
Pro. Health unto your majesty.

                  [Exeunt Prophilus, Hemophil, and Groneas.
Amyc. What! Tecnicus is gone?
Arm. He is, to Delphos;
  And to your royal hands presents this box.
Amyc. Unseal it, good Armostes; therein lie
  The secrets of the oracle; out with it;

                      [Armostes takes out the scroll.
  Apollo live our patron! Read, Armostes.
Arm. 'The plot in which the Vine takes root
  Begins to dry from head to foot;
  The stock, soon withering, want of sap
  Doth cause to quail the budding grape:
  But, from the neighbouring Elm, a dew
  Shall drop, and feed the plot anew.'
Amyc. That is the oracle; what exposition
  Makes the philosopher?
Arm. This brief one, only.

       'The plot is Sparta, the dried Vine the king;
       The quailing grape his daughter; but the thing
       Of most importance, not to be revealed,
       Is a near prince, the Elm: the rest concealed.

                            'TECNICUS.'

Amyc. Enough; although the opening of this riddle
   Be but itself a riddle, yet we construe
   How near our labouring age draws to a rest:
   But must Calantha quail too? that young grape
   Untimely budded! I could mourn for her;
   Her tenderness hath yet deserved no rigour
   So to be crossed by fate.
Arm. You misapply, sir,
   With favour let me speak it, what Apollo
   Hath clouded in hid sense; I here conjecture
   Her marriage with some neighbouring prince, the dew
   Of which befriending Elm shall ever strengthen
   Your subjects with a sovereignty of power.
Crot. Besides, most gracious lord, the pith of oracles
   Is to be then digested, when the events
   Expound their truth, not brought as soon to light
   As uttered; Truth is child of Time; and herein
   I find no scruple, rather cause of comfort,
   With unity of kingdoms.
Amyc. May it prove so,
   For weal of this dear nation!—Where is Ithocles?—
   Armostes, Crotolon, when this wither'd Vine
   Of my frail carcase, on the funeral pile,
   Is fired into its ashes, let that young man
   Be hedged about still with your cares and loves;
   Much owe I to his worth, much to his service.—
   Let such as wait come in now!
Arm. All attend here!

    Enter Ithocles, Calantha, Prophilus, Orgilus, Euphranea,
              Hemophil, and Groneas

Cal. Dear sir! king! father!
Ith. Oh, my royal master!
Amyc. Cleave not my heart, sweet twins of my life's solace,
   With your forejudging fears: there is no physic
   So cunningly restorative to cherish
   The fall of age, or call back youth and vigour,
   As your consents in duty; I will shake off
   This languishing disease of time, to quicken
   Fresh pleasures in these drooping hours of sadness:
   Is fair Euphranea married yet to Prophilus?
Crot. This morning, gracious lord.
Org. This very morning;

Which, with your highness' leave, you may observe too.
Our sister looks, methinks, mirthful and sprightly,
As if her chaster fancy could already
Expound the riddle of her gain in losing
A trifle, maids know only that they know not.
Pish! prithee, blush not; 'tis but honest change
Of fashion in the garment, loose for straight,
And so the modest maid is made a wife.
Shrewd business—is 't not, sister?

Euph. You are pleasant.

Amyc. We thank thee, Orgilus, this mirth becomes thee.
But wherefore sits the court in such a silence?
A wedding without revels is not seemly.

Cal. Your late indisposition, sir, forbade it.

Amyc. Be it thy charge, Calantha, to set forward
The bridal sports, to which I will be present;
If not, at least consenting: mine own Ithocles,
I have done little for thee yet.

Ith. You have built me,
To the full height I stand in.

Cal. Now or never!—   [*Aside.*
May I propose a suit?

Amyc. Demand, and have it.

Cal. Pray, sir, give me this young man, and no further
Account him yours, than he deserves in all things
To be thought worthy mine; I will esteem him
According to his merit.

Amyc. Still thou 'rt my daughter,
Still grow'st upon my heart.   Give me thine hand.
                                              [*To Ithocles.*

Calantha, take thine own; in noble actions
Thou 'lt find him firm and absolute.   I would not
Have parted with thee, Ithocles, to any
But to a mistress, who is all what I am.

Ith. A change, great king, most wished for, 'cause the same.

Cal. Thou art mine.—Have I now kept my word?

Ith. Divinely.

Org. Rich fortunes guard, the favour of a princess,
Rock thee, brave man, in ever crowned plenty!—
You are minion of the time; be thankful for it.
Ho! here 's a swing in destiny—apparent!
The youth is up on tiptoe, yet may stumble.   [*Aside.*

Amyc. On to your recreations!—Now convey me

Unto my bed-chamber; none on his forehead
Wear a distemper'd look.

All. The gods preserve you!

Cal. Sweet, be not from my sight.

Ith. My whole felicity!

> [*Amyclas is carried out.—Exeunt all but Ithocles, detained
> by Orgilus.*

Org. Shall I be bold, my lord?

Ith. Thou canst not, Orgilus.
Call me thine own; for Prophilus must henceforth
Be all thy sister's; friendship, though it cease not
In marriage, yet is oft at less command
Than when a single freedom can dispose it.

Org. Most right, my most good lord, my most great lord,
My gracious princely lord, I might add royal.

Ith. Royal! A subject royal?

Org. Why not, pray, sir?
The sovereignty of kingdoms, in their nonage,
Stooped to desert, not birth; there's as much merit
In clearness of affection, as in puddle
Of generation; you have conquered love
Even in the loveliest: if I greatly err not,
The son of Venus hath bequeathed his quiver
To Ithocles to manage, by whose arrows
Calantha's breast is opened.

Ith. Can it be possible?

Org. I was myself a piece of a suitor once,
And forward in preferment too; so forward
That, speaking truth, I may without offence, sir,
Presume to whisper, that my hopes, and (hark ye!)
My certainty of marriage stood assured
With as firm footing (by your leave), as any's,
Now, at this very instant—but——

Ith. 'Tis granted:
And for a league of privacy between us,
Read o'er my bosom and partake a secret;
The princess is contracted mine.

Org. Still, why not?
I now applaud her wisdom: when your kingdom
Stands seated in your will, secure and settled,
I dare pronounce you will be a just monarch;
Greece must admire and tremble.

Ith. Then the sweetness

Of so imparadised a comfort, Orgilus!
It is to banquet with the gods.
Org. The glory
Of numerous children, potency of nobles,
Bent knees, hearts paved to tread on!
Ith. With a friendship
So dear, so fast as thine.
Org. I am unfitting
For office; but for service——
Ith. We 'll distinguish
Our fortunes merely in the title; partners
In all respects else but the bed.—
Org. The bed?
Forefend it, Jove's own jealousy!—till lastly
We slip down in the common earth together.
And there our beds are equal; save some monument
To show this was the king, and this the subject——

　　　　　　　　　　　　　　　[*Soft sad music.*

List, what sad sounds are these? extremely sad ones.
Ith. Sure from Penthea's lodgings.
Org. Hark! a voice too.

A Song (*within*)

'Oh, no more, no more, too late
　　Sighs are spent; the burning tapers
Of a life as chaste as fate,
　　Pure as are unwritten papers,
Are burnt out: no heat, no light
Now remains; 'tis ever night.
　　Love is dead; let lovers' eyes,
　　　　Lock'd in endless dreams,
　　　　Th' extremes of all extremes,
　　Ope no more, for now Love dies.
Now Love dies,—implying
Love's martyrs must be ever, ever dying.'

Ith. Oh, my misgiving heart!
Org. A horrid stillness
Succeeds this deathful air; let 's know the reason:
Tread softly; there is mystery in mourning.　　　[*Exeunt.*

Scene IV

Penthea discovered in a chair, veiled; Christalla and Philema at her feet mourning.   Enter two Servants, with two other chairs, one worked by clockwork.

Enter Ithocles and Orgilus

1 *Serv.* [*Aside to Org.*] 'Tis done; that on her right hand.
Org. Good! begone   [*Exeunt Servants.*
Ith. Soft peace enrich this room!
Org. How fares the lady?
Phil. Dead.
Chris. Dead!
Phil. Starved!
Chris. Starved!
Ith. Me miserable!
Org. Tell us
   How parted she from life?
Phil. She called for music,
   And begged some gentle voice to tune a farewell
   To life and griefs; Christalla touched the lute,
   I wept the funeral song.
Chris. Which scarce was ended,
   But her last breath sealed up these hollow sounds:
   'O cruel Ithocles, and injured Orgilus!'
   So down she drew her veil, so died.
Ith. So died!
Org. Up! you are messengers of death, go from us;
                         [*Christalla and Philema rise.*
   Here's woe enough to court without a prompter.
   Away; and,—hark ye! till you see us next,
                         [*Exeunt Christalla and Philema.*
   No syllable that she is dead.—Away,
   Keep a smooth brow.—
                         [*My lord.—*
Ith. Mine only sister!
   Another is not left me.
Org. Take that chair,
   I'll seat me here in this: between us sits
   The object of our sorrows; some few tears
   We'll part among us: I perhaps can mix
   One lamentable story to prepare them.—
   There, there! sit there, my lord!

Ith. Yes, as you please. [*Sits down, the chair closes upon him.*
  What means this treachery?
Org. Caught! you are caught,
  Young master! 'tis thy throne of coronation,
  Thou fool of greatness! See I take this veil off;
  Survey a beauty withered by the flames
  Of an insulting Phaeton, her brother.
Ith. Thou mean'st to kill me basely?
Org. I foreknew
  The last act of her life, and trained thee hither,
  To sacrifice a tyrant to a turtle.
  You dreamt of kingdoms, did you! how to bosom
  The delicacies of a youngling princess!
  How with this nod to grace that subtle courtier,
  How with that frown to make this noble tremble,
  And so forth; whilst Penthea's groans and tortures,
  Her agonies, her miseries, afflictions,
  Ne'er touched upon your thought! as for my injuries,
  Alas! they were beneath your royal pity;
  But yet they lived, thou proud man, to confound thee!
  Behold thy fate; this steel! [*Draws a dagger.*
Ith. Strike home! A courage
  As keen as thy revenge shall give it welcome,
  But prithee faint not; if the wound close up,
  Tent it with double force, and search it deeply.
  Thou look'st that I should whine, and beg compassion,
  As loath to leave the vainness of my glories;
  A statelier resolution arms thy confidence,
  To cozen thee of honour; neither could I,
  With equal trial of unequal fortune,
  By hazard of a duel; 'twere a bravery
  Too mighty for a slave intending murder.
  On to the execution, and inherit
  A conflict with my horrors.
Org. By Apollo,
  Thou talk'st a goodly language! for requital
  I will report thee to thy mistress richly;
  And take this peace along: some few short minutes
  Determined, my resolves shall quickly follow
  Thy wrathful ghost; then, if we tug for mastery,
  Penthea's sacred eyes shall lend new courage.
  Give me thy hand—be healthful in thy parting
  From lost mortality! thus, thus I free it. [*Stabs him.*

Ith. Yet, yet, I scorn to shrink.
Org. Keep up thy spirit:
   I will be gentle even in blood; to linger
   Pain, which I strive to cure, were to be cruel. [*Stabs him again.*
Ith. Nimble in vengeance, I forgive thee.   Follow
   Safety, with best success; oh, may it prosper!—
   Penthea, by thy side thy brother bleeds;
   The earnest of his wrongs to thy forced faith.
   Thoughts of ambition, or delicious banquet
   With beauty, youth, and love, together perish
   In my last breath, which on the sacred altar
   Of a long-looked-for peace—now—moves—to heaven.
                                        [*Dies.*

Org. Farewell, fair spring of manhood! henceforth welcome
   Best expectation of a noble sufferance!
   I 'll lock the bodies safe, till what must follow
   Shall be approved.—Sweet twins, shine stars for ever!—
   In vain they build their hopes, whose life is shame,
   No monument lasts but a happy name!
                   [*Locks the door and exit.*

ACT V

SCENE I

Enter Bassanes

Bass. Athens—to Athens I have sent, the nursery
   Of Greece for learning, and the fount of knowledge;
   For here, in Sparta, there 's not left amongst us
   One wise man to direct; we are all turn'd madcaps.
   'Tis said Apollo is the god of herbs,
   Then certainly he knows the virtue of them:
   To Delphos I have sent too; if there can be
   A help for nature, we are sure yet.

Enter Orgilus

Org. Honour
   Attend thy counsels ever.
Bass. I beseech thee,
   With all my heart, let me go from thee quietly;

I will not aught to do with thee, of all men.
The doubles of a hare,—or, in a morning,
Salutes from a splay-footed witch,—to drop
Three drops of blood at th' nose just, and no more,—
Croaking of ravens, or the screech of owls,
Are not so boding mischief, as thy crossing
My private meditations: shun me, prithee;
And if I cannot love thee heartily,
I 'll love thee as well as I can.

Org. Noble Bassanes,
Mistake me not.

Bass. Phew! then we shall be troubled.
Thou wert ordained my plague—heaven make me thankful,
And give me patience too, heaven, I beseech thee!

Org. Accept a league of amity: for henceforth,
I vow, by my best genius, in a syllable,
Never to speak vexation; I will study
Service and friendship, with a zealous sorrow
For my past incivility towards you.

Bass. Heyday, good words, good words! I must believe 'em,
And be a coxcomb for my labour.

Org. Use not
So hard a language; your misdoubt is causeless:
For instance, if you promise to put on
A constancy of patience, such a patience
As chronicle or history ne'er mentioned,
As follows not example, but shall stand
A wonder, and a theme for imitation,
The first, the index pointing to a second,
I will acquaint you with an unmatched secret,
Whose knowledge to your griefs shall set a period.

Bass. Thou canst not, Orgilus; 'tis in the power
Of the gods only; yet, for satisfaction,
Because I note an earnest in thine utterance,
Unforced, and naturally free, be resolute,
The virgin-bays shall not withstand the lightning
With a more careless danger, than my constancy
The full of thy relation; could it move
Distraction in a senseless marble statue,
It should find me a rock: I do expect now
Some truth of unheard moment.

Org. To your patience
You must add privacy, as strong in silence

As mysteries locked up in Jove's own bosom.

Bass. A skull hid in the earth a treble age,
  Shall sooner prate.

Org. Lastly, to such direction
  As the severity of a glorious action
  Deserves to lead your wisdom and your judgment,
  You ought to yield obedience.

Bass. With assurance
  Of will and thankfulness.

Org. With manly courage
  Please then to follow me.

Bass. Where'er, I fear not.   [*Exeunt.*

SCENE II

A Flourish.   Enter Euphranea, led by Groneas and Hemophil;
  Prophilus, led by Christalla and Philema; Nearchus sup-
  porting Calantha; Crotolon and Amelus.

Cal. We miss our servant Ithocles, and Orgilus;
  On whom attend they?

Crot. My son, gracious princess,
  Whisper'd some new device, to which these revels
  Should be but usher; wherein I conceive
  Lord Ithocles and he himself are actors.

Cal. A fair excuse for absence: as for Bassanes,
  Delights to him are troublesome; Armostes
  Is with the king?

Crot. He is.

Cal. On to the dance!
  Cousin, hand you the bride; the bridegroom must be
  Entrusted to my courtship.   Be not jealous,
  Euphranea; I shall scarcely prove a temptress.—
  Fall to our dance.

The Revels

Music.   Nearchus dances with Euphranea, Prophilus with
  Calantha, Christalla with Hemophil, Philema with Groneas.

  They dance the First Change ; during which Armostes enters.

Arm. [*Whispers Calantha.*] The king your father's dead.

Cal. To the other change.

Arm. Is 't possible?

They dance the Second Change

Enter Bassanes

Bass. [*Whispers Calantha.*] Oh, madam!
   Penthea, poor Penthea's starved.
Cal. Beshrew thee!
   Lead to the next.
Bass. Amazement dulls my senses.

They dance the Third Change

Enter Orgilus

Org. [*Whispers Calantha.*] Brave Ithocles is murdered, murdered
      cruelly.
Cal. How dull this music sounds! Strike up more sprightly;
   Our footings are not active like our heart,
   Which treads the nimbler measure.
Org. I am thunderstruck!

The Last Change

Cal. So! let us breathe a while.—[*Music ceases.*]—Hath not this
      motion
   Raised fresher colours on our cheeks?
Near. Sweet princess,
   A perfect purity of blood enamels
   The beauty of your white.
Cal. We all look cheerfully:
   And cousin, 'tis methinks a rare presumption
   In any who prefer our lawful pleasures
   Before their own sour censure, to interrupt
   The custom of this ceremony bluntly.
Near. None dares, lady.
Cal. Yes, yes; some hollow voice delivered to me
   Now that the king was dead.
Arm. The king is dead:
   That fatal news was mine; for in mine arms
   He breath'd his last, and with his crown bequeathed you
   Your mother's wedding ring; which here I tender.
Crot. Most strange!
Cal. Peace crown his ashes! We are queen then.
Near. Long live Calantha! Sparta's sovereign queen
All. Long live the queen!
Cal. What whispered Bassanes?
Bass. That my Penthea, miserable soul,
   Was starved to death.

S 899

Cal. She is happy; she hath finished
    A long and painful process.—A third murmur
    Pierced mine unwilling ears.
Org. That Ithocles
    Was murdered; rather butchered, had not bravery
    Of an undaunted spirit, conquering terror,
    Proclaimed his last act triumph over ruin.
Arm. How! murdered!
Cal. By whose hand?
Org. By mine; this weapon
    Was instrument to my revenge; the reasons
    Are just, and known; quit him of these, and then
    Never lived gentleman of greater merit,
    Hope or abiliment to steer a kingdom.
Crot. Fie, Orgilus!
Euph. Fie, brother!
Cal. You have done it?
Bass. How it was done, let him report, the forfeit
    Of whose allegiance to our laws doth covet
    Rigour of justice; but, that done it is,
    Mine eyes have been an evidence of credit
    Too sure to be convinced.   Armostes, rend not
    Thine arteries with hearing the bare circumstances
    Of these calamities: thou hast lost a nephew,
    A niece, and I a wife: continue man still;
    Make me the pattern of digesting evils,
    Who can outlive my mighty ones, not shrinking
    At such a presence as would sink a soul
    Into what's most of death, the worst of horrors.
    But I have sealed a covenant with sadness,
    And enter'd into bonds without condition,
    To stand these tempests calmly; mark me, nobles,
    I do not shed a tear, not for Penthea!
    Excellent misery!
Cal. We begin our reign
    With a first act of justice! thy confession,
    Unhappy Orgilus, dooms thee a sentence;
    But yet thy father's or thy sister's presence
    Shall be excus'd.   Give, Crotolon, a blessing
    To thy lost son; Euphranea, take a farewell,
    And both be gone.
Crot. [*To Orgilus.*] Confirm thee, noble sorrow
    In worthy resolution!

Euph. Could my tears speak,
  My griefs were slight.
Org. All goodness dwell amongst ye!
  Enjoy my sister, Prophilus; my vengeance
  Aim'd never at thy prejudice.
Cal. Now withdraw.
                    [*Exeunt Crotolon, Prophilus, and Euphranea.*
  Bloody relater of thy stains in blood,
  For that thou hast reported him, whose fortunes
  And life by thee are both at once snatched from him,
  With honourable mention, make thy choice
  Of what death likes thee best; there 's all our bounty,
  But to excuse delays, let me, dear cousin,
  Entreat you and these lords see execution,
  Instant, before you part.
Near. Your will commands us.
Org. One suit, just queen, my last: vouchsafe your clemency,
  That by no common hand I be divided
  From this my humble frailty.
Cal. To their wisdoms
  Who are to be spectators of thine end,
  I make the reference: those that are dead,
  Are dead; had they not now died, of necessity
  They must have paid the debt they owed to nature,
  One time or other.—Use dispatch, my lords;
  We 'll suddenly prepare our coronation.
                    [*Exeunt Calantha, Philema, and Christalla.*
Arm. 'Tis strange, these tragedies should never touch on
  Her female pity.
Bass. She has a masculine spirit:
  And wherefore should I pule, and, like a girl,
  Put finger in the eye? let 's be all toughness,
  Without distinction betwixt sex and sex.
Near. Now, Orgilus, thy choice?
Org. To bleed to death.
Arm. The executioner?
Org. Myself, no surgeon;
  I am well skilled in letting blood.   Bind fast
  This arm, that so the pipes may from their conduits
  Convey a full stream; here 's a skilful instrument:
                    [*Shows his dagger.*
  Only I am a beggar to some charity
  To speed me in this execution,

By lending th' other prick to th' other arm,
When this is bubbling life out.
Bass. I am for you,
   It most concerns my art, my care, my credit;
   Quick, fillet both his arms.
Org. Gramercy, friendship!
   Such courtesies are real, which flow cheerfully
   Without an expectation of requital.
   Reach me a staff in this hand.—[*They give him a staff.*]—If a
      proneness,
   Or custom in my nature, from my cradle,
   Had been inclined to fierce and eager bloodshed,
   A coward guilt, hid in a coward quaking,
   Would have betrayed me to ignoble flight,
   And vagabond pursuit of dreadful safety:
   But look upon my steadiness, and scorn not
   The sickness of my fortune; which, since Bassanes
   Was husband to Penthea, had lain bed-rid.
   We trifle time in words:—thus I show cunning
   In opening of a vein too full, too lively.
                 [*Pierces the vein with his dagger.*
Arm. Desperate courage!
Near. Honourable infamy!
Hem. I tremble at the sight.
Gron. Would I were loose!
Bass. It sparkles like a lusty wine new broach'd;
   The vessel must be sound from which it issues.
   Grasp hard this other stick—I 'll be as nimble—
   But pray thee, look not pale—Have at ye! stretch out
   Thine arm with vigour, and unshaken virtue. [*Opens the vein.*
   Good! oh, I envy not a rival, fitted
   To conquer in extremities: this pastime
   Appears majestical; some high-tuned poem,
   Hereafter, shall deliver to posterity
   The writer's glory, and his subject's triumph.
   How is 't, man?—droop not yet.
Org. I feel no palsies.
   On a pair-royal do I wait in death:
   My sovereign, as his liegeman; on my mistress,
   As a devoted servant; and on Ithocles,
   As if no brave, yet no unworthy enemy:
   Nor did I use an engine to entrap
   His life, out of a slavish fear to combat

Youth, strength, or cunning; but for that I durst not
Engage the goodness of a cause on fortune,
By which his name might have outfaced my vengeance.
Oh, Tecnicus, inspired with Phœbus' fire!
I call to mind thy augury, 'twas perfect;
Revenge proves its own executioner.
When feeble man is bending to his mother,
The dust he was first framed on, thus he totters——
Bass. Life's fountain is dried up.
Org. So falls the standard
Of my prerogative in being a creature!
A mist hangs o'er mine eyes, the sun's bright splendour
Is clouded in an everlasting shadow:
Welcome, thou ice, that sit'st about my heart,
No heat can ever thaw thee.   [*Dies.*
Near. Speech hath left him.
Bass. He hath shook hands with time; his funeral urn
Shall be my charge; remove the bloodless body.
The coronation must require attendance;
That past, my few days can be but one mourning.   [*Exeunt.*

Scene III

*An altar, covered with white : two lights of virgin wax upon it.—
Recorders, during which enter attendants, bearing Ithocles on
a hearse, in a rich robe, with a crown on his head ; and place
him on the one side of the altar.   After which, enter Calantha
in white, crowned, attended by Euphranea, Philema, and
Christalla, also in white : Nearchus, Armostes, Crotolon,
Prophilus, Amelus, Bassanes, Hemophil, and Groneas.*

*Calantha kneels before the altar, the ladies kneeling behind her; the
rest stand off.   The Recorders cease during her devotions.
Soft music.   Calantha and the rest rise, doing obeisance to
the altar.*

Cal. Our orisons are heard; the gods are merciful.
Now tell me, you, whose loyalties pay tribute
To us your lawful sovereign, how unskilful
Your duties, or obedience is, to render

Subjection to the sceptre of a virgin,
Who have been ever fortunate in princes
Of masculine and stirring composition?
A woman has enough to govern wisely
Her own demeanours, passions, and divisions.
A nation warlike, and inured to practice
Of policy and labour, cannot brook
A feminate authority; we therefore
Command your counsel, how you may advise us
In choosing of a husband, whose abilities
Can better guide this kingdom.

Near. Royal lady,
Your law is in your will.

Arm. We have seen tokens
Of constancy too lately, to mistrust it.

Crot. Yet, if your highness settle on a choice,
By your own judgment both allowed and liked of,
Sparta may grow in power, and proceed
To an increasing height.

Cal. Hold you the same mind?

Bass. Alas, great mistress! reason is so clouded
With the thick darkness of my infinite woes,
That I forecast nor dangers, hopes, or safety.
Give me some corner of the world to wear out
The remnant of the minutes I must number,
Where I may hear no sounds, but sad complaints
Of virgins, who have lost contracted partners;
Of husbands howling that their wives were ravished
By some untimely fate; of friends divided
By churlish opposition; or of fathers
Weeping upon their children's slaughtered carcases;
Or daughters, groaning o'er their fathers' hearses,
And can I dwell there, and with these keep consort
As musical as theirs.   What can you look for
From an old, foolish, peevish, doting man,
But craziness of age?

Cal. Cousin of Argos.

Near. Madam.

Cal. Were I presently
To choose you for my lord, I'll open freely
What articles I would propose to treat on,
Before our marriage.

Near. Name them, virtuous lady.

Cal. I would presume you would retain the royalty
   Of Sparta in her own bounds; then in Argos
   Armostes might be viceroy; in Messene
   Might Crotolon bear sway; and Bassanes——
Bass. I, queen? alas! what I?
Cal. Be Sparta's marshal;
   The multitudes of high employments could not
   But set a peace to private griefs.   These gentlemen,
   Groneas and Hemophil, with worthy pensions,
   Should wait upon your person, in your chamber;
   I would bestow Christalla on Amelus,
   She 'll prove a constant wife; and Philema
   Should into Vesta's temple.
Bass. This is a testament!
   It sounds not like conditions on a marriage.
Near. All this should be performed.
Cal. Lastly, for Prophilus;
   He should be, cousin, solemnly invested
   In all those honours, titles, and preferments
   Which his dear friend, and my neglected husband,
   Too short a time enjoyed.
Pro. I am unworthy
   To live in your remembrance.
Euph. Excellent lady!
Near. Madam, what means that word, 'neglected husband'?
Cal. Forgive me: now I turn to thee, thou shadow
   Of my contracted lord! Bear witness all,
   I put my mother's wedding-ring upon
   His finger; 'twas my father's last bequest.
                    [*Places a ring on the finger of Ithocles.*
   Thus I new-marry him, whose wife I am;
   Death shall not separate us.   Oh, my lords,
   I but deceived your eyes with antic gesture,
   When one news straight came huddling on another,
   Of death! and death! and death! still I danced forward:
   But it struck home, and here, and in an instant.
   Be such mere women, who, with shrieks and outcries,
   Can vow a present end to all their sorrows,
   Yet live to [court] new pleasures, and outlive them:
   They are the silent griefs which cut the heart-strings;
   Let me die smiling.
Near. 'Tis a truth too ominous.

Cal. One kiss on these cold lips, my last!—[*Kisses Ithocles.*]—
    crack, crack—
  Argos now 's Sparta's king. Command the voices
  Which wait at th' altar, now to sing the song
  I fitted for my end.
Near. Sirs, the song!

Dirge

Chorus.   Glories, pleasures, pomps, delights, and ease,
                    Can but please
           [The] outward senses, when the mind
           Is [or] untroubled, or by peace refined.

First voice. Crowns may flourish and decay,
           Beauties shine, but fade away.

Second.   Youth may revel, yet it must
           Lie down in a bed of dust.

Third.   Earthly honours flow and waste,
           Time alone doth change and last.

Chorus.   Sorrows mingled with contents, prepare
                  Rest for care;
           Love only reigns in death; though art
           Can find no comfort for a Broken Heart.

Arm. Look to the queen!
Bass. Her 'heart is broke' indeed.
  Oh, royal maid, 'would thou hadst missed this part!
  Yet 'twas a brave one. I must weep to see
  Her smile in death.
Arm. Wise Tecnicus! thus said he:

      'When Youth is ripe, and Age from time doth part,
      The lifeless Trunk shall wed the Broken Heart'.

  'Tis here fulfilled.
Near. I am your king.
All. Long live
  Nearchus, King of Sparta!
Near. Her last will
  Shall never be digressed from; wait in order
  Upon these faithful lovers, as becomes us.—
  The counsels of the gods are never known,
  Till men can call the effects of them their own.   [*Exeunt.*

Epilogue

WHERE noble judgments and clear eyes are fixed
To grace endeavour, there sits truth, not mixed
With ignorance; those censures may command
Belief, which talk not, till they understand.
Let some say, *This was flat*; some, *Here the scene
Fell from its height*; another, *That the mean
Was ill observed, in such a growing passion,
As it transcended either state or fashion.*
Some few may cry, *'Twas pretty well*, or so,
But—— and there shrug in silence: yet we know
Our writer's aim was, in the whole, addressed
Well to deserve of ALL, but please the BEST:
Which granted, by th' allowance of this strain,
The BROKEN HEART may be pieced up again.

'TIS PITY SHE'S A WHORE

To The Truly Noble

JOHN, EARL OF PETERBOROUGH, LORD MORDAUNT, BARON OF TURVEY

My Lord,

Where a truth of merit hath a general warrant, there love is but a debt, acknowledgment a justice. Greatness cannot often claim virtue by inheritance; yet, in this, yours appears most eminent, for that you are not more rightly heir to your fortunes than glory shall be to your memory. Sweetness of disposition ennobles a freedom of birth; in both, your lawful interest adds honour to your own name, and mercy to my presumption. Your noble allowance of these first fruits of my leisure, in the action, emboldens my confidence of your as noble construction in this presentment; especially since my service must ever owe particular duty to your favours, by a particular engagement. The gravity of the subject may easily excuse the lightness of the title, otherwise I had been a severe judge against mine own guilt. Princes have vouchsafed grace to trifles offered from a purity of devotion; your lordship may likewise please to admit into your good opinion, with these weak endeavours, the constancy of affection from the sincere lover of your deserts in honour.

JOHN FORD.

DRAMATIS PERSONÆ

BONAVENTURA, a friar.
A CARDINAL, Nuncio to the Pope.
SORANZO, a nobleman.
FLORIO, ⎫
DONADO, ⎬ citizens of Parma.
GRIMALDI, a Roman gentleman.
GIOVANNI, son to FLORIO.
BERGETTO, nephew to DONADO.
RICHARDETTO, a supposed physician.
VASQUES, servant to SORANZO.
POGGIO, servant to BERGETTO.
Banditti.

ANNABELLA, daughter to FLORIO.
HIPPOLITA, wife to RICHARDETTO.
PHILOTIS, his niece.
PUTANA, tutoress to ANNABELLA.

Officers, Attendants, Servants, etc.

THE SCENE—PARMA

ACT I

Scene I

Enter Friar and Giovanni

Friar. Dispute no more in this; for know, young man,
   These are no school points; nice philosophy
   May tolerate unlikely arguments,
   But Heaven admits no jest: wits that presumed
   On wit too much, by striving how to prove
   There was no God, with foolish grounds of art,
   Discover'd first the nearest way to hell;
   And fill'd the world with devilish atheism.
   Such questions, youth, are fond: far better 'tis
   To bless the sun, than reason why it shines;
   Yet He thou talk'st of, is above the sun.—
   No more! I may not hear it.
Gio. Gentle father,
   To you I have unclasp'd my burden'd soul,
   Emptied the storehouse of my thoughts and heart,
   Made myself poor of secrets; have not left
   Another word untold, which hath not spoke
   All what I ever durst, or think, or know;
   And yet is here the comfort I shall have?
   Must I not do what all men else may,—love?
Friar. Yes, you may love, fair son.
Gio. Must I not praise
   That beauty, which, if fram'd anew, the gods
   Would make a god of, if they had it there;
   And kneel to it, as I do kneel to them?
Friar. Why, foolish madman!—
Gio. Shall a peevish sound,
   A customary form, from man to man,
   Of brother and of sister, be a bar
   'Twixt my perpetual happiness and me?
   Say that we had one father, say one womb
   (Curse to my joys!) gave both us life and birth;

Are we not, therefore, each to other bound
So much the more by nature? by the links
Of blood, of reason? nay, if you will have it,
Even of religion, to be ever one,
One soul, one flesh, one love, one heart, one all?

Friar. Have done, unhappy youth! for thou art lost.

Gio. Shall, then, for that I am her brother born,
My joys be ever banished from her bed?
No, father; in your eyes I see the change
Of pity and compassion; from your age,
As from a sacred oracle, distils
The life of counsel: tell me, holy man,
What cure shall give me ease in these extremes?

Friar. Repentance, son, and sorrow for this sin:
For thou hast mov'd a Majesty above,
With thy unranged (almost) blasphemy.

Gio. Oh, do not speak of that, dear confessor.

Friar. Art thou, my son, that miracle of wit,
Who once, within these three months, wert esteem'd
A wonder of thine age, throughout Bononia?
How did the university applaud
Thy government, behaviour, learning, speech,
Sweetness, and all that could make up a man!
I was proud of my tutelage, and chose
Rather to leave my books, than part with thee;
I did so:—but the fruits of all my hopes
Are lost in thee, as thou art in thyself.
O Giovanni! hast thou left the schools
Of knowledge, to converse with lust and death?
For death waits on thy lust.   Look through the world,
And thou shalt see a thousand faces shine
More glorious than this idol thou ador'st:
Leave her, and take thy choice, 'tis much less sin;
Though in such games as those, they lose that win.

Gio. It were more easy to stop the ocean
From floats and ebbs, than to dissuade my vows.

Friar. Then I have done, and in thy wilful flames
Already see thy ruin; Heaven is just.—
Yet hear my counsel.

Gio. As a voice of life.

Friar. Hie to thy father's house, there lock thee fast
Alone within thy chamber; then fall down
On both thy knees, and grovel on the ground;

Cry to thy heart; wash every word thou utter'st
In tears (and if 't be possible) of blood:
Beg Heaven to cleanse the leprosy of lust
That rots thy soul; acknowledge what thou art,
A wretch, a worm, a nothing; weep, sigh, pray
Three times a day, and three times every night:
For seven days space do this; then, if thou find'st
No change in thy desires, return to me;
I 'll think on remedy.   Pray for thyself
At home, whilst I pray for thee here.—Away!
My blessing with thee! we have need to pray.
Gio. All this I 'll do, to free me from the rod
    Of vengeance; else I 'll swear my fate 's my god.

                                            [*Exeunt.*

SCENE II

Enter Grimaldi and Vasques, with their swords drawn

Vas. Come, sir, stand to your tackling; if you prove craven,
    I 'll make you run quickly.
Grim. Thou art no equal match for me.
Vas. Indeed I never went to the wars to bring home news; nor
    I cannot play the mountebank for a meal's meat, and swear I
    got my wounds in the field.   See you these grey hairs? they 'll
    not flinch for a bloody nose.   Wilt thou to this gear?
Grim. Why, slave, think'st thou I 'll balance my reputation
    with a cast-suit? Call thy master, he shall know that I dare——
Vas. Scold like a cot-quean: that 's your profession.   Thou
    poor shadow of a soldier, I will make thee know my master
    keeps servants, thy betters in quality and performance.
    Com'st thou to fight or prate?
Grim. Neither, with thee.   I am a Roman and a gentleman; one
    that have got mine honour with expense of blood.
Vas. You are a lying coward, and a fool.   Fight, or by these
    hilts I 'll kill thee: brave my lord! You 'll fight?
Grim. Provoke me not, for if thou dost——
Vas. Have at you.   [*They fight, Grimaldi is worsted.*

Enter Florio, Donado, and Soranzo, from opposite sides

Flo. What mean these sudden broils so near my doors?
    Have you not other places, but my house,
    To vent the spleen of your disorder'd bloods?

Must I be haunted still with such unrest,
As not to eat, or sleep in peace at home?
Is this your love, Grimaldi? Fie! 'tis naught.
Don. And, Vasques, I may tell thee, 'tis not well
To broach these quarrels; you are ever forward
In seconding contentions.

Enter above Annabella and Putana

Flo. What's the ground?
Sor. That, with your patience, signiors, I'll resolve:
This gentleman, whom fame reports a soldier,
(For else I know not) rivals me in love
To Signior Florio's daughter; to whose ears
He still prefers his suit, to my disgrace;
Thinking the way to recommend himself,
Is to disparage me in his report.—
But know, Grimaldi, though, maybe, thou art
My equal in thy blood, yet this betrays
A lowness in thy mind; which, wert thou noble,
Thou would'st as much disdain, as I do thee
For this unworthiness; and on this ground
I will'd my servant to correct his tongue,
Holding a man so base no match for me.
Vas. And had not your sudden coming prevented us, I had let
my gentleman blood under the gills; I should have worm'd
you, sir, for running mad.
Grim. I'll be reveng'd, Soranzo.
Vas. On a dish of warm broth to stay your stomach—do,
honest innocence, do! spoon-meat is a wholesomer diet than
a Spanish blade.
Grim. Remember this!   [*Exit.*
Sor. I fear thee not, Grimaldi.
Flo. My Lord Soranzo, this is strange to me;
Why you should storm, having my word engaged:
Owing her heart, what need you doubt her ear?
Losers may talk, by law of any game.
Vas. Yet the villainy of words, Signior Florio, may be such, as
would make any unspleened dove choleric. Blame not my
lord in this.
Flo. Be you more silent;
I would not for my wealth, my daughter's love
Should cause the spilling of one drop of blood.
Vasques, put up: let's end this fray in wine.   [*Exeunt.*

Put. How like you this, child? here 's threatening, challenging, quarrelling, and fighting, on every side, and all is for your sake; you had need look to yourself, charge, you 'll be stolen away sleeping else shortly.

Ann. But, tutoress, such a life gives no content
To me, my thoughts are fix'd on other ends.
Would you would leave me!

Put. Leave you! no marvel else; leave me no leaving, charge: this is love outright. Indeed, I blame you not; you have choice fit for the best lady in Italy.

Ann. Pray do not talk so much.

Put. Take the worst with the best, there 's Grimaldi the soldier, a very well-timber'd fellow. They say he 's a Roman, nephew to the Duke Montferrato; they say he did good service in the wars against the Milanese; but, 'faith, charge, I do not like him, an 't be for nothing but for being a soldier: not one amongst twenty of your skirmishing captains but have some privy maim or other, that mars their standing upright. I like him the worse, he crinkles so much in the hams: though he might serve if there were no more men, yet he 's not the man I would choose.

Ann. Fie, how thou prat'st!

Put. As I am a very woman, I like Signior Soranzo well; he is wise, and what is more, rich; and what is more than that, kind; and what is more than all this, a nobleman: such a one, were I the fair Annabella myself, I would wish and pray for. Then he is bountiful; besides, he is handsome, and by my troth, I think, wholesome, and that 's news in a gallant of three-and-twenty: liberal, that I know; loving, that you know; and a man sure, else he could never have purchased such a good name with Hippolita, the lusty widow, in her husband's lifetime. An 'twere but for that report, sweetheart, would he were thine! Commend a man for his qualities, but take a husband as he is a plain, sufficient, naked man; such a one is for your bed, and such a one is Signior Soranzo, my life for 't.

Ann. Sure the woman took her morning's draught too soon.

Enter Bergetto and Poggio

Put. But look, sweetheart, look what thing comes now! Here 's another of your ciphers to fill up the number: Oh, brave old ape in a silken coat! Observe.

Ber. Didst thou think, Poggio, that I would spoil my new clothes, and leave my dinner, to fight!

Pog. No, sir, I did not take you for so arrant a baby.

Ber. I am wiser than so: for I hope, Poggio, thou never heard'st of an elder brother that was a coxcomb; didst, Poggio?

Pog. Never indeed, sir, as long as they had either land or money left them to inherit.

Ber. Is it possible, Poggio? Oh, monstrous! Why, I 'll undertake, with a handful of silver, to buy a headful of wit at any time: but, sirrah, I have another purchase in hand; I shall have the wench, mine uncle says. I will but wash my face, and shift socks; and then have at her, i' faith.—Mark my pace, Poggio!   [*Passes over the stage.*

Pog. Sir,—I have seen an ass and a mule trot the Spanish pavin with a better grace, I know not how often.

         [*Aside, and following him.*

Ann. This idiot haunts me too.

Put. Ay, ay, he needs no description. The rich magnifico that is below with your father, charge, Signior Donado, his uncle, for that he means to make this, his cousin, a golden calf, thinks that you will be a right Israelite, and fall down to him presently: but I hope I have tutored you better. They say a fool's bauble is a lady's play-fellow; yet you, having wealth enough, you need not cast upon the dearth of flesh, at any rate. Hang him, innocent!

Giovanni passes over the stage

Ann. But see, Putana, see! what blessed shape
Of some celestial creature now appears!—
What man is he, that with such sad aspèct
Walks careless of himself?

Put. Where?

Ann. Look below.

Put. Oh, 'tis your brother, sweet.

Ann. Ha!

Put. 'Tis your brother.

Ann. Sure 'tis not he; this is some woeful thing
Wrapp'd up in grief, some shadow of a man.
Alas! he beats his breast, and wipes his eyes,
Drown'd all in tears: methinks I hear him sigh;
Let 's down, Putana, and partake the cause.
I know my brother, in the love he bears me,

Will not deny me partage in his sadness;
My soul is full of heaviness and fear.

[*Aside, and exit with Putana.*

Scene III

Gio. Lost! I am lost! my fates have doom'd my death:
The more I strive, I love; the more I love,
The less I hope: I see my ruin certain.
What judgment or endeavours could apply
To my incurable and restless wounds,
I thoroughly have examined, but in vain.
Oh, that it were not in religion sin
To make our love a god, and worship it!
I have even wearied heaven with pray'rs, dried up
The spring of my continual tears, even starv'd
My veins with daily fasts: what wit or art
Could counsel, I have practised; but, alas!
I find all these but dreams, and old men's tales,
To fright unsteady youth; I am still the same:
Or I must speak, or burst. 'Tis not, I know,
My lust, but 'tis my fate, that leads me on.
Keep fear and low faint-hearted shame with slaves!
I 'll tell her that I love her, though my heart
Were rated at the price of that attempt.
Oh me! she comes.

Enter Annabella and Putana

Ann. Brother!
Gio. If such a thing
As courage dwell in men, ye heavenly powers,
Now double all that virtue in my tongue! [*Aside.*
Ann. Why, brother,
Will you not speak to me?
Gio. Yes; how do you, sister?
Ann. Howe'er I am, methinks you are not well.
Put. Bless us! why are you so sad, sir?
Gio. Let me entreat you, leave us a while, Putana.
Sister, I would be private with you.
Ann. Withdraw, Putana.
Put. I will.—If this were any other company for her, I should

think my absence an office of some credit; but I will leave
them together.   [*Aside, and exit.*

Gio. Come, sister, lend your hand; let 's walk together;
  I hope you need not blush to walk with me;
  Here 's none but you and I.

Ann. How 's this?

Gio. I' faith, I mean no harm.

Ann. Harm?

Gio. No, good faith.
  How is it with thee?

Ann. I trust he be not frantic.—   [*Aside.*
  I am very well, brother.

Gio. Trust me, but I am sick; I fear so sick,
  'Twill cost my life.

Ann. Mercy forbid it! 'tis not so, I hope.

Gio. I think you love me, sister.

Ann. Yes, you know I do.

Gio. I know it, indeed—you are very fair.

Ann. Nay, then I see you have a merry sickness.

Gio. That 's as it proves.   The poets feign, I read,
  That Juno for her forehead did exceed
  All other goddesses; but I durst swear
  Your forehead exceeds hers, as hers did theirs.

Ann. 'Troth, this is pretty.

Gio. Such a pair of stars
  As are thine eyes, would, like Promethean fire,
  If gently glanced, give life to senseless stones.

Ann. Fie upon you!

Gio. The lily and the rose, most sweetly strange,
  Upon your dimple cheeks do strive for change:
  Such lips would tempt a saint: such hands as those
  Would make an anchorite lascivious.

Ann. Do you mock me, or flatter me?

Gio. If you would see a beauty more exact
  Than art can counterfeit, or nature frame,
  Look in your glass, and there behold your own.

Ann. Oh, you are a trim youth!

Gio. Here!   [*Offers his dagger to her.*

Ann. What to do?

Gio. And here 's my breast; strike home!
  Rip up my bosom, there thou shalt behold
  A heart, in which is writ the truth I speak——
  Why stand you?

Ann. Are you earnest?

Gio. Yes, most earnest.
  You cannot love?

Ann. Whom?

Gio. Me.   My tortured soul
  Hath felt affliction in the heat of death.
  Oh, Annabella, I am quite undone!
  The love of thee, my sister, and the view
  Of thy immortal beauty, have untuned
  All harmony both of my rest and life.
  Why do you not strike?

Ann. Forbid it, my just fears!
  If this be true, 'twere fitter I were dead.

Gio. True! Annabella; 'tis no time to jest.
  I have too long suppressed my hidden flames,
  That almost have consum'd me; I have spent
  Many a silent night in sighs and groans;
  Ran over all my thoughts, despised my fate,
  Reason'd against the reasons of my love,
  Done all that smooth-cheek'd virtue could advise,
  But found all bootless: 'tis my destiny
  That you must either love, or I must die.

Ann. Comes this in sadness from you?

Gio. Let some mischief
  Befall me soon, if I dissemble aught.

Ann. You are my brother Giovanni.

Gio. You
  My sister Annabella; I know this.
  And could afford you instance why to love
  So much the more for this; to which intent
  Wise nature first in your creation meant
  To make you mine; else 't had been sin and foul
  To share one beauty to a double soul.
  Nearness in birth and blood, doth but persuade
  A nearer nearness in affection.
  I have ask'd counsel of the holy church,
  Who tells me I may love you; and, 'tis just,
  That, since I may, I should; and will, yes will:
  Must I now live, or die?

Ann. Live; thou hast won
  The field, and never fought: what thou hast urged,
  My captive heart had long ago resolv'd.
  I blush to tell thee,—but I 'll tell thee now—

For every sigh that thou hast spent for me,
I have sigh'd ten; for every tear, shed twenty:
And not so much for that I loved, as that
I durst not say I loved, nor scarcely think it.
Gio. Let not this music be a dream, ye gods,
For pity's sake, I beg you!
Ann. On my knees,   [*She kneels.*
Brother, even by our mother's dust, I charge you,
Do not betray me to your mirth or hate;
Love me, or kill me, brother.
Gio. On my knees,   [*He kneels.*
Sister, even by my mother's dust I charge you,
Do not betray me to your mirth or hate;
Love me, or kill me, sister.
Ann. You mean good sooth, then?
Gio. In good troth, I do;
And so do you, I hope: say, I'm in earnest.
Ann. I'll swear it, I.
Gio. And I; and by this kiss,   [*Kisses her.*
(Once more, yet once more; now let's rise) [*They rise*] by this,
I would not change this minute for Elysium.
What must we now do?
Ann. What you will.
Gio. Come then;
After so many tears as we have wept,
Let's learn to court in smiles, to kiss, and sleep.   [*Exeunt.*

Scene IV

Enter Florio and Donado

Flo. Signior Donado, you have said enough,
I understand you; but would have you know,
I will not force my daughter 'gainst her will.
You see I have but two, a son and her;
And he is so devoted to his book,
As I must tell you true, I doubt his health:
Should he miscarry, all my hopes rely
Upon my girl.   As for worldly fortune,
I am, I thank my stars, bless'd with enough.
My care is, how to match her to her liking;

I would not have her marry wealth, but love,
And if she like your nephew, let him have her;
Here 's all that I can say.

Don. Sir, you say well,
Like a true father; and, for my part, I,
If the young folks can like, ('twixt you and me)
Will promise to assure my nephew presently
Three thousand florins yearly, during life,
And, after I am dead, my whole estate.

Flo. 'Tis a fair proffer, sir; meantime your nephew
Shall have free passage to commence his suit:
If he can thrive, he shall have my consent;
So for this time I 'll leave you, signior.   [*Exit.*

Don. Well,
Here 's hope yet, if my nephew would have wit;
But he is such another dunce, I fear
He 'll never win the wench.   When I was young,
I could have done 't, i' faith, and so shall he,
If he will learn of me; and, in good time,
He comes himself.—   [*Enter Bergetto and Poggio.*
How now, Bergetto, whither away so fast?

Ber. Oh, uncle! I have heard the strangest news that ever came
out of the mint; have I not, Poggio?

Pog. Yes, indeed, sir.

Don. What news, Bergetto?

Ber. Why, look ye, uncle, my barber told me just now, that
there is a fellow come to town, who undertakes to make a mill
go without the mortal help of any water or wind, only with
sandbags; and this fellow hath a strange horse, a most excellent
beast, I 'll assure you, uncle, my barber says; whose head, to
the wonder of all Christian people, stands just behind where
his tail is.   Is 't not true, Poggio?

Pog. So the barber swore, forsooth.

Don. And you are running thither?

Ber. Ay, forsooth, uncle.

Don. Wilt thou be a fool still?   Come, sir, you shall not go; you
have more mind of a puppet-play than on the business I told
you: why, thou great baby, wilt never have wit? wilt make
thyself a May-game to all the world?

Pog. Answer for yourself, master.

Ber. Why, uncle, should I sit at home still, and not go abroad
to see fashions like other gallants?

Don. To see hobby-horses! what wise talk, I pray, had you with Annabella, when you were at Signior Florio's house?

Ber. Oh, the wench!—Uds sa'me, uncle, I tickled her with a rare speech, that I made her almost burst her belly with laughing.

Don. Nay, I think so; and what speech was 't?

Ber. What did I say, Poggio?

Pog. Forsooth, my master said, that he loved her almost as well as he loved parmasent; and swore (I'll be sworn for him) that she wanted but such a nose as his was, to be as pretty a young woman as any was in Parma.

Don. Oh, gross!

Ber. Nay, uncle;—then she ask'd me, whether my father had more children than myself? and I said no; 'twere better he should have had his brains knock'd out first.

Don. This is intolerable.

Ber. Then said she, will Signior Donado, your uncle, leave you all his wealth?

Don. Ha! that was good; did she harp upon that string?

Ber. Did she harp upon that string! ay, that she did. I answered, 'Leave me all his wealth? why, woman, he hath no other wit; if he had, he should hear on 't to his everlasting glory and confusion: I know, quoth I, I am his white boy, and will not be gull'd'; and with that she fell into a great smile, and went away. Nay, I did fit her.

Don. Ah, sirrah, then I see there's no changing of nature. Well, Bergetto, I fear thou wilt be a very ass still.

Ber. I should be sorry for that, uncle.

Don. Come, come you home with me: since you are no better a speaker, I'll have you write to her after some courtly manner, and enclose some rich jewel in the letter.

Ber. Ay marry, that will be excellent.

Don. Peace, innocent!
 Once in my time I'll set my wits to school,
 If all fail, 'tis but the fortune of a fool.

Ber. Poggio, 'twill do, Poggio!   [*Exeunt.*

ACT II

SCENE I

Enter Giovanni and Annabella

Gio. Come, Annabella, no more Sister now,
　　But Love, a name more gracious; do not blush,
　　Beauty's sweet wonder, but be proud to know
　　That yielding thou hast conquer'd, and inflamed
　　A heart, whose tribute is thy brother's life.
Ann. And mine is his.　Oh, how these stolen contents
　　Would print a modest crimson on my cheeks,
　　Had any but my heart's delight prevail'd!
Gio. I marvel why the chaster of your sex
　　Should think this pretty toy call'd maidenhead,
　　So strange a loss; when, being lost, 'tis nothing,
　　And you are still the same.
Ann. 'Tis well for you;
　　Now you can talk.
Gio. Music as well consists
　　In th' ear, as in the playing.
Ann. Oh, you are wanton!—
　　Tell on 't, you were best; do.
Gio. Thou wilt chide me then.
　　Kiss me—so! thus hung Jove on Leda's neck,
　　And suck'd divine ambrosia from her lips.
　　I envy not the mightiest man alive;
　　But hold myself, in being king of thee,
　　More great than were I king of all the world:
　　But I shall lose you, sweetheart.
Ann. But you shall not.
Gio. You must be married, mistress.
Ann. Yes! to whom?
Gio. Some one must have you.
Ann. You must.
Gio. Nay, some other.
Ann. Now prithee do not speak so; without jesting
　　You 'll make me weep in earnest.
Gio. What, you will not!
　　But tell me, sweet, canst thou be dared to swear
　　That thou wilt live to me, and to no other?

Ann. By both our loves I dare; for didst thou know,
My Giovanni, how all suitors seem
To my eyes hateful, thou wouldst trust me then.
Gio. Enough, I take thy word: sweet, we must part;
Remember what thou vow'st; keep well my heart.
Ann. Will you be gone?
Gio. I must.
Ann. When to return?
Gio. Soon.
Ann. Look you do.
Gio. Farewell.   [*Exit.*
Ann. Go where thou wilt, in mind I'll keep thee here,
And where thou art, I know I shall be there.
Guardian!

Enter Putana

Put. Child, how is 't, child? well, thank heav'n, ha?
Ann. Oh, guardian, what a paradise of joy
Have I passed over!
Put. Nay, what a paradise of joy have you passed under! why,
now I commend thee, charge.   Fear nothing, sweetheart;
what though he be your brother? your brother 's a man, I hope;
and I say still, if a young wench feel the fit upon her, let her
take anybody, father or brother, all is one.
Ann. I would not have it known for all the world.
Put. Nor I indeed; for the speech of the people; else 'twere
nothing.
Flo. [*Within.*] Daughter Annabella!
Ann. Oh, me! my father,——Here, sir:—reach my work.
Flo. [*Within.*] What are you doing?
Ann. So; let him come now.

*Enter Florio, followed by Richardetto as a Doctor of Physic, and
Philotis, with a lute*

Flo. So hard at work! that 's well; you lose no time.
Look, I have brought you company; here 's one,
A learned doctor, lately come from Padua,
Much skill'd in physic; and, for that I see
You have of late been sickly, I entreated
This reverend man to visit you some time.
Ann. You are very welcome, sir.
Rich. I thank you, mistress:
Loud fame in large report hath spoke your praise,

As well for virtue as perfection;
For which I have been bold to bring with me
A kinswoman of mine, a maid, for song
And music, one perhaps will give content;
Please you to know her.
Ann. They are parts I love,
And she for them most welcome.
Phi. Thank you, lady.
Flo. Sir, now you know my house, pray make not strange;
And if you find my daughter need your art,
I 'll be your paymaster.
Rich. Sir, what I am
She shall command.
Flo. You shall bind me to you.
Daughter, I must have conference with you
About some matters that concern us both.
Good master doctor, please you but walk in,
We 'll crave a little of your cousin's cunning;
I think my girl hath not quite forgot
To touch an instrument; she could have done 't;
We 'll hear them both.
Rich. I 'll wait upon you, sir.   [*Exeunt.*

SCENE II

Enter Soranzo, with a book

' Love's measure is extreme, the comfort pain;
   The life unrest, and the reward disdain.'

What 's here? look 't o'er again.—'Tis so; so writes
This smooth licentious poet in his rhymes:
But, Sannazar, thou ly'st; for, had thy bosom
Felt such oppression as is laid on mine,
Thou wouldst have kiss'd the rod that made the[e] smart.
To work then, happy muse, and contradict
What Sannazar hath in his envy writ.   [*Writes.*

' Love 's measure is the mean, sweet his annoys;
   His pleasures life, and his reward all joys.'

Had Annabella liv'd when Sannazar
Did, in his brief Encomium, celebrate

Venice, that queen of cities, he had left
That verse which gain'd him such a sum of gold,
And for one only look from Annabel,
Had writ of her, and her diviner cheeks.
Oh, how my thoughts are——

Vas. [*Within.*] Pray forbear; in rules of civility, let me give
notice on 't: I shall be tax'd of my neglect of duty and service.

Sor. What rude intrusion interrupts my peace?
Can I be nowhere private?

Vas. [*Within.*] Troth, you wrong your modesty.

Sor. What 's the matter, Vasques? who is 't?

Enter Hippolita and Vasques

Hip. 'Tis I;
Do you know me now? Look, perjur'd man, on her
Whom thou and thy distracted lust have wrong'd.
Thy sensual rage of blood hath made my youth
A scorn to men and angels; and shall I
Be now a foil to thy unsated change?
Thou know'st, false wanton, when my modest fame
Stood free from stain or scandal, all the charms
Of hell or sorcery could not prevail
Against the honour of my chaster bosom.
Thine eyes did plead in tears, thy tongue in oaths,
Such, and so many, that a heart of steel
Would have been wrought to pity, as was mine;
And shall the conquest of my lawful bed,
My husband's death, urg'd on by his disgrace,
My loss of womanhood, be ill-rewarded
With hatred and contempt? No; know, Soranzo,
I have a spirit doth as much distaste
The slavery of fearing thee, as thou
Dost loathe the memory of what hath passed.

Sor. Nay, dear Hippolita——

Hip. Call me not dear,
Nor think with supple words to smooth the grossness
Of my abuses; 'tis not your new mistress,
Your goodly madam-merchant, shall triumph
On my dejection; tell her thus from me,
My birth was nobler, and by much more free.

Sor. You are too violent.

Hip. You are too double
In your dissimulation. Seest thou this,

This habit, these black mourning weeds of care?
'Tis thou art cause of this; and hast divorced
My husband from his life, and me from him,
And made me widow in my widowhood.

Sor. Will you yet hear?

Hip. More of thy perjuries?
Thy soul is drown'd too deeply in those sins;
Thou need'st not add to th' number.

Sor. Then I 'll leave you;
You are past all rules of sense.

Hip. And thou of grace.

Vas. Fie, mistress, you are not near the limits of reason; if my
lord had a resolution as noble as virtue itself, you take the
course to unedge it all.   Sir, I beseech you do not perplex her;
griefs, alas, will have a vent: I dare undertake Madam
Hippolita will now freely hear you.

Sor. Talk to a woman frantic!—Are these the fruits of your love?

Hip. They are the fruits of thy untruth, false man!
Didst thou not swear, whilst yet my husband liv'd,
That thou wouldst wish no happiness on earth
More than to call me wife? didst thou not vow,
When he should die, to marry me? for which
The devil in my blood, and thy protests,
Caus'd me to counsel him to undertake
A voyage to Ligorne, for that we heard
His brother there was dead, and left a daughter
Young and unfriended, whom, with much ado,
I wish'd him to bring hither: he did so,
And went; and, as thou know'st, died on the way.
Unhappy man, to buy his death so dear,
With my advice! yet thou, for whom I did it,
Forget'st thy vows, and leav'st me to my shame.

Sor. Who could help this?

Hip. Who? perjur'd man! thou couldst,
If thou hadst faith or love.

Sor. You are deceived:
The vows I made, if you remember well,
Were wicked and unlawful; 'twere more sin
To keep them than to break them: as for me,
I cannot mask my penitence.   Think thou
How much thou hast digress'd from honest shame,
In bringing of a gentleman to death,
Who was thy husband; such a one as he,

So noble in his quality, condition,
Learning, behaviour, entertainment, love,
As Parma could not show a braver man.

Vas. You do not well; this was not your promise.

Sor. I care not; let her know her monstrous life.
Ere I 'll be servile to so black a sin,
I 'll be a curse.—Woman, come here no more;
Learn to repent, and die; for by my honour,
I hate thee and thy lust: you have been too foul.   [*Exit.*

Vas. This part has been scurvily play'd.   [*Aside.*

Hip. How foolishly this beast contemns his fate,
And shuns the use of that, which I more scorn
Than I once lov'd, his love! but let him go,
My vengeance shall give comfort to his woe.   [*Going.*

Vas. Mistress, mistress, Madam Hippolita; pray, a word or two.

Hip. With me, sir?

Vas. With you, if you please.

Hip. What is 't?

Vas. I know you are infinitely moved now, and you think you
have cause; some I confess you have, but sure not so much
as you imagine.

Hip. Indeed!

Vas. Oh, you were miserably bitter, which you followed even to
the last syllable; 'faith, you were somewhat too shrewd: by
my life, you could not have took my lord in a worse time
since I first knew him; to-morrow, you shall find him a new
man.

Hip. Well, I shall wait his leisure.

Vas. Fie, this is not a hearty patience; it comes sourly from you;
'troth, let me persuade you for once.

Hip. I have it, and it shall be so; thanks opportunity—[*Aside.*]
—Persuade me! to what?

Vas. Visit him in some milder temper. Oh, if you could but
master a little your female spleen, how might you win him!

Hip. He will never love me. Vasques, thou hast been a too
trusty servant to such a master, and I believe thy reward in
the end will fall out like mine.

Vas. So perhaps too.

Hip. Resolve thyself it will. Had I one so true, so truly honest,
so secret to my counsels, as thou hast been to him and his, I
should think it a slight acquittance, not only to make him
master of all I have, but even of myself.

Vas. Oh, you are a noble gentlewoman!

Hip. Wilt thou feed always upon hopes? well, I know thou art
    wise, and seest the reward of an old servant daily, what it is.

Vas. Beggary and neglect.

Hip. True; but, Vasques, wert thou mine, and wouldst be
    private to me and my designs, I here protest, myself, and all
    what I can else call mine, should be at thy dispose.

Vas. Work you that way, old mole? then I have the wind of
    you—[*Aside.*]—I were not worthy of it by any desert that
    could lie—within my compass; if I could——

Hip. What then?

Vas. I should then hope to live in these my old years with
    rest and security.

Hip. Give me thy hand: now promise but thy silence,
    And help to bring to pass a plot I have;
    And here, in sight of Heaven, that being done,
    I make thee lord of me and mine estate.

Vas. Come, you are merry; this is such a happiness that I can
    neither think nor believe.

Hip. Promise thy secrecy, and 'tis confirm'd.

Vas. Then here I call our good genii for witnesses, whatsoever
    your designs are, or against whomsoever, I will not only be a
    special actor therein, but never disclose it till it be effected.

Hip. I take thy word, and, with that, thee for mine;
    Come then, let 's more confer of this anon.—
    On this delicious bane my thought shall banquet,
    Revenge shall sweeten what my griefs have tasted.
                        [*Aside, and exit with Vasques.*

Scene III

Enter Richardetto and Philotis

Rich. Thou seest, my lovely niece, these strange mishaps,
    How all my fortunes turn to my disgrace;
    Wherein I am but as a looker-on,
    Whilst others act my shame, and I am silent.

Phi. But, uncle, wherein can this borrow'd shape
    Give you content?

Rich. I 'll tell thee, gentle niece;
    Thy wanton aunt in her lascivious riots
    Lives now secure, thinks I am surely dead,
    In my late journey to Ligorne for you;

As I have caus'd it to be rumour'd out.
Now would I see with what an impudence
She gives scope to her loose adultery,
And how the common voice allows hereof;
Thus far I have prevail'd.

Phi. Alas, I fear
You mean some strange revenge.

Rich. Oh, be not troubled,
Your ignorance shall plead for you in all——
But to our business.—What! you learn'd for certain,
How Signior Florio means to give his daughter
In marriage to Soranzo?

Phi. Yes, for certain.

Rich. But how find you young Annabella's love
Inclined to him?

Phi. For aught I could perceive,
She neither fancies him nor any else.

Rich. There's mystery in that, which time must show.
She us'd you kindly?

Phi. Yes.

Rich. And crav'd your company?

Phi. Often.

Rich. 'Tis well; it goes as I could wish.
I am the doctor now, and as for you,
None knows you; if all fail not, we shall thrive.
But who comes here?—I know him; 'tis Grimaldi,
A Roman and a soldier, near allied
Unto the Duke of Montferrato, one
Attending on the nuncio of the Pope
That now resides in Parma; by which means
He hopes to get the love of Annabella.

Enter Grimaldi

Grim. Save you, sir.

Rich. And you, sir.

Grim. I have heard
Of your approved skill, which through the city
Is freely talk'd of, and would crave your aid.

Rich. For what, sir?

Grim. Marry, sir, for this——
But I would speak in private.

Rich. Leave us, cousin.   [*Philotis retires.*

Grim. I love fair Annabella, and would know

Whether in arts there may not be receipts
To move affection.
Rich. Sir, perhaps there may;
  But these will nothing profit you.
Grim. Not me?
Rich. Unless I be mistook, you are a man
  Greatly in favour with the cardinal.
Grim. What of that?
Rich. In duty to his grace,
  I will be bold to tell you, if you seek
  To marry Florio's daughter, you must first
  Remove a bar 'twixt you and her.
Grim. Who 's that?
Rich. Soranzo is the man that hath her heart,
  And while he lives, be sure you cannot speed.
Grim. Soranzo! what, mine enemy? is it he?
Rich. Is he your enemy?
Grim. The man I hate
  Worse than confusion; I will tell him straight.——
Rich. Nay, then take my advice,
  Even for his grace's sake the cardinal;
  I 'll find a time when he and she do meet,
  Of which I 'll give you notice; and, to be sure
  He shall not 'scape you, I 'll provide a poison
  To dip your rapier's point in; if he had
  As many heads as Hydra had, he dies.
Grim. But shall I trust thee, doctor?
Rich. As yourself;
  Doubt not in aught.—[*Exit Grimaldi.*]—Thus shall the fates
    decree,
  By me Soranzo falls, that ruin'd me.   [*Exeunt.*

SCENE IV

Enter Donado, with a letter, Bergetto, and Poggio

Don. Well, sir, I must be content to be both your secretary and
  your messenger myself. I cannot tell what this letter may
  work; but, as sure as I am alive, if thou come once to talk with
  her, I fear thou wilt mar whatsoever I make.
Ber. You make, uncle! why am not I big enough to carry mine
  own letter, I pray?

Don. Ay, ay, carry a fool's head of thy own! why, thou dunce, wouldst thou write a letter, and carry it thyself?

Ber. Yes, that I would, and read it to her with mine own mouth; for you must think, if she will not believe me myself when she hears me speak, she will not believe another's handwriting. Oh, you think I am a blockhead, uncle. No, sir, Poggio knows I have indited a letter myself; so I have.

Pog. Yes truly, sir, I have it in my pocket.

Don. A sweet one, no doubt; pray let 's see it.

Ber. I cannot read my own hand very well, Poggio; read it, Poggio.

Don. Begin.

Pog. [*Reads.*] 'Most dainty and honey-sweet mistress, I could call you fair, and lie as fast as any that loves you; but my uncle being the elder man, I leave it to him, as more fit for his age, and the colour of his beard. I am wise enough to tell you I can board where I see occasion; or if you like my uncle's wit better than mine, you shall marry me; if you like mine better than his, I will marry you, in spite of your teeth. So commending my best parts to you, I rest

Yours, upwards and downwards, or you may choose.

BERGETTO.'

Ber. Ah, ha! here 's stuff, uncle!

Don. Here 's stuff indeed—to shame us all. Pray whose advice did you take in this learned letter?

Pog. None, upon my word, but mine own.

Ber. And mine, uncle, believe it, nobody's else; 'twas mine own brain, I thank a good wit for 't.

Don. Get you home, sir, and look you keep within doors till I return.

Ber. How? that were a jest indeed! I scorn it, i' faith.

Don. What! you do not?

Ber. Judge me, but I do now.

Pog. Indeed, sir, 'tis very unhealthy.

Don. Well, sir, if I hear any of your apish running to motions and fopperies, till I come back, you were as good not; look to 't.

[*Exit.*

Ber. Poggio, shall 's steal to see this horse with the head in 's tail?

Pog. Ay, but you must take heed of whipping.

Ber. Dost take me for a child, Poggio? Come, honest Poggio.

[*Exeunt.*

SCENE V

Enter Friar and Giovanni

Friar. Peace! thou hast told a tale, whose every word
  Threatens eternal slaughter to the soul;
  I 'm sorry I have heard it: would mine ears
  Had been one minute deaf, before the hour
  That thou cam'st to me! Oh, young man, castaway,
  By the religious number of mine order,
  I day and night have wak'd my aged eyes
  Above my strength, to weep on thy behalf:
  But Heaven is angry, and be thou resolv'd,
  Thou art a man remark'd to taste a mischief.
  Look for 't; though it come late, it will come sure.
Gio. Father, in this you are uncharitable;
  What I have done, I 'll prove both fit and good.
  It is a principle which you have taught,
  When I was yet your scholar, that the frame
  And composition of the mind doth follow
  The frame and composition of [the] body.
  So, where the body's furniture is *beauty*,
  The mind's must needs be *virtue*; which allow'd,
  Virtue itself is reason but refined,
  And love the quintessence of that: this proves
  My sister's beauty, being rarely fair,
  Is rarely virtuous; chiefly in her love,
  And chiefly, in that love, her love to me:
  If hers to me, then so is mine to her;
  Since in like causes are effects alike.
Friar. Oh, ignorance in knowledge! long ago,
  How often have I warn'd thee this before?
  Indeed, if we were sure there were no Deity,
  Nor heaven nor hell; then to be led alone
  By nature's light (as were philosophers
  Of elder times) might instance some defence.
  But 'tis not so: then, madman, thou wilt find,
  That nature is in Heaven's positions blind.
Gio. Your age o'errules you; had you youth like mine,
  You 'd make her love your heaven, and her divine.
Friar. Nay, then I see thou 'rt too far sold to hell:
  It lies not in the compass of my prayers

    To call thee back, yet let me counsel thee;
    Persuade thy sister to some marriage.
Gio. Marriage? why that 's to damn her; that 's to prove
    Her greedy of variety of lust.
Friar. Oh, fearful! if thou wilt not, give me leave
    To shrive her, lest she should die unabsolved.
Gio. At your best leisure, father: then she 'll tell you,
    How dearly she doth prize my matchless love;
    Then you will know what pity 'twere we two
    Should have been sunder'd from each other's arms.
    View well her face, and in that little round
    You may observe a world's variety;
    For colour, lips; for sweet perfumes, her breath;
    For jewels, eyes; for threads of purest gold,
    Hair; for delicious choice of flowers, cheeks!
    Wonder in every portion of that throne.—
    Hear her but speak, and you will swear the spheres
    Make music to the citizens in heaven.—
    But, father, what is else for pleasure fram'd,
    Lest I offend your ears, shall go unnam'd.
Friar. The more I hear, I pity thee the more;
    That one so excellent should give those parts
    All to a second death.   What I can do,
    Is but to pray; and yet—I could advise thee,
    Wouldst thou be ruled.
Gio. In what?
Friar. Why leave her yet:
    The throne of mercy is above your trespass;
    Yet time is left you both——
Gio. To embrace each other,
    Else let all time be struck quite out of number;
    She is like me, and I like her, resolv'd.
Friar. No more! I 'll visit her;—this grieves me most,
    Things being thus, a pair of souls are lost.   [*Exeunt.*

Scene VI

Enter Florio, Donado, Annabella, and Putana

Flo. Where is Giovanni?

Ann. Newly walk'd abroad,
And, as I heard him say, gone to the friar,
His reverend tutor.

Flo. That 's a blessed man,
A man made up of holiness; I hope
He 'll teach him how to gain another world.

Don. Fair gentlewoman, here 's a letter, sent
To you from my young cousin; I dare swear
He loves you in his soul; would you could hear
Sometimes, what I see daily, sighs and tears,
As if his breast were prison to his heart.

Flo. Receive it, Annabella.

Ann. Alas, good man!   [*Takes the letter.*

Don. What 's that she said?

Put. An 't please you, sir, she said, 'Alas, good man!' Truly
I do commend him to her every night before her first sleep,
because I would have her dream of him; and she hearkens to
that most religiously.

Don. Say'st so? God a' mercy, Putana! there is something for
thee — [*Gives her money*] — and prithee do what thou canst
on his behalf; it shall not be lost labour, take my word for it.

Put. Thank you most heartily, sir; now I have a feeling of your
mind, let me alone to work.

Ann. Guardian.

Put. Did you call?

Ann. Keep this letter.

Don. Signior Florio, in any case bid her read it instantly.

Flo. Keep it! for what? pray read it me hereright.

Ann. I shall, sir.   [*She reads the letter.*

Don. How do you find her inclined, signior?

Flo. Troth, sir, I know not how; not all so well
As I could wish.

Ann. Sir, I am bound to rest your cousin's debtor.
The jewel I 'll return; for if he love,
I 'll count that love a jewel.

Don. Mark you that?
Nay, keep them both, sweet maid.

Ann. You must excuse me,
   Indeed I will not keep it.
Flo. Where 's the ring,
   That which your mother, in her will, bequeath'd,
   And charged you on her blessing not to give it
   To any but your husband? send back that.
Ann. I have it not.
Flo. Ha! have it not; where is it?
Ann. My brother in the morning took it from me,
   Said he would wear it to-day.
Flo. Well, what do you say
   To young Bergetto's love! are you content to
   Match with him? speak.
Don. There is the point, indeed.
Ann. What shall I do? I must say something now.   [*Aside.*
Flo. What say? why do you not speak?
Ann. Sir, with your leave—
   Please you to give me freedom?
Flo. Yes, you have [it].
Ann. Signior Donado, if your nephew mean
   To raise his better fortunes in his match,
   The hope of me will hinder such a hope:
   Sir, if you love him, as I know you do,
   Find one more worthy of his choice than me;
   In short, I 'm sure I shall not be his wife.
Don. Why here 's plain dealing; I commend thee for 't;
   And all the worst I wish thee, is, heaven bless thee!
   Your father yet and I will still be friends;
   Shall we not, Signior Florio?
Flo. Yes; why not?
   Look, here your cousin comes.

Enter Bergetto and Poggio

Don. Oh, coxcomb! what doth he make here?
Ber. Where is my uncle, sirs?
Don. What is the news now?
Ber. Save you, uncle, save you! You must not think I come for
   nothing, masters; and how, and how is it? what, you have
   read my letter? ah, there I—tickled you, i' faith.
Pog. But 'twere better you had tickled her in another place.
Ber. Sirrah sweetheart, I 'll tell thee a good jest; and riddle
   what it is.
Ann. You say you 'll tell me.

Ber. As I was walking just now in the street, I met a swaggering fellow would needs take the wall of me; and because he did thrust me, I very valiantly call'd him rogue; he hereupon bade me draw, I told him I had more wit than so: but when he saw that I would not, he did so maul me with the hilts of his rapier, that my head sung whilst my feet caper'd in the kennel.

Don. Was ever the like ass seen!

Ann. And what did you all this while?

Ber. Laugh at him for a gull, till I saw the blood run about mine ears, and then I could not choose but find in my heart to cry; till a fellow with a broad beard (they say he is a new-come doctor) call'd me into his house, and gave me a plaster, look you, here 'tis;—and, sir, there was a young wench wash'd my face and hands most excellently; i' faith I shall love her as long as I live for it—did she not, Poggio?

Pog. Yes, and kiss'd him too.

Ber. Why la now, you think I tell a lie, uncle, I warrant.

Don. Would he that beat thy blood out of thy head, had beaten some wit into it! for I fear thou never wilt have any.

Ber. Oh, uncle, but there was a wench would have done a man's heart good to have look'd on her. By this light, she had a face methinks worth twenty of you, Mistress Annabella.

Don. Was ever such a fool born?

Ann. I am glad she liked you, sir.

Ber. Are you so? by my troth I thank you, forsooth.

Flo. Sure it was the doctor's niece, that was last day with us here.

Ber. 'Twas she, 'twas she.

Don. How do you know that, Simplicity?

Ber. Why does he not say so? if I should have said no, I should have given him the lie, uncle, and so have deserv'd a dry beating again; I 'll none of that.

Flo. A very modest well-behav'd young maid, as I have seen.

Don. Is she indeed?

Flo. Indeed she is, if I have any judgment.

Don. Well, sir, now you are free: you need not care for sending letters now; you are dismiss'd, your mistress here will none of you.

Ber. No! why, what care I for that? I can have wenches enough in Parma for half a crown apiece; cannot I, Poggio?

Pog. I 'll warrant you, sir.

Don. Signior Florio, I thank you for your free recourse you gave for my admittance; and to you, fair maid, that jewel I will give you against your marriage. Come, will you go, sir?

Ber. Ay, marry will I.   Mistress, farewell, mistress; I 'll come
again to-morrow—farewell, mistress.

> [*Exeunt Donado, Bergetto, and Poggio.*

Enter Giovanni

Flo. Son, where have you been? what alone, alone still?
I would not have it so; you must forsake
This over-bookish humour.   Well; your sister
Hath shook the fool off.
Gio. 'Twas no match for her.
Flo. 'Twas not indeed; I meant it nothing less;
Soranzo is the man I only like;
Look on him, Annabella.   Come, 'tis supper-time,
And it grows late.   [*Exit.*
Gio. Whose jewel 's that?
Ann. Some sweetheart's.
Gio. So I think.
Ann. A lusty youth,
Signior Donado, gave it me to wear
Against my marriage.
Gio. But you shall not wear it;
Send it him back again.
Ann. What, you are jealous?
Gio. That you shall know anon, at better leisure:
Welcome sweet night! the evening crowns the day.   [*Exeunt.*

ACT III

Scene I

Enter Bergetto and Poggio

Ber. Does my uncle think to make me a baby still? No, Poggio;
he shall know I have a sconce now.
Pog. Ay, let him not bob you off like an ape with an apple.
Ber. 'Sfoot, I will have the wench, if he were ten uncles, in
despite of his nose, Poggio.
Pog. Hold him to the grindstone, and give not a jot of ground;
she hath in a manner promised you already.

Ber. True, Poggio; and her uncle, the doctor, swore I should marry her.

Pog. He swore; I remember.

Ber. And I will have her, that 's more: didst see the codpiece-point she gave me, and the box of marmalade?

Pog. Very well; and kiss'd you, that my chops water'd at the sight on 't: there is no way but to clap up a marriage in hugger-mugger.

Ber. I will do it; for I tell thee, Poggio, I begin to grow valiant methinks, and my courage begins to rise.

Pog. Should you be afraid of your uncle?

Ber. Hang him, old doting rascal! no; I say I will have her.

Pog. Lose no time then.

Ber. I will beget a race of wise men and constables that shall cart whores at their own charges; and break the duke's peace ere I have done, myself.—Come away. [*Exeunt.*

SCENE II

Enter Florio, Giovanni, Soranzo, Annabella, Putana, and Vasques

Flo. My Lord Soranzo, though I must confess
The proffers that are made me have been great,
In marriage of my daughter; yet the hope
Of your still rising honours has prevail'd
Above all other jointures: here she is;
She knows my mind; speak for yourself to her,
And hear you, daughter, see you use him nobly:
For any private speech, I 'll give you time.
Come, son, and you the rest; let them alone;
Agree [they] as they may.

Sor. I thank you, sir.

Gio. Sister, be not all woman, think on me. [*Aside to Annabella.*

Sor. Vasques.

Vas. My lord.

Sor. Attend me without.
[*Exeunt all but Soranzo and Annabella.*

Ann. Sir, what 's your will with me?

Sor. Do you not know
What I should tell you?

Ann. Yes; you 'll say you love me.

Sor. And I will swear it too; will you believe it?
Ann. 'Tis no point of faith.

       Enter Giovanni, in the gallery above

Sor. Have you not will to love?
Ann. Not you.
Sor. Whom then?
Ann. That 's as the fates infer.
Gio. Of those I 'm regent now.
Sor. What mean you, sweet?
Ann. To live and die a maid.
Sor. Oh, that 's unfit.
Gio. Here 's one can say that 's but a woman's note.
Sor. Did you but see my heart, then would you swear——
Ann. That you were dead.
Gio. That 's true, or somewhat near it.
Sor. See you these true love's tears?
Ann. No.
Gio. Now she winks.
Sor. They plead to you for grace.
Ann. Yet nothing speak.
Sor. Oh, grant my suit.
Ann. What is 't?
Sor. To let me live——
Ann. Take it.
Sor. Still yours.
Ann. That is not mine to give.
Gio. One such another word would kill his hopes.
Sor. Mistress, to leave those fruitless strifes of wit,
   Know I have lov'd you long, and lov'd you truly;
   Not hope of what you have, but what you are,
   Hath drawn me on; then let me not in vain
   Still feel the rigour of your chaste disdain:
   I 'm sick, and sick to the heart.
Ann. Help, aqua vitæ!
Sor. What mean you?
Ann. Why, I thought you had been sick.
Sor. Do you mock my love?
Gio. There, sir, she was too nimble.
Sor. 'Tis plain; she laughs at me.—[*Aside.*]—These scornful taunts
   Neither become your modesty nor years.

Ann. You are no looking-glass; or if you were,
  I would dress my language by you.
Gio. I am confirm'd.
Ann. To put you out of doubt, my lord, methinks
  Your common sense should make you understand,
  That if I lov'd you, or desired your love,
  Some way I should have given you better taste:
  But since you are a nobleman, and one
  I would not wish should spend his youth in hopes,
  Let me advise you to forbear your suit,
  And think I wish you well, I tell you this.
Sor. Is 't you speak this?
Ann. Yes, I myself; yet know,
  (Thus far I give you comfort,) if mine eyes
  Could have pick'd out a man, amongst all those
  That sued to me, to make a husband of,
  You should have been that man; let this suffice,
  Be noble in your secrecy, and wise.
Gio. Why, now I see she loves me.
Ann. One word more.
  As ever virtue liv'd within your mind,
  As ever noble courses were your guide,
  As ever you would have me know you lov'd me,
  Let not my father know hereof by you;
  If I hereafter find that I must marry,
  It shall be you or none.
Sor. I take that promise.
Ann. Oh, oh, my head!
Sor. What 's the matter, not well?
Ann. Oh, I begin to sicken.
Gio. Heaven forbid!   [*Exit from above.*
Sor. Help, help, within there, ho!
                        [*Enter Florio, Giovanni, and Putana.*
  Look to your daughter, Signior Florio.
Flo. Hold hér up, she swoons.
Gio. Sister, how do you?
Ann. Sick,—brother, are you there?
Flo. Convey her to bed instantly, whilst I send for a physician;
  quickly, I say.
Put. Alas, poor child!   [*Exeunt all but Soranzo.*
                    Re-enter Vasques
Vas. My lord.
Sor. Oh, Vasques! now I doubly am undone,

Both in my present and my future hopes:
She plainly told me that she could not love,
And thereupon soon sicken'd; and I fear
Her life 's in danger.

Vas. By 'r lady, sir, and so is yours, if you knew all.—[*Aside.*]—
'Las, sir, I am sorry for that; may be, 'tis but the maids-
sickness, an overflux of youth; and then, sir, there is no such
present remedy as present marriage.   But hath she given you
an absolute denial?

Sor. She hath, and she hath not; I 'm full of grief;
But what she said, I 'll tell thee as we go.   [*Exeunt.*

Scene III

Enter Giovanni and Putana

Put. Oh, sir, we are all undone, quite undone, utterly undone,
and shamed for ever: your sister, oh, your sister!

Gio. What of her? for heaven's sake, speak; how does she?

Put. Oh, that ever I was born to see this day!

Gio. She is not dead, ha? is she?

Put. Dead! no, she is quick;—'tis worse, she is with child. You
know what you have done; heaven forgive you! 'tis too late
to repent now, heaven help us!

Gio. With child? how dost thou know 't?

Put. How do I know 't? am I at these years ignorant what the
meanings of qualms and water-pangs be? of changing of
colours, queasiness of stomachs, pukings, and another thing
that I could name? Do not, for her and your credit's sake,
spend the time in asking how, and which way, 'tis so: she is
quick, upon my word; if you let a physician see her water,
you are undone.

Gio. But in what case is she?

Put. Prettily amended: 'twas but a fit, which I soon espied, and
she must look for often henceforward.

Gio. Commend me to her, bid her take no care;
Let not the doctor visit her, I charge you;
Make some excuse, till I return.—Oh, me!
I have a world of business in my head.
Do not discomfort her—
How do these news perplex me! If my father

Come to her, tell him she 's recover'd well;
Say 'twas but some ill diet—d' ye hear, woman?
Look you to 't.
Put. I will, sir.   [*Exeunt.*

Scene IV

Enter Florio and Richardetto

Flo. And how do you find her, sir?
Rich. Indifferent well;
   I see no danger, scarce perceive she 's sick,
   But that she told me, she had lately eaten
   Melons, and, as she thought, those disagreed
   With her young stomach.
Flo. Did you give her aught?
Rich. An easy surfeit-water, nothing else;
   You need not doubt her health; I rather think
   Her sickness is a fullness of her blood—
   You understand me?
Flo. I do; you counsel well;
   And once, within these few days, will so order it,
   She shall be married ere she know the time.
Rich. Yet let not haste, sir, make unworthy choice;
   That were dishonour.
Flo. Master doctor, no;
   I will not do so neither: in plain words,
   My Lord Soranzo is the man I mean.
Rich. A noble and a virtuous gentleman.
Flo. As any is in Parma: not far hence,
   Dwells Father Bonaventure, a grave friar,
   Once tutor to my son; now at his cell
   I 'll have them married.
Rich. You have plotted wisely.
Flo. I 'll send one straight to speak with him to-night.
Rich. Soranzo 's wise; he will delay no time.
Flo. It shall be so.

Enter Friar and Giovanni

Friar. Good peace be here, and love!
Flo. Welcome, religious friar; you are one
   That still bring blessing to the place you come to.

Gio. Sir, with what speed I could, I did my best
　　To draw this holy man from forth his cell,
　　To visit my sick sister; that with words
　　Of ghostly comfort, in this time of need,
　　He might absolve her, whether she live or die.
Flo. 'Twas well done, Giovanni; thou herein
　　Hast show'd a Christian's care, a brother's love:
　　Come, father, I 'll conduct you to her chamber,
　　And one thing would entreat you.
Friar. Say on, sir.
Flo. I have a father's dear impression,
　　And wish, before I fall into my grave,
　　That I might see her married, as 'tis fit;
　　A word from you, grave man, will win her more
　　Than all our best persuasions.
Friar. Gentle sir,
　　All this I 'll say, that Heaven may prosper her.　　　　[*Exeunt.*

Scene V

Enter Grimaldi

Grim. Now if the doctor keep his word, Soranzo,
　　Twenty to one you miss your bride.　I know
　　'Tis an unnoble act, and not becomes
　　A soldier's valour; but in terms of love,
　　Where merit cannot sway, policy must:
　　I am resolv'd, if this physician
　　Play not on both hands, then Soranzo falls.

Enter Richardetto

Rich. You are come as I could wish; this very night
　　Soranzo, 'tis ordain'd must be affied
　　To Annabella, and, for aught I know,
　　Married.
Grim. How!
Rich. Yet your patience;
　　The place, 'tis Friar Bonaventure's cell.
　　Now I would wish you to bestow this night
　　In watching thereabouts; 'tis but a night:
　　If you miss now, to-morrow I 'll know all.

Grim. Have you the poison?
Rich. Here 'tis, in this box;
 Doubt nothing, this will do 't; in any case,
 As you respect your life, be quick and sure.
Grim. I 'll speed him.
Rich. Do.—Away; for 'tis not safe
 You should be seen much here,—ever my love!
Grim. And mine to you.   [*Exit.*
Rich. So! if this hit, I 'll laugh and hug revenge;
 And they that now dream of a wedding-feast,
 May chance to mourn the lusty bridegroom's ruin:
 But to my other business—Niece Philotis!

Enter Philotis

Phi. Uncle.
Rich. My lovely niece,
 You have bethought you?
Phi. Yes,—and, as you counsell'd,
 Fashion'd my heart to love him; but he swears
 He will to-night be married; for he fears
 His uncle else, if he should know the drift,
 Will hinder all, and call his coz to shrift.
Rich. To-night? why best of all; but let me see,
 I—ha!—yes,—so it shall be; in disguise
 We 'll early to the friar's—I have thought on 't.
Phi. Uncle, he comes.

Enter Bergetto and Poggio

Rich. Welcome, my worthy coz.
Ber. Lass, pretty lass, come buss, lass! A-ha, Poggio!
            [*Kisses her.*
Rich. There 's hope of this yet.   [*Aside.*
 You shall have time enough; withdraw a little,
 We must confer at large.
Ber. Have you not sweetmeats, or dainty devices for me?
Phi. You shall [have] enough, sweetheart.
Ber. Sweetheart! mark that, Poggio. By my troth I cannot
 choose but kiss thee once more for that word, *sweetheart.*
 Poggio, I have a monstrous swelling about my stomach,
 whatsoever the matter be.
Pog. You shall have physic for 't, sir.
Rich. Time runs apace.
 X 899

Ber. Time 's a blockhead.

Rich. Be ruled; when we have done what 's fit to do,
  Then you may kiss your fill, and bed her too.   [*Exeunt.*

Scene VI

*Annabella's chamber. A table with wax lights : Annabella at
confession before the Friar ; she weeps and wrings her hands*

Friar. I am glad to see this penance; for, believe me,
  You have unripp'd a soul so foul and guilty,
  As I must tell you true, I marvel how
  The earth hath borne you up; but weep, weep on,
  These tears may do you good; weep faster yet,
  Whilst I do read a lecture.

Ann. Wretched creature!

Friar. Ay, you are wretched, miserably wretched,
  Almost condemn'd alive.   There is a place,
  List, daughter! in a black and hollow vault,
  Where day is never seen; there shines no sun,
  But flaming horror of consuming fires,
  A lightless sulphur, chok'd with smoky fogs
  Of an infected darkness: in this place
  Dwell many thousand thousand sundry sorts
  Of never-dying deaths: there damned souls
  Roar without pity; there are gluttons fed
  With toads and adders; there is burning oil
  Pour'd down the drunkard's throat; the usurer
  Is forced to sup whole draughts of molten gold;
  There is the murderer for ever stabb'd,
  Yet can he never die; there lies the wanton
  On racks of burning steel, whilst in his soul
  He feels the torment of his raging lust.——

Ann. Mercy! oh, mercy!

Friar. There stand these wretched things,
  Who have dream'd out whole years in lawless sheets
  And secret incests, cursing one another:
  Then you will wish each kiss your brother gave,
  Had been a dagger's point; then you shall hear
  How he will cry, 'Oh, would my wicked sister
  Had first been damn'd, when she did yield to lust!'——

But soft, methinks I see repentance work
New motions in your heart; say, how is 't with you?
Ann. Is there no way left to redeem my miseries?
Friar. There is, despair not; Heaven is merciful,
And offers grace even now. 'Tis thus agreed:
First, for your honour's safety, that you marry
My Lord Soranzo; next, to save your soul,
Leave off this life, and henceforth live to him.
Ann. Ah me!
Friar. Sigh not; I know the baits of sin
Are hard to leave; oh, 'tis a death to do 't.
Remember what must come: are you content?
Ann. I am.
Friar. I like it well; we 'll take the time.
Who 's near us there?

Enter Florio and Giovanni

Flo. Did you call, father?
Friar. Is Lord Soranzo come?
Flo. He stays below.
Friar. Have you acquainted him at full?
Flo. I have,
And he is overjoy'd.
Friar. And so are we:
Bid him come near.
Gio. My sister weeping?—Ha!
I fear this friar's falsehood.—[*Aside.*]—I will call him.   [*Exit.*
Flo. Daughter, are you resolv'd?
Ann. Father, I am.

Re-enter Giovanni, with Soranzo and Vasques

Flo. My Lord Soranzo, here
Give me your hand; for that, I give you this.
                  [*Joins their hands.*
Sor. Lady, say you so too?
Ann. I do, and vow
To live with you and yours.
Friar. Timely resolv'd;
My blessing rest on both! more to be done,
You may perform it on the morning sun.   [*Exeunt.*

Scene VII

Enter Grimaldi with his rapier drawn, and a dark lantern

Grim. 'Tis early night as yet, and yet too soon
    To finish such a work; here I will lie
    To listen who comes next.   *[He lies down.*

Enter Bergetto and Philotis disguised : and followed, at a distance,
            by Richardetto and Poggio

Ber. We are almost at the place, I hope, sweetheart.
Grim. I hear them near, and heard one say 'sweetheart'.
    'Tis he; now guide my hand, some angry justice,
    Home to his bosom.—Now have at you, sir!
           [Stabs Bergetto, and exit.
Ber. Oh, help, help! here's a stitch fallen in my guts; oh for a
    flesh-tailor quickly—Poggio!
Phi. What ails my love?
Ber. I am sure I cannot piss forward and backward, and yet I
    am wet before and behind; lights! lights! ho, lights!
Phi. Alas, some villain here has slain my love.
Rich. Oh, Heaven forbid it; raise up the next neighbours
    Instantly, Poggio, and bring lights.   *[Exit Poggio.*
    How is 't, Bergetto? slain! It cannot be;
    Are you sure you are hurt?
Ber. Oh, my belly seethes like a porridge-pot; some cold water,
    I shall boil over else: my whole body is in a sweat, that you
    may wring my shirt; feel here—why, Poggio!

Re-enter Poggio, with Officers, and lights

Pog. Here; alas! how do you?
Rich. Give me a light. What's here? all blood! Oh, sirs,
    Signior Donado's nephew now is slain.
    Follow the murderer with all the haste
    Up to the city, he cannot be far hence;
    Follow, I beseech you.
Officers. Follow, follow, follow.   *[Exeunt.*
Rich. Tear off thy linen, coz, to stop his wounds;
    Be of good comfort, man.
Ber. Is all this mine own blood? nay, then, good night with me.
    Poggio, commend me to my uncle, dost hear? bid him, for my

sake, make much of this wench: oh—I am going the wrong
way sure, my belly aches so—oh, farewell, Poggio! Oh!—oh!—
                                                      [*Dies.*
Phi. Oh, he is dead.
Pog. How! dead!
Rich. He 's dead indeed;
  'Tis now too late to weep: let 's have him home,
  And, with what speed we may, find out the murderer.
Pog. Oh, my master! my master! my master!   [*Exeunt.*

Scene VIII

Enter Vasques and Hippolita

Hip. Betroth'd?
Vas. I saw it.
Hip. And when 's the marriage-day?
Vas. Some two days hence.
Hip. Two days! why, man, I would but wish two hours,
  To send him to his last, and lasting sleep;
  And, Vasques, thou shalt see I 'll do it bravely.
Vas. I do not doubt your wisdom, nor, I trust, you my secrecy;
  I am infinitely yours.
Hip. I will be thine in spite of my disgrace.
  So soon? O wicked man! I durst be sworn,
  He 'd laugh to see me weep.
Vas. And that 's a villainous fault in him.
Hip. No, let him laugh; I am arm'd in my resolves:
  Be thou still true.
Vas. I should get little by treachery against so hopeful a pre-
  ferment, as I am like to climb to——
Hip. Even to—my bosom, Vasques. Let my youth
  Revel in these new pleasures; if we thrive,
  He now hath but a pair of days to live.   [*Exeunt.*

Scene IX

Enter Florio, Donado, Richardetto, Poggio, and Officers

Flo. 'Tis bootless now to show yourself a child.
  Signior Donado, what is done, is done;
  Spend not the time in tears, but seek for justice.

Rich. I must confess, somewhat I was in fault,
  That had not first acquainted you what love
  Passed 'twixt him and my niece; but, as I live,
  His fortune grieves me as it were mine own.
Don. Alas, poor creature, he meant no man harm,
  That I am sure of.
Flo. I believe that, too.
  But stay, my masters; are you sure you saw
  The murderer pass here?
Officer. An it please you, sir, we are sure we saw a ruffian, with
  a naked weapon in his hand all bloody, get into my lord
  cardinal's grace's gate; that we are sure of; but for fear of
  his grace (bless us!) we durst go no farther.
Don. Know you what manner of man he was?
Officer. Yes, sure, I know the man; they say he is a soldier: he
  that lov'd your daughter, sir, an 't please ye; 'twas he for
  certain.
Flo. Grimaldi, on my life.
Officer. Ay, ay, the same.
Rich. The cardinal is noble; he no doubt
  Will give true justice.
Don. Knock someone at the gate.
Pog. I 'll knock, sir.   [*Knocks.*
Serv. [*Within.*] What would ye?
Flo. We require speech with the lord cardinal
  About some present business; pray inform
  His grace that we are here.

Enter Cardinal, followed by Grimaldi

Card. Why how now, friends! what saucy mates are you,
  That know nor duty nor civility?
  Are we a person fit to be your host;
  Or is our house become your common inn,
  To beat our doors at pleasure? What such haste
  Is yours, as that it cannot wait fit times?
  Are you the masters of this commonwealth,
  And know no more discretion? Oh, your news
  Is here before you: you have lost a nephew,
  Donado, last night by Grimaldi slain:
  Is that your business? well, sir, we have knowledge on 't,
  Let that suffice.
Grim. In presence of your grace,
  In thought, I never meant Bergetto harm:

But, Florio, you can tell, with how much scorn
Soranzo, back'd with his confederates,
Hath often wrong'd me; I to be reveng'd,
(For that I could not win him else to fight)
Had thought, by way of ambush, to have kill'd him,
But was, unluckily, therein mistook;
  Else he had felt what late Bergetto did:
And though my fault to him were merely chance,
Yet humbly I submit me to your grace,   *[Kneeling.*
To do with me as you please.
Card. Rise up, Grimaldi.   *[He rises.*
  You citizens of Parma, if you seek
For justice, know, as nuncio from the Pope,
For this offence I here receive Grimaldi
Into His Holiness' protection:
He is no common man, but nobly born,
Of princes' blood, though you, Sir Florio,
Thought him too mean a husband for your daughter.
If more you seek for, you must go to Rome,
For he shall thither; learn more wit for shame.—
Bury your dead:—away, Grimaldi—leave 'em!
          [Exeunt Cardinal and Grimaldi.
Don. Is this a churchman's voice? dwells justice here?
Flo. Justice is fled to heaven, and comes no nearer.
  Soranzo?—was 't for him? Oh, impudence!
Had he the face to speak it, and not blush?
Come, come, Donado, there 's no help in this,
When cardinals think murder 's not amiss:
Great men may do their wills, we must obey,
But Heaven will judge them for 't, another day.   *[Exeunt.*

ACT IV

SCENE I

Enter the Friar, Giovanni, Annabella, Philotis, Soranzo, Donado,
Florio, Richardetto, Putana, and Vasques

Friar. These holy rites perform'd, now take your times
  To spend the remnant of the day in feast;
  Such fit repasts are pleasing to the saints,
  Who are your guests, though not with mortal eyes
  To be beheld.—Long prosper in this day,
  You happy couple, to each other's joy!

Sor. Father, your prayer is heard; the hand of goodness
  Hath been a shield for me against my death;
  And, more to bless me, hath enrich'd my life
  With this most precious jewel; such a prize
  As earth hath not another like to this.
  Cheer up, my love; and, gentlemen, my friends,
  Rejoice with me in mirth: this day we 'll crown
  With lusty cups to Annabella's health.

Gio. Oh, torture! were the marriage yet undone,
  Ere I 'd endure this sight, to see my love
  Clipped by another, I would dare confusion,
  And stand the horror of ten thousand deaths.   [*Aside.*

Vas. Are you not well, sir?

Gio. Prithee, fellow, wait;
  I need not thy officious diligence.

Flo. Signior Donado, come, you must forget
  Your late mishaps, and drown your cares in wine.

Sor. Vasques!

Vas. My lord.

Sor. Reach me that weighty bowl.
  Here, brother Giovanni, here 's to you,
  Your turn comes next, though now a bachelor;
  Here 's to your sister's happiness, and mine!
                            [*Drinks, and offers him the bowl.*

Gio. I cannot drink.

Sor. What!

Gio. 'Twill indeed offend me.

Ann. Pray do not urge him, if he be not willing.   [*Hautboys.*

Flo. How now! what noise is this?

Vas. Oh, sir, I had forgot to tell you; certain young maidens of
　　Parma, in honour to Madam Annabella's marriage, have sent
　　their loves to her in a masque, for which they humbly crave
　　your patience and silence.
Sor. We are much bound to them; so much the more,
　　As it comes unexpected: guide them in.

*Enter Hippolita, followed by Ladies in white robes, with garlands
　　of willows, all masked*

Music and a Dance

Sor. Thanks, lovely virgins! now might we but know
　　To whom we have been beholding for [this] love,
　　We shall acknowledge it.
Hip. Yes, you shall know:
　　What think you now?　　　　　　　　　　　　[*Unmasks.*
Omnes. Hippolita!
Hip. 'Tis she;
　　Be not amaz'd; nor blush, young lovely bride,
　　I come not to defraud you of your man:
　　'Tis now no time to reckon up the talk
　　What Parma long hath rumour'd of us both;
　　Let rash report run on! the breath that vents it
　　Will, like a bubble, break itself at last.
　　But now to you, sweet creature:—lend your hand—
　　Perhaps it hath been said, that I would claim
　　Some interest in Soranzo, now your lord;
　　What I have right to do, his soul knows best:
　　But in my duty to your noble worth,
　　Sweet Annabella, and my care of you,
　　Here, take, Soranzo, take this hand from me,
　　I 'll once more join, what by the Holy Church
　　Is finished and allow'd.—Have I done well?
Sor. You have too much engaged us.
Hip. One thing more.
　　That you may know my single charity,
　　Freely I here remit all interest
　　I e'er could claim, and give you back your vows;
　　And to confirm 't,—reach me a cup of wine—
　　　　　　　　　　　　[*Vasques gives her a poisoned cup.*
　　My Lord Soranzo, in this draught I drink
　　Long rest t' ye!—[*She drinks*]—look to it, Vasques.　[*Aside.*
Vas. Fear nothing—

Sor. Hippolita, I thank you; and will pledge
  This happy union as another life.
  Wine, there!

Vas. You shall have none; neither shall you pledge her.

Hip. How!

Vas. Know now, mistress she-devil, your own mischievous
  treachery hath kill'd you; I must not marry you.

Hip. Villain!

Omnes. What's the matter?

Vas. Foolish woman, thou art now like a firebrand, that hath
  kindled others and burnt thyself:—*troppo sperar, inganna,*—
  thy vain hope hath deceived thee; thou art but dead; if thou
  hast any grace, pray.

Hip. Monster!

Vas. Die in charity, for shame.—This thing of malice, this
  woman, hath privately corrupted me with promise of [mar-
  riage,] under this politic reconciliation, to poison my lord,
  whilst she might laugh at his confusion on his marriage-day.
  I promised her fair; but I knew what my reward should have
  been, and would willingly have spared her life, but that I was
  acquainted with the danger of her disposition; and now have
  fitted her a just payment in her own coin: there she is, she
  hath yet——and end thy days in peace, vile woman; as for
  life, there's no hope, think not on 't.

Omnes. Wonderful justice!

Rich. Heaven, thou art righteous.

Hip. Oh, 'tis true,
  I feel my minute coming.   Had that slave
  Kept promise,—Oh, my torment!—thou, this hour,
  Hadst died, Soranzo—heat above hell-fire!—
  Yet, ere I pass away—cruel, cruel flames!—
  Take here my curse amongst you; may thy bed
  Of marriage be a rack unto thy heart,
  Burn blood, and boil in vengeance—Oh, my heart,
  My flame's intolerable—may'st thou live
  To father bastards; may her womb bring forth
  Monsters—and die together in your sins,
  Hated, scorn'd, and unpitied!—oh—oh——   [*Dies.*

Flo. Was e'er so vile a creature!

Rich. Here's the end
  Of lust and pride.

Ann. It is a fearful sight.

Sor. Vasques, I know thee now a trusty servant,

And never will forget thee.——Come, my love,
We 'll home, and thank the heavens for this escape.
Father and friends, we must break up this mirth;
It is too sad a feast.
Don. Bear hence the body.
Friar. [*Aside to Giovanni.*] Here 's an ominous change!
Mark this, my Giovanni, and take heed!—
I fear the event; that marriage seldom 's good,
Where the bride-banquet so begins in blood.   [*Exeunt.*

SCENE II

Enter Richardetto and Philotis

Rich. My wretched wife, more wretched in her shame
Than in her wrongs to me, hath paid too soon
The forfeit of her modesty and life.
And I am sure, my niece, though vengeance hover,
Keeping aloof yet from Soranzo's fall,
Yet he will fall, and sink with his own weight.
I need not now (my heart persuades me so)
To further his confusion; there is One
Above begins to work; for, as I hear,
Debates already 'twixt his wife and him
Thicken and run to head; she, as 'tis said,
Slightens his love, and he abandons hers:
Much talk I hear.   Since things go thus, my niece,
In tender love and pity of your youth,
My counsel is, that you should free your years
From hazard of these woes, by flying hence
To fair Cremona, there to vow your soul
In holiness, a holy votaress;
Leave me to see the end of these extremes.
All human worldly courses are uneven,
No life is blessed but the way to heaven.
Phi. Uncle, shall I resolve to be a nun?
Rich. Ay, gentle niece; and in your hourly prayers
Remember me, your poor unhappy uncle.
Hie to Cremona now, as fortune leads,
Your home your cloister, your best friends your beads;

Your chaste and single life shall crown your birth,
Who dies a virgin, lives a saint on earth.
Phi. Then farewell, world, and worldly thoughts, adieu!
Welcome, chaste vows, myself I yield to you.   [*Exeunt.*

SCENE III

Enter Soranzo unbraced, and dragging in Annabella

Sor. Come, strumpet, famous whore! were every drop
Of blood that runs in thy adulterous veins
A life, this sword (dost see 't?) should in one blow
Confound them all. Harlot, rare, notable harlot,
That with thy brazen face maintain'st thy sin,
Was there no man in Parma to be bawd
To your loose cunning whoredom else but I?
Must your hot itch and pleurisy of lust,
The heyday of your luxury, be fed
Up to a surfeit, and could none but I
Be pick'd out to be cloak to your close tricks,
Your belly-sports?—Now I must be the dad
To all that gallimaufry that is stuff'd
In thy corrupted bastard-bearing womb!—
Why, must I?
Ann. Beastly man! Why?—'tis thy fate.
I sued not to thee; for, but that I thought
Your over-loving lordship would have run
Mad on denial, had you lent me time,
I would have told you in what case I was:
But you would needs be doing.
Sor. Whore of whores!
Darest thou tell me this?
Ann. Oh, yes; why not?
You were deceived in me; 'twas not for love
I chose you, but for honour; yet know this,
Would you be patient yet, and hide your shame,
I 'd see whether I could love you.
Sor. Excellent quean!
Why, art thou not with child?
Ann. What needs all this,
When 'tis superfluous? I confess I am.

Sor. Tell me by whom.

Ann. Soft, 'twas not in my bargain.
Yet somewhat, sir, to stay your longing stomach
I am content t' acquaint you with; THE man,
The more than man, that got this sprightly boy,—
(For 'tis a boy, [and] therefore glory, sir,
Your heir shall be a son)——

Sor. Damnable monster!

Ann. Nay, an you will not hear, I 'll speak no more.

Sor. Yes, speak, and speak thy last.

Ann. A match, a match!
This noble creature was in every part
So angel-like, so glorious, that a woman,
Who had not been but human, as was I,
Would have kneel'd to him, and have begg'd for love.—
You! why you are not worthy once to name
His name without true worship, or, indeed,
Unless you kneel'd, to hear another name him.

Sor. What was he call'd?

Ann. We are not come to that;
Let it suffice, that you shall have the glory
To father what so brave a father got.
In brief, had not this chance fall'n out as it doth,
I never had been troubled with a thought
That you had been a creature;—but for marriage,
I scarce dream yet of that.

Sor. Tell me his name.

Ann. Alas, alas, there 's all! will you believe?

Sor. What?

Ann. You shall never know.

Sor. How!

Ann. Never; if
You do, let me be curs'd.

Sor. Not know it, strumpet! I 'll rip up thy heart,
And find it there.

Ann. Do, do.

Sor. And with my teeth,
Tear the prodigious lecher joint by joint.

Ann. Ha, ha, ha! the man 's merry.

Sor. Dost thou laugh?
Come, whore, tell me your lover, or by truth
I 'll hew thy flesh to shreds; who is 't?

Ann. Che morte piu dolce che morire per amore?   [*Sings.*

Sor. Thus will I pull thy hair, and thus I 'll drag
　　Thy lust be-leper'd body through the dust——
　　　　　　　　　　　　　　　　　[Hales her up and down.
　　Yet tell his name.

Ann. Morendo in grazia dee morire senza dolore ?　　　*[Sings.*

Sor. Dost thou triumph? the treasure of the earth
　　Shall not redeem thee; were there kneeling kings
　　Did beg thy life, or angels did come down
　　To plead in tears, yet should not all prevail
　　Against my rage: dost thou not tremble yet?

Ann. At what? to die! no, be a gallant hangman;
　　I dare thee to the worst: strike, and strike home;
　　I leave revenge behind, and thou shalt feel it.

Sor. Yet tell me ere thou diest, and tell me truly,
　　Knows thy old father this?

Ann. No, by my life.

Sor. Wilt thou confess, and I will spare thy life?

Ann. My life! I will not buy my life so dear.

Sor. I will not slack my vengeance.　　　*[Draws his sword.*

Enter Vasques

Vas. What do you mean, sir?

Sor. Forbear, Vasques; such a damned whore
　　Deserves no pity.

Vas. Now the gods forefend!
　　And would you be her executioner, and kill her in your rage,
　　too? Oh, 'twere most unmanlike; she is your wife, what
　　faults have been done by her before she married you, were not
　　against you: alas! poor lady, what hath she committed, which
　　any lady in Italy in the like case would not? Sir, you must
　　be ruled by your reason, and not by your fury; that were
　　inhuman and beastly.

Sor. She shall not live.

Vas. Come, she must: you would have her confess the authors
　　of her present misfortunes, I warrant you; 'tis an unconscion-
　　able demand, and she should lose the estimation that I, for
　　my part, hold of her worth, if she had done it: why, sir,
　　you ought not, of all men living, to know it. Good sir, be
　　reconciled; alas, good gentlewoman!

Ann. Pish, do not beg for me, I prize my life
　　As nothing; if the man will needs be mad,
　　Why let him take it.

Sor. Vasques, hear'st thou this?

Vas. Yes, and commend her for it; in this she shows the noble-
ness of a gallant spirit, and beshrew my heart, but it becomes
her rarely.—[*Aside to Soranzo.*]—Sir, in any case smother
your revenge; leave the scenting out your wrongs to me; be
ruled, as you respect your honour, or you mar all.—[*Aloud.*]—
Sir, if ever my service were of any credit with you, be not so
violent in your distractions: you are married now; what a
triumph might the report of this give to other neglected
suitors! 'tis as manlike to bear extremities, as godlike to
forgive.

Sor. Oh, Vasques, Vasques, in this piece of flesh,
    This faithless face of hers, had I laid up
    The treasure of my heart. Hadst thou been virtuous,
    Fair, wicked woman, not the matchless joys
    Of life itself, had made me wish to live
    With any saint but thee: deceitful creature,
    How hast thou mock'd my hopes, and in the shame
    Of thy lewd womb even buried me alive!
    I did too dearly love thee.

Vas. This is well; follow this temper with some passion; be brief
    and moving, 'tis for the purpose.   [*Aside to Soranzo.*

Sor. Be witness to my words thy soul and thoughts;
    And tell me, didst not think that in my heart
    I did too superstitiously adore thee?

Ann. I must confess, I know lov'd me well.

Sor. And wouldst thou use me thus! O Annabella!
    Be thou assured, whoe'er the villain was
    That thus hath tempted thee to this disgrace,
    Well he might lust, but never loved like me.
    He doted on the picture that hung out
    Upon thy cheeks, to please his humorous eye;
    For on the part I lov'd, which was thy heart,
    And, as I thought, thy virtues.

Ann. Oh, my lord!
    These words wound deeper than your sword could do.

Vas. Let me not ever take comfort, but I begin to weep myself,
    so much I pity him; why, madam, I knew, when his rage was
    overpast, what it would come to.

Sor. Forgive me, Annabella: though thy youth
    Hath tempted thee above thy strength to folly,
    Yet will I not forget what I should be,
    And what I am, a husband; in that name
    Is hid divinity: if I do find

That thou wilt yet be true, here I remit
All former faults, and take thee to my bosom.

Vas. By my troth, and that 's a point of noble charity.

Ann. Sir, on my knees——

Sor. Rise up, you shall not kneel.
Get you to your chamber, see you make no show
Of alteration; I 'll be with you straight:
My reason tells me now, that "'tis as common
To err in frailty as to be a woman'.
Go to your chamber.   [*Exit Annabella.*

Vas. So! this was somewhat to the matter: what do you think
of your heaven of happiness now, sir?

Sor. I carry hell about me, all my blood
Is fired in swift revenge.

Vas. That may be; but know you how, or on whom? Alas!
to marry a great woman, being made great in the stock to
your hand, is a usual sport in these days; but to know what
ferret it was that hunted your coney-burrow,—there is the
cunning.

Sor. I 'll make her tell herself, or——

Vas. Or what? you must not do so; let me yet persuade your
sufferance a little while: go to her, use her mildly; win her,
if it be possible, to a voluntary, to a weeping tune; for the
rest, if all hit, I will not miss my mark. Pray, sir, go in; the
next news I tell you shall be wonders.

Sor. Delay in vengeance gives a heavier blow!   [*Exit.*

Vas. Ah, sirrah, here 's work for the nonce! I had a suspicion
of a bad matter in my head a pretty while ago; but after my
madam's scurvy looks here at home, her waspish perverseness,
and loud fault-finding, then I remembered the proverb, that
'where hens crow, and cocks hold their peace, there are sorry
houses'. 'Sfoot, if the lower parts of a she-tailor's cunning
can cover such a swelling in the stomach, I 'll never blame a
false stitch in a shoe whilst I live again. Up, and up so quick?
and so quickly too? 'twere a fine policy to learn by whom:
this must be known; and I have thought on 't——
            [*Enter Putana, in tears.*
Here 's the way, or none.—What, crying, old mistress! alas,
alas, I cannot blame you; we have a lord, Heaven help us, is
so mad as the devil himself, the more shame for him.

Put. Oh, Vasques, that ever I was born to see this day! Doth
he use thee so too, sometimes, Vasques?

Vas. Me? why he makes a dog of me; but if some were of my

mind, I know what we would do.   As sure as I am an honest man, he will go near to kill my lady with unkindness: say she be with child, is that such a matter for a young woman of her years to be blamed for?

Put. Alas, good heart, it is against her will full sore.

Vas. I durst be sworn, all his madness is for that she will not confess whose 'tis, which he will know; and when he doth know it, I am so well acquainted with his humour, that he will forget all strait: well, I could wish she would in plain terms tell all, for that 's the way, indeed.

Put. Do you think so?

Vas. Foh, I know it; provided that he did not win her to it by force.   He was once in a mind that you could tell, and meant to have wrung it out of you; but I somewhat pacified him from that; yet sure you know a great deal.

Put. Heaven forgive us all! I know a little, Vasques.

Vas. Why should you not? who else should? Upon my conscience she loves you dearly; and you would not betray her to any affliction for the world.

Put. Not for all the world, by my faith and troth, Vasques.

Vas. 'Twere pity of your life if you should; but in this you should both relieve her present discomforts, pacify my lord, and gain yourself everlasting love and preferment.

Put. Dost think so, Vasques?

Vas. Nay, I know it; sure it was some near and entire friend.

Put. 'Twas a dear friend indeed; but——

Vas. But what? fear not to name him: my life between you and danger: 'faith, I think it was no base fellow.

Put. Thou wilt stand between me and harm?

Vas. 'Uds pity, what else? you shall be rewarded too, trust me.

Put. 'Twas even no worse than her own brother.

Vas. Her brother Giovanni, I warrant you!

Put. Even he, Vasques; as brave a gentleman as ever kiss'd fair lady.   Oh, they love most perpetually.

Vas. A brave gentleman indeed! why therein I commend her choice—better and better—[*Aside.*] You are sure 'twas he?

Put. Sure; and you shall see he will not be long from her too.

Vas. He were to blame if he would; but may I believe thee?

Put. Believe me! why, dost think I am a Turk or a Jew? No, Vasques, I have known their dealings too long, to belie them now.

Vas. Where are you? there, within, sirs!

Enter Banditti

Put. How now, what are these?

Vas. You shall know presently. Come, sirs, take me this old damnable hag, gag her instantly, and put out her eyes, quickly, quickly!

Put. Vasques! Vasques!

Vas. Gag her, I say; 'sfoot, do you suffer her to prate? what do you fumble about? let me come to her. I'll help your old gums, you toad-bellied bitch! [*They gag her.*] Sirs, carry her closely into the coal-house, and put out her eyes instantly; if she roars, slit her nose; do you hear, be speedy and sure.

[*Exeunt Banditti with Putana.*

Why this is excellent, and above expectation—her own brother! Oh, horrible! to what a height of liberty in damnation hath the devil trained our age! her brother, well! there's yet but a beginning; I must to my lord, and tutor him better in his points of vengeance: now I see how a smooth tale goes beyond a smooth tail; but soft—what thing comes next? Giovanni! as I could wish; my belief is strengthened, 'tis as firm as winter and summer.

Enter Giovanni

Gio. Where's my sister?

Vas. Troubled with a new sickness, my lord; she's somewhat ill.

Gio. Took too much of the flesh, I believe.

Vas. Troth, sir, and you I think have even hit it; but my virtuous lady——

Gio. Where is she?

Vas. In her chamber; please you visit her; she is alone. [*Giovanni gives him money.*] Your liberality hath doubly made me your servant, and ever shall, ever——

[*Exit Giovanni, re-enter Soranzo.*

Sir, I am made a man; I have plied my cue with cunning and success; I beseech you let us be private.

Sor. My lady's brother's come; now he'll know all.

Vas. Let him know it; I have made some of them fast enough. How have you dealt with my lady?

Sor. Gently, as thou hast counsell'd; oh, my soul
Runs circular in sorrow for revenge;
But, Vasques, thou shalt know——

Vas. Nay, I will know no more, for now comes your turn to know; I would not talk so openly with you—let my young master take time enough, and go at pleasure; he is sold to

death, and the devil shall not ransom him.—Sir, I beseech you,
your privacy.

Sor. No conquest can gain glory of my fear.   [*Exeunt.*

ACT V

SCENE I

Annabella appears at a window, above

Ann. Pleasures, farewell, and all ye thriftless minutes
    Wherein false joys have spun a weary life!
    To these my fortunes now I take my leave.
    Thou, precious Time, that swiftly rid'st in post
    Over the world, to finish up the race
    Of my last fate, here stay thy restless course,
    And bear to ages that are yet unborn
    A wretched, woeful woman's tragedy!
    My conscience now stands up against my lust,
    With depositions character'd in guilt,   [*Enter Friar, below.*
    And tells me I am lost: now I confess;
    Beauty that clothes the outside of the face,
    Is cursed if it be not cloth'd with grace.
    Here like a turtle, (mew'd up in a cage)'
    Unmated, I converse with air and walls,
    And descant on my vile unhappiness.
    O Giovanni! that hast had the spoil
    Of thine own virtues, and my modest fame;
    Would thou hadst been less subject to those stars
    That luckless reign'd at my nativity!
    Oh, would the scourge, due to my black offence,
    Might pass from thee, that I alone might feel
    The torment of an uncontrolled flame!
Friar. What 's this I hear?
Ann. That man, that blessed friar,
    Who join'd in ceremonial knot my hand
    To him whose wife I now am, told me oft,
    I trod the path to death, and show'd me how.
    But they who sleep in lethargies of lust,
    Hug their confusion, making Heaven unjust;
    And so did I.

Friar. Here 's music to the soul!

Ann. Forgive me, my good Genius, and this once
 Be helpful to my ends; let some good man
 Pass this way, to whose trust I may commit
 This paper, double lined with tears and blood;
 Which being granted, here I sadly vow
 Repentance, and a leaving of that life
 I long have died in.

Friar. Lady, Heaven hath heard you,
 And hath by providence ordain'd that I
 Should be his minister for your behoof.

Ann. Ha, what are you?

Friar. Your brother's friend, the friar;
 Glad in my soul that I have liv'd to hear
 This free confession 'twixt your peace and you:
 What would you, or to whom? fear not to speak.

Ann. Is Heaven so bountiful?—then I have found
 More favour than I hoped; here, holy man——

                              [*Throws down a letter.*

 Commend me to my brother, give him that,
 That letter; bid him read it, and repent.
 Tell him that I, imprison'd in my chamber,
 Barr'd of all company, even of my guardian,
 (Which gives me cause of much suspect) have time
 To blush at what hath passed; bid him be wise,
 And not believe the friendship of my lord;
 I fear much more than I can speak: good Father,
 The place is dangerous, and spies are busy.
 I must break off.——You 'll do 't?

Friar. Be sure I will,
 And fly with speed:——my blessing ever rest
 With thee, my daughter; live, to die more blest!   [*Exit.*

Ann. Thanks to the heavens, who have prolong'd my breath
 To this good use! now I can welcome death.

                              [*Withdraws from the window.*

SCENE II

Enter Soranzo and Vasques

Vas. Am I to be believed now? first, marry a strumpet that
 cast herself away upon you but to laugh at your horns! to
 feast on your disgrace, riot in your vexations, cuckold you

in your bride-bed, waste your estate upon panders and
bawds!——

Sor. No more, I say, no more.

Vas. A cuckold is a goodly tame beast, my lord!

Sor. I am resolv'd; urge not another word;
My thoughts are great, and all as resolute
As thunder; in meantime, I 'll cause our lady
To deck herself in all her bridal robes;
Kiss her, and fold her gently in my arms.
Begone—yet hear you, are the banditti ready
To wait in ambush?

Vas. Good sir, trouble not yourself about other business than
your own resolution; remember that time lost cannot be
recalled.

Sor. With all the cunning words thou canst, invite
The states of Parma to my birthday's feast:
Haste to my brother-rival and his father,
Entreat them gently, bid them not to fail;
Be speedy, and return.

Vas. Let not your pity betray you, till my coming back; think
upon incest and cuckoldry.

Sor. Revenge is all the ambition I aspire,
To that I 'll climb or fall; my blood 's on fire.   [*Exeunt.*

Scene III

Enter Giovanni

Gio. Busy opinion is an idle fool,
That, as a school-rod keeps a child in awe,
Frights th' unexperienced temper of the mind:
So did it me; who, ere my precious sister
Was married, thought all taste of love would die
In such a contract; but I find no change
Of pleasure in this formal law of sports.
She is still one to me, and every kiss
As sweet and as delicious as the first
I reap'd, when yet the privilege of youth
Entitled her a virgin.   Oh, the glory
Of two united hearts like hers and mine!
Let poring bookmen dream of other worlds;
My world, and all of happiness, is here,
And I 'd not change it for the best to come:

A life of pleasure is Elysium.—   [*Enter Friar.*
Father, you enter on the jubilee
Of my retired delights; now I can tell you,
The hell you oft have prompted, is nought else
But slavish and fond superstitious fear;
And I could prove it too——

Friar. Thy blindness slays thee:
Look there, 'tis writ to thee.   [*Gives him the letter.*

Gio. From whom?

Friar. Unrip the seals and see;
The blood 's yet seething hot, that will anon
Be frozen harder than congealed coral.—
Why d' ye change colour, son?

Gio. 'Fore heaven, you make
Some petty devil factor 'twixt my love
And your religion-masked sorceries.
Where had you this?

Friar. Thy conscience, youth, is sear'd,
Else thou wouldst stoop to warning.

Gio. 'Tis her hand,
I know 't; and 'tis all written in her blood.
She writes I know not what. *Death!* I 'll not fear
An armed thunderbolt aim'd at my heart.
She writes, we are discover'd—pox on dreams
Of low faint-hearted cowardice!—discover'd?
The devil we are! which way is 't possible?
Are we grown traitors to our own delights?
Confusion take such dotage! 'tis but forged;
This is your peevish chattering, weak old man!—
Now, sir, what news bring you?

Enter Vasques

Vas. My lord, according to his yearly custom, keeping this day
a feast in honour of his birthday, by me invites you thither.
Your worthy father, with the Pope's reverend nuncio, and
other magnificoes of Parma, have promised their presence;
will 't please you to be of the number?

Gio. Yes, tell [him] I *dare* come.

Vas. Dare come?

Gio. So I said; and tell him more, I *will* come.

Vas. These words are strange to me.

Gio. Say, I will come.

Vas. You will not miss?

Gio. Yet more! I 'll come, sir.   Are you answered?
Vas. So I 'll say——my service to you.   [*Exit.*
Friar. You will not go, I trust.
Gio. Not go! for what?
Friar. Oh, do not go; this feast, I 'll gage my life,
  Is but a plot to train you to your ruin;
  Be ruled, you shall not go.
Gio. Not go! stood Death
  Threatening his armies of confounding plagues,
  With hosts of dangers hot as blazing stars,
  I would be there; not go! yes, and resolve
  To strike as deep in slaughter as they all;
  For I will go.
Friar. Go where thou wilt;—I see
  The wildness of thy fate draws to an end,
  To a bad fearful end:—I must not stay
  To know thy fall; back to Bononia I
  With speed will haste, and shun this coming blow.
  Parma, farewell; would I had never known thee,
  Or aught of thine! Well, young man, since no prayer
  Can make thee safe, I leave thee to despair.   [*Exit.*
Gio. Despair, or tortures of a thousand hells,
  All 's one to me; I have set up my rest.
  Now, now, work serious thoughts on baneful plots;
  Be all a man, my soul; let not the curse
  Of old prescription rend from me the gall
  Of courage, which enrolls a glorious death:
  If I must totter like a well-grown oak,
  Some under-shrubs shall in my weighty fall
  Be crush'd to splits; with me they all shall perish!   [*Exit.*

SCENE IV

Enter Soranzo, Vasques with masks, and Banditti

Sor. You will not fail, or shrink in the attempt?
Vas. I will undertake for their parts; be sure, my masters, to
  be bloody enough, and as unmerciful as if you were preying
  upon a rich booty on the very mountains of Liguria: for your
  pardons, trust to my lord; but for reward, you shall trust none
  but your own pockets.
Band. We 'll make a murder.

Sor. Here 's gold,—[*Gives them money.*]—here 's more; want
　　nothing; what you do
　Is noble, and an act of brave revenge:
　I 'll make you rich, banditti, and all free.

Omnes. Liberty! liberty!

Vas. Hold, take every man a vizard; when you are withdrawn,
　　keep as much silence as you can possibly. You know the
　　watchword, till which be spoken, move not; but when you
　　hear that, rush in like a stormy flood: I need not instruct you
　　in your own profession.

Omnes. No, no, no.

Vas. In, then; your ends are profit and preferment.—Away!
　　　　　　　　　　　　　　　　　　　　[*Exeunt Banditti.*

Sor. The guests will all come, Vasques?

Vas. Yes, sir. And now let me a little edge your resolution:
　　you see nothing is unready to this great work, but a great
　　mind in you; call to your remembrance your disgraces, your
　　loss of honour, Hippolita's blood, and arm your courage in
　　your own wrongs; so shall you best right those wrongs in
　　vengeance, which you may truly call your own.

Sor. 'Tis well; the less I speak, the more I burn,
　And blood shall quench that flame.

Vas. Now you begin to turn Italian. This beside; when my
　　young incest-monger comes, he will be sharp set on his old
　　bit: give him time enough, let him have your chamber and bed
　　at liberty; let my hot hare have law ere he be hunted to his
　　death, that, if it be possible, he post to hell in the very act
　　of his damnation.

Sor. It shall be so; and see, as we would wish,
　He comes himself first——　　　　　　　　[*Enter Giovanni.*
　Welcome, my much-lov'd brother;
　Now I perceive you honour me; you are welcome——
　But where 's my father?

Gio. With the other states,
　Attending on the nuncio of the Pope,
　To wait upon him hither. How 's my sister?

Sor. Like a good housewife, scarcely ready yet;
　You were best walk to her chamber.

Gio. If you will.

Sor. I must expect my honourable friends;
　Good brother, get her forth.

Gio. You are busy, sir.　　　　　　　　　　　　　[*Exit.*

Vas. Even as the great devil himself would have it! let him go

and glut himself in his own destruction—[*Flourish.*]—Hark,
the nuncio is at hand; good sir, be ready to receive him.

Enter Cardinal, Florio, Donado, Richardetto, and Attendants

Sor. Most reverend lord, this grace hath made me proud,
  That you vouchsafe my house; I ever rest
  Your humble servant for this noble favour.
Card. You are our friend, my lord; His Holiness
  Shall understand how zealously you honour
  Saint Peter's vicar in his substitute:
  Our special love to you.
Sor. Signiors, to you
  My welcome, and my ever best of thanks
  For this so memorable courtesy.
  Pleaseth your grace, walk near?
Card. My lord, we come
  To celebrate your feast with civil mirth,
  As ancient custom teacheth: we will go.
Sor. Attend his grace there.   Signiors, keep your way.
                                                        [*Exeunt.*

SCENE V

Annabella, richly dressed, and Giovanni

Gio. What, chang'd so soon! hath your new sprightly lord
  Found out a trick in night-games more than we
  Could know, in our simplicity?—Ha! is 't so?
  Or does the fit come on you, to prove treacherous
  To your past vows and oaths?
Ann. Why should you jest
  At my calamity, without all sense
  Of the approaching dangers you are in?
Gio. What dangers half so great as thy revolt?
  Thou art a faithless sister, else thou know'st,
  Malice, or any treachery beside,
  Would stoop to my bent brows; why, I hold fate
  Clasp'd in my fist, and could command the course
  Of time's eternal motion, hadst thou been
  One thought more steady than an ebbing sea.
  And what? you 'll now be honest, that 's resolv'd?
Ann. Brother, dear brother, know what I have been,
  And know that now there 's but a dining-time

'Twixt us and our confusion; let's not waste
These precious hours in vain and useless speech.
Alas! these gay attires were not put on
But to some end; this sudden solemn feast
Was not ordain'd to riot in expense;
I that have now been chamber'd here alone,
Barr'd of my guardian, or of any else,
Am not for nothing at an instant freed
To fresh access.   Be not deceiv'd, my brother,
This banquet is an harbinger of death
To you and me; resolve yourself it is,
And be prepared to welcome it.

Gio. Well, then;
The schoolmen teach that all this globe of earth
Shall be consumed to ashes in a minute.

Ann. So I have read too.

Gio. But 'twere somewhat strange
To see the waters burn; could I believe
This might be true, I could believe as well
There might be hell or heaven.

Ann. That's most certain.

Gio. A dream, a dream! else in this other world
We should know one another.

Ann. So we shall.

Gio. Have you heard so?

Ann. For certain.

Gio. But do you think,
That I shall see you there? You look on me.—
May we kiss one another, prate, or laugh,
Or do as we do here?

Ann. I know not that;
But—brother, for the present, what d' ye mean
To free yourself from danger? some way think
How to escape; I'm sure the guests are come.

Gio. Look up, look here; what see you in my face?

Ann. Distraction and a troubled conscience.

Gio. Death, and a swift repining wrath:—yet look;
What see you in mine eyes?

Ann. Methinks you weep.

Gio. I do indeed; these are the funeral tears
Shed on your grave; these furrow'd up my cheeks
When first I lov'd and knew not how to woo.
Fair Annabella, should I here repeat

The story of my life, we might lose time.
Be record all the spirits of the air,
And all things else that are, that day and night,
Early and late, the tribute which my heart
Hath paid to Annabella's sacred love,
Hath been these tears, which are her mourners now!
Never till now did Nature do her best,
To show a matchless beauty to the world,
Which in an instant, ere it scarce was seen,
The jealous destinies required again.
Pray, Annabella, pray! since we must part,
Go thou, white in thy soul, to fill a throne
Of innocence and sanctity in heaven.
Pray, pray, my sister!
Ann. Then I see your drift——
Ye blessed angels guard me!
Gio. So say I;
Kiss me.   If ever aftertimes should hear
Of our fast-knit affections, though perhaps
The laws of conscience and of civil use
May justly blame us, yet when they but know
Our loves, that love will wipe away that rigour,
Which would in other incests be abhorr'd.
Give me your hand: how sweetly life doth run
In these well-colour'd veins! how constantly
These palms do promise health! but I could chide
With Nature for this cunning flattery—
Kiss me again—forgive me.
Ann. With my heart.
Gio. Farewell!
Ann. Will you be gone?
Gio. Be dark, bright sun,
And make this midday night, that thy gilt rays
May not behold a deed, will turn their splendour
More sooty than the poets feign their Styx!
One other kiss, my sister.
Ann. What means this?
Gio. To save thy fame, and kill thee in a kiss.   [*Stabs her.*
Thus die, and die by me, and by my hand!
Revenge is mine; honour doth love command.
Ann. Oh, brother, by your hand!
Gio. When thou art dead
I 'll give my reasons for 't; for to dispute

With thy (even in thy death) most lovely beauty,
Would make me stagger to perform this act
Which I most glory in.

Ann. Forgive him, Heaven—and me my sins! farewell,
Brother unkind, unkind,—mercy, great Heaven, oh—oh! [*Dies.*

Gio. She's dead, alas, good soul! The hapless fruit
That in her womb received its life from me,
Hath had from me a cradle and a grave.
I must not dally—this sad marriage-bed
In all her best, bore her alive and dead.
Soranzo, thou hast miss'd thy aim in this!
I have prevented now thy reaching plots,
And kill'd a love, for whose each drop of blood
I would have pawn'd my heart.   Fair Annabella,
How over-glorious art thou in thy wounds,
Triúmphing over infamy and hate!
Shrink not, courageous hand, stand up, my heart,
And boldly act my last, and greater part!   [*The scene closes.*

SCENE VI

A banquet.   Enter the Cardinal, Florio, Donaldo, Soranzo,
Richardetto, Vasques, and Attendants

Vas. [*Apart to Soranza.*] Remember, sir, what you have to do;
be wise and resolute.

Sor. Enough—my heart is fix'd.—Pleaseth your grace
To taste these coarse confections: though the use
Of such set entertainments more consists
In custom, than in cause, yet, reverend sir,
I am still made your servant by your presence.

Card. And we your friend.

Sor. But where's my brother Giovanni?

Enter Giovanni, with a heart upon his dagger

Gio. Here, here, Soranzo! trimm'd in reeking blood,
That triumphs over death! proud in the spoil
Of love and vengeance! fate, or all the powers
That guide the motions of immortal souls,
Could not prevent me.

Card. What means this?

Flo. Son Giovanni!

Sor. Shall I be forestall'd?   [*Aside.*

Gio. Be not amazed: if your misgiving hearts
    Shrink at an idle sight, what bloodless fear
    Of coward passion would have seiz'd your senses,
    Had you beheld the rape of life and beauty
    Which I have acted?—my sister, oh, my sister!
Flo. Ha! what of her?
Gio. The glory of my deed
    Darken'd the midday sun, made noon as night.
    You came to feast, my lords, with dainty fare,
    I came to feast too; but I digg'd for food
    In a much richer mine, than gold or stone
    Of any value balanced; 'tis a heart,
    A heart, my lords, in which is mine entomb'd:
    Look well upon 't; do you know it?
Vas. What strange riddle 's this?   *[Aside.*
Gio. 'Tis Annabella's heart, 'tis; why do you startle?
    I vow 'tis hers;—this dagger's point plough'd up
    Her fruitful womb, and left to me the fame
    Of a most glorious executioner.
Flo. Why, madman, art thyself?
Gio. Yes, father; and, that times to come may know,
    How, as my fate, I honour'd my revenge,
    List, father; to your ears I will yield up
    How much I have deserv'd to be your son.
Flo. What is 't thou say'st?
Gio. Nine moons have had their changes,
    Since I first thoroughly view'd, and truly lov'd,
    Your daughter and my sister.
Flo. How? Alas, my lords,
    He is a frantic madman!
Gio. Father, no.
    For nine months space, in secret, I enjoy'd
    Sweet Annabella's sheets; nine months I lived
    A happy monarch of her heart and her;
    Soranzo, thou know'st this; thy paler cheek
    Bears the confounding print of thy disgrace;
    For her too fruitful womb too soon betray'd
    The happy passage of our stolen delights,
    And made her mother to a child unborn.
Card. Incestuous villain!
Flo. Oh, his rage belies him.
Gio. It does not, 'tis the oracle of truth;
    I vow it is so.

Sor. I shall burst with fury——
    Bring the strumpet forth!
Vas. I shall, sir.   *[Exit.*
Gio. Do, sir; have you all no faith
    To credit yet my triumphs? here I swear
    By all that you call sacred, by the love
    I bore my Annabella whilst she lived,
    These hands have from her bosom ripp'd this heart.—
                      [Re-enter Vasques.
    Is 't true or no, sir?
Vas. 'Tis most strangely true.
Flo. Cursed man—have I lived to——   *[Dies.*
Card. Hold up, Florio.
    Monster of children! see what thou hast done,
    Broke thy old father's heart! is none of you
    Dares venture on him?
Gio. Let them! Oh, my father,
    How well his death becomes him in his griefs!
    Why this was done with courage; now survives
    None of our house but I, gilt in the blood
    Of a fair sister and a hapless father.
Sor. Inhuman scorn of men, hast thou a thought
    T' outlive thy murders?   *[Draws.*
Gio. Yes, I tell thee yes;
    For in my fists I bear the twists of life.
    Soranzo, see this heart, which was thy wife's;
    Thus I exchange it royally for thine.   *[They fight.*
    And thus and thus! now brave revenge is mine. *[Soranzo falls.*
Vas. I cannot hold any longer. You, sir, are you grown
    insolent in your butcheries? have at you.
Gio. Come, I am arm'd to meet thee.   *[They fight.*
Vas. No! will it not be yet? if this will not, another shall. Not
    yet? I shall fit you anon——Vengeance!

The Banditti rush in

Gio. Welcome! come more of you; whate'er you be,
    I dare your worst——   *[They surround and wound him.*
    Oh, I can stand no longer; feeble arms,
    Have you so soon lost strength?   *[Falls.*
Vas. Now, you are *welcome*, sir!—Away, my masters, all is done;
    shift for yourselves, your reward is your own; shift for your-
    selves.   *[Aside to Banditti.*
Band. Away, away!   *[Exeunt.*

Vas. How do you, my lord? See you this? [*Pointing to Giovanni.*]
how is 't?

Sor. Dead; but in death well pleas'd, that I have liv'd
To see my wrongs reveng'd on that black devil.—
Oh, Vasques, to thy bosom let me give
My last of breath; let not that lecher live——
Oh!——   [*Dies.*

Vas. The reward of peace and rest be with [you], my ever
dearest lord and master!

Gio. Whose hand gave me this wound?

Vas. Mine, sir; I was your first man; have you enough?

Gio. I thank thee, thou hast done for me
But what I would have else done on myself.
Art sure thy lord is dead?

Vas. Oh, impudent slave!
As sure as I am sure to see thee die.

Card. Think on thy life and end, and call for mercy.

Gio. Mercy? why, I have found it in this justice.

Card. Strive yet to cry to Heaven.

Gio. Oh, I bleed fast.
Death, thou 'rt a guest long look'd for, I embrace
Thee and thy wounds; oh, my last minute comes!
Where'er I go, let me enjoy this grace,
Freely to view my Annabella's face.   [*Dies.*

Don. Strange miracle of justice!

Card. Raise up the city, we shall be murder'd all!

Vas. You need not fear, you shall not; this strange task being
ended, I have paid the duty to the son, which I have vowed
to the father.

Card. Speak, wretched villain, what incarnate fiend
Hath led thee on to this?

Vas. Honesty, and pity of my master's wrongs: for know, my
lord, I am by birth a Spaniard, brought forth my country in my
youth by Lord Soranzo's father; whom, whilst he lived, I
served faithfully; since whose death I have been to this man,
as I was to him.   What I have done, was duty, and I repent
nothing, but that the loss of my life had not ransomed his.

Card. Say, fellow, know'st thou any yet unnam'd,
Of council in this incest?

Vas. Yes, an old woman, sometime guardian to this murder'd
lady.

Card. And what 's become of her?

Vas. Within this room she is; whose eyes, after her confession,

I caused to be put out, but kept alive, to confirm what from
Giovanni's own mouth you have heard.   Now, my lord, what
I have done you may judge of; and let your own wisdom be a
judge in your own reason.

Card. Peace! first this woman, chief in these effects,
My sentence is, that forthwith she be ta'en
Out of the city, for example's sake,
There to be burnt to ashes.

Don. 'Tis most just.

Card. Be it your charge, Donado, see it done.

Don. I shall.

Vas. What for me? if death, 'tis welcome; I have been honest
to the son, as I was to the father.

Card. Fellow, for thee, since what thou didst was done
Not for thyself, being no Italian,
We banish thee for ever; to depart
Within three days: in this we do dispense
With grounds of reason, not of thine offence.

Vas. 'Tis well; this conquest is mine, and I rejoice that a
Spaniard outwent an Italian in revenge.   [*Exit.*

Card. Take up these slaughter'd bodies, see them buried;
And all the gold and jewels, or whatsoever,
Confiscate by the canons of the Church,
We seize upon to the Pope's proper use.

Rich. [*Discovers himself.*] Your grace's pardon; thus long I
liv'd disguised,
To see the effect of pride and lust at once
Brought both to shameful ends.

Card. What! Richardetto, whom we thought for dead?

Don. Sir, was it you——

Rich. Your friend.

Card. We shall have time
To talk at large of all; but never yet
Incest and murder have so strangely met.
Of one so young, so rich in nature's store,
Who could not say, 'TIS PITY SHE 'S A WHORE?   [*Exeunt.*